STUDIES IN WORDS

Canto is a new imprint offering a range of titles,
classic and more recent, across a broad spectrum of
subject areas and interests. History, literature,
biography, archaeology, politics, religion,
psychology, philosophy and science are all
represented in Canto's specially selected list of
titles, which now offers some of the best and most
accessible of Cambridge publishing to a wider
readership.

TO
STANLEY AND
JOAN BENNETT

STUDIES IN WORDS

BY

C. S. LEWIS

SECOND EDITION

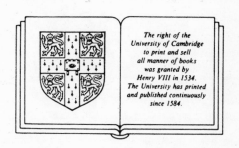

The right of the
University of Cambridge
to print and sell
all manner of books
was granted by
Henry VIII in 1534.
The University has printed
and published continuously
since 1584.

CAMBRIDGE UNIVERSITY PRESS

CAMBRIDGE

NEW YORK PORT CHESTER

MELBOURNE SYDNEY

Published by the Press Syndicate of the University of Cambridge
The Pitt Building, Trumpington Street, Cambridge CB2 1TP
40 West 20th Street, New York, NY 10011, USA
10 Stamford Road, Oakleigh, Melbourne 3166, Australia

Library of Congress Catalogue Card Number 66–10799

First published 1960
Second edition 1967
Reprinted 1967, 1972
Reiussed in paperback 1974
Reprinted 1975, 1976, 1987
Canto edition 1990

Printed in Great Britain by
Billing & Sons Ltd, Worcester

ISBN 0 521 05547 4 hardback
ISBN 0 521 39831 2 paperback

CONTENTS

PREFACE

THIS book is based on lectures given at Cambridge during the last few years and is primarily addressed to students. I have indeed hoped that others also might find it of interest but I must warn them what it is not. It is not an essay in the higher linguistics. The ultimate nature of language and the theory of meaning are not here my concern. The point of view is merely lexical and historical. My words are studied as an aid to more accurate reading and chosen for the light they throw on ideas and sentiments. The notes on some common types of semantic change given in the first chapter are a rough and ready attempt at practical guidance; if any deeper issues are raised by implication, this was not my intention.

C. S. L.

CAMBRIDGE
June 1959

1

INTRODUCTION

THIS book has grown out of a practice which was at first my necessity and later my hobby; whether at last it has attained the dignity of a study, others must decide. In my young days when I had to take my pupils through Anglo-Saxon and Middle English texts neither they nor I could long be content to translate a word in the sense which its particular context demanded while leaving the different senses it bore in other places to be memorised, without explanation, as if they were wholly different words. Natural curiosity and mnemonic thrift drove us, as it drives others, to link them up and to see, where possible, how they could have radiated out from a central meaning. Once embarked, it was impossible not to be curious about the later senses of those which survived into Modern English. Margins and notebooks thus became steadily fuller. One saw increasingly that sixteenth- and even nineteenth-century texts needed such elucidation not very much more rarely, and in a more subtle way, than those of the eleventh or twelfth; for in the older books one knows what one does not understand but in the later one discovers, often after years of contented misreading, that one has been interpolating senses later than those the author intended. And all the while one seems to be learning not only about words. In the end the habit becomes second nature; the slightest semantic discomfort in one's reading rouses one, like a terrier, to the game. No doubt I thus learned rather laboriously from my own reading some things that could have been learned more quickly from the *N.E.D.* But I would advise everyone to do the same so far—a serious qualification—as his time allows. One understands a word much better if one has met it alive, in its native habitat. So far as is possible our knowledge should be checked and supplemented, not derived, from the dictionary.

At the same time a prospective reader may reasonably ask what difference there will be, for him, between reading one of my chapters and looking up one of my words in the dictionary. The answer is that I offer both less and more. Less, because I do not even attempt to be exhaustive; as regards the greater words I am already too old to hope for that. I offer more, first, because I drive words of different languages abreast. I depart from classical English philology by having no concern with sounds, nor with derivations simply as such. I am concerned solely with the semantic relations of, say, *natura* and *nature*; the fact that one is 'derived' from the other is for my purpose unimportant. That is why *phusis* and *kind* come in with just as good a title as *natura*. Something will be said later about what I think can be gained from such a procedure. And secondly, I have been able to say more about the history of thought and sentiment which underlies the semantic biography of a word than would have been possible or proper in a dictionary. I have of course checked my results by the *N.E.D.* It has often given me the perfect example for which I had searched my own *waste what precedes us*

reading in vain; often (*pereant qui ante nos!*) mortified me by anticipating the beautiful example I had already found for myself; and sometimes given what I thought, perhaps with foolish partiality, to be not so good an example as mine. In a few places, not without diffidence, I have ventured to dissent from it.

The readers I have principally in view are students. One of my aims is to facilitate, as regards certain words, a more accurate reading of old books; and therefore to encourage everyone to similar exploration of many other words. I am sometimes told that there are people who want a study of literature wholly free from philology; that is, from the love and knowledge of words. Perhaps no such people exist. If they do, they are either crying for the moon or else resolving on a lifetime of persistent and carefully guarded delusion. If we read an old poem with insufficient regard for change in the overtones, and even the dictionary meanings, of words since its date—if, in fact, we are content with whatever effect the words accidentally produce in our modern minds—then of course we do not read the poem the old writer intended. What we get may still be, in our opinion, a poem; but it will be our poem, not his. If we call this *tout court* 'reading' the old poet, we are deceiving ourselves. If we reject as 'mere philology' every attempt to restore for us his real poem, we are safeguarding the deceit. Of course any man is entitled to say he prefers the poems he makes for himself out of his mistranslations to the poems the writers intended. I have no quarrel with him. He need have none with me. Each to his taste.

3

And to avoid this, knowledge is necessary. Intelligence and sensibility by themselves are not enough. This is well illustrated by an example within my own experience. In the days of the old School Certificate we once set as a gobbet from *Julius Caesar*

> Is Brutus sick and is it physical
> To walk unbraced and suck up the humours
> Of the dank morning [1]

and one boy explained *physical* as 'sensible, sane; the opposite of "mental" or mad'. It would be crass to laugh at that boy's ignorance without also admiring his extreme cleverness. The ignorance is laughable because it could have been avoided. But if that ignorance had been inevitable—as similar ignorances often are when we are dealing with an ancient book—if so much linguistic history were lost that we did not and could not know the sense 'mad' for *mental* and the antithesis of *mental–physical* to be far later than Shakespeare's time, then his suggestion would deserve to be hailed as highly intelligent. We should indeed probably accept it, at least provisionally, as correct. For it makes excellent sense of the passage and also accounts for the meaning it gives to *physical* by a semantic process which—if we did not know that chronology ruled it out—we should regard as very possible.

So far from being secured against such errors, the highly intelligent and sensitive reader will, without knowledge, be most in danger of them. His mind bubbles over with

[1] II, i, 261.

4

possible meanings. He has ready to hand un-thought-of metaphors, highly individual shades of feeling, subtle associations, ambiguities—every manner of semantic gymnastics—which he can attribute to his author. Hence the difficulty of 'making sense' out of a strange phrase will seldom be for him insuperable. Where the duller reader simply does not understand, he misunderstands—triumphantly, brilliantly. But it is not enough to make sense. We want to find the sense the author intended. 'Brilliant' explanations of a passage often show that a clever, insufficiently informed man has found one more mare's nest. The wise reader, far from boasting an ingenuity which will find sense in what looks like nonsense, will not accept even the most slightly strained meaning until he is quite sure that the history of the word does not permit something far simpler. The smallest semantic discomfort rouses his suspicions. He notes the key word and watches for its recurrence in other texts. Often they will explain the whole puzzle.

By driving words from different languages abreast I have been able to bring out something which interests me far more than derivations. We find in the history, say, of *phusis*, *natura*, and *kind*, or again in that of *eleutherios*, *liberalis*, *free*, and *frank*, similar or even identical semantic operations being performed quite independently. The speakers who achieved them belonged to different stocks and lived in different countries at different periods, and they started with different linguistic tools. In an age when the linguistic analysts have made us afraid that our thought may be almost wholly conditioned by our speech this seems to me encouraging. Apparently there is at least some independence. There is something, either in the structure of the mind or in the things it thinks about, which can produce the same results under very different conditions.

After hearing one chapter of this book when it was still a lecture, a man remarked to me 'You have made me afraid to say anything at all'. I know what he meant. Prolonged thought *about* the words which we ordinarily use to think *with* can produce a momentary aphasia. I think it is to be welcomed. It is well we should become aware of what we are doing when we speak, of the ancient, fragile, and (well used) immensely potent instruments that words are.

This implies that I have an idea of what is good and bad language. I have. Language is an instrument for communication. The language which can with the greatest ease make the finest and most numerous distinctions of meaning is the best. It is better to have *like* and *love* than to have *aimer* for both. It was better to have the older English distinction between 'I haven't got indigestion' (I am not suffering from it at the moment) and 'I don't have indigestion' (I am not a dyspeptic) than to level both, as America has now taught most Englishmen to do, under 'I don't have'.

In the following pages we shall see good words, or good senses of words, losing their edge or, more rarely, recovering it or getting a new edge that serves some different purpose. I have tried not to obtrude the moral, but I should be glad if I sent any reader away with a new sense of responsibility to the language. It is unnecessary defeatism to believe that we can do nothing about it. Our conversation will have little effect; but if we get into print—perhaps especially if we are leader-writers, reviewers, or reporters—we can help to strengthen or weaken some disastrous vogue word; can encourage a good, and resist a bad, gallicism or Americanism. For many things the press prints today will be taken up by the great mass of speakers in a few years.

Verbicide, the murder of a word, happens in many ways. Inflation is one of the commonest; those who taught us to say *awfully* for 'very', *tremendous* for 'great', *sadism* for 'cruelty', and *unthinkable* for 'undesirable' were verbicides. Another way is verbiage, by which I here mean the use of a word as a promise to pay which is never going to be kept. The use of *significant* as if it were an absolute, and with no intention of ever telling us what the thing is significant of, is an example. So is *diametrically* when it is used merely to put *opposite* into the superlative. Men often commit verbicide because they want to snatch a word as a party banner, to appropriate its 'selling quality'. Verbicide was committed when we exchanged *Whig* and *Tory* for *Liberal* and *Conservative*. But the greatest cause of verbicide is the fact that most people are obviously far more anxious to express their approval and disapproval of things than to describe them. Hence the tendency of words to become less descriptive and more evaluative; then to become evaluative, while still retaining some hint of the sort of goodness or badness implied; and to end up by being purely evaluative—useless synonyms for *good* or for *bad*. We shall see this happening to the word *villain* in a later chapter. *Rotten*, paradoxically has become so completely a synonym for 'bad' that we now have to say *bad* when we mean 'rotten'.

I am not suggesting that we can by an archaising purism repair any of the losses that have already occurred. It may not, however, be entirely useless to resolve that we ourselves will never commit verbicide. If modern critical usage seems to be initiating a process which might finally make *adolescent* and *contemporary* mere synonyms for *bad* and *good*—and stranger things have happened—we should banish them from our vocabulary. I am tempted to adapt the couplet we see in some parks—

> Let no one say, and say it to your shame,
> That there was meaning here before you came.

I will close this chapter with a 'statement', as the musicians say, of certain themes which will recur in those that follow.

I. THE EFFECTS OF RAMIFICATION

As everyone knows, words constantly take on new meanings. Since these do not necessarily, nor even usually, obliterate the old ones, we should picture this process not on the analogy of an insect undergoing metamorphoses but rather on that of a tree throwing out new branches, which themselves throw out subordinate branches; in fact, as ramification. The new branches sometimes overshadow and kill the old ones but by no means always. We shall again and again find the earliest senses of a word flourishing for centuries despite a vast over-growth of later senses which might have been expected to kill them.

The philologist's dream is to diagrammatise all the meanings of a word so as to have a perfect semantic tree of it; every twig traced to its branch, every branch traced back to the trunk. That this can seldom, if ever, be perfectly achieved does not matter much; all studies end in doubts. But there is apparently some real danger of forgetting that the overwhelming majority of those who use the word neither know nor care anything about the tree. And even those who do know something of it most often use the word without thinking about it. Just in the same way, all men use their muscles when they move but most men do not know or care what muscles they are using; and even anatomists, who do know, are not usually thinking of this during a game of tennis. When we use one word in many different senses we avail our-selves of the results produced by semantic ramification. We can do this successfully without being aware of them.

That is why I cannot agree with Professor Empson's suggestion[1] that when we say 'Use your sense, man!' we are implying that the intellectual effort demanded is as easy as the reception of a sense-impression—in other words that we are using *sense* (i.e. sense-perception) meta-phorically. Particular objections will be found in a later chapter: the ramification which produced for the word *sense* the two meanings (gumption and sense-perception) is well over two thousand years old, and need not have

[1] *The Structure of Complex Words* (1951), p. 257.

9

had anything to do with metaphor. It is handed to the modern speaker 'on a plate'. And that is the general principle I am here concerned with. If we neglect the semantic history of a word we shall be in danger of attributing to ordinary speakers an individual semantic agility which in reality they neither have nor need. It is perfectly true that we hear very simple people daily using several different senses of one word with perfect accuracy —like a dancer in a complicated dance. But this is not because they understand either the relation between them or their history.

Each new speaker learns his native language chiefly by imitation, partly by those hurried scraps of amateur lexicography which his elders produce in answer to the frequent question 'What does that mean?' He does not at first—how should he?—distinguish between different senses of one word and different words. They all have to be learned in the same way. Memory and the faculty of imitation, not semantic gymnastics, enable him to speak about *sentences* in a Latin exercise and *sentences* of imprisonment, about a cardboard *box* and a *box* at the theatre. He does not even ask which are different words and which merely different senses. Nor, for the most part, do we. How many adults know whether *bows* of ships and *bows* taught by the dancing master—or *down* (a hill) and *down* (*deorsum*)—or a boys' *school* and a *school* of porpoises— are accidental homophones (like *neat* and *neat* or *arms* and *arms*) or products of ramification?

A child may, of course, be philologically minded. If so, it may construct imaginary semantic trees for itself. But it does so to explain the usages it has already learned; the usage is not a result of the theory. As a child I—probably like many others—evolved the theory that a candle-stick was so called 'because it makes the candle *stick* up'. But that wasn't why I called it a candlestick. I called it a candlestick because everyone else did.

II. THE INSULATING POWER OF THE CONTEXT

It is this most important principle that enables speakers to give half a dozen different meanings to a single word with very little danger of confusion. If ambiguity (in Professor Empson's sense) were not balanced by this power, communication would become almost impossible. There is, I understand, a species of modern poetry which is so written that it cannot be fully received unless all the possible senses of words are operative in the reader's mind. Whether there was any such poetry before the present century—whether all old poetry thus read is misread— are questions we need not discuss here. What seems to me certain is that in ordinary language the sense of a word is governed by the context and this sense normally excludes all others from the mind. When we see the notice 'Wines and Spirits' we do not think about angels, devils, ghosts and fairies—nor about the 'spirits' of the older medical theory. When someone speaks about the Stations of the Cross we do not think about railway stations nor about our station in life.

The proof of this is that the sudden intrusion of any irrelevant sense—in other words the voluntary or involuntary pun—is funny. It is funny because it is unexpected. There is a semantic explosion because the two meanings rush together from a great distance; one of them was not in our consciousness at all till that moment. If it had been, there would be no detonation. This comes out very clearly in those numerous stories which decorum forbids me to recall (in print); stories where some august person such as a headmistress or a bishop, on a platform, gravely uses a word in one sense, blissfully forgetful of some other and very unsuitable sense—producing a ludicrous indecency. It will usually be found that the audience, like the speaker, had till then quite forgotten it too. For the shouts of open, or the sibilations of suppressed, laughter do not usually begin at once but after several seconds. The obscene intruder, the uninvited semantic guest, has taken that time to come up from the depths where he lay asleep, off duty.

It is of course the insulating power of the context which enables old senses to persist, uncontaminated by newer ones. Thus *train* (of a dress) and *train* (on the railway), or *civil* (courteous) and *civil* (not military), or *magazine* (a store) and *magazine* (a periodical), do not interfere with one another because they are unlikely to occur in the same context. They live happily by keeping out of each other's way.

III. THE DANGEROUS SENSE

When a word has several meanings historical circumstances often make one of them dominant during a particular period. Thus *station* is now more likely to mean a railway-station than anything else; *evolution*, more likely to bear its biological sense than any other. When I was a boy *estate* had as its dominant meaning 'land belonging to a large landowner', but the meaning 'land covered with small houses' is dominant now.

The dominant sense of any word lies uppermost in our minds. Wherever we meet the word, our natural impulse will be to give it that sense. When this operation results in nonsense, of course, we see our mistake and try over again. But if it makes tolerable sense our tendency is to go merrily on. We are often deceived. In an old author the word may mean something different. I call such senses dangerous senses because they lure us into misreadings. in examining a word I shall often have to distinguish one of its meanings as its *dangerous sense*, and I shall symbolise this by writing the word (in italics) with the letters *d.s.* after it.

Thus, since 'safety' is the *dangerous sense* of the word *security* the symbol *security* (*d.s.*) would stand for '*security* in the sense of safety'. Similarly *philosophy* (*d.s.*) means '*philosophy* in the sense of metaphysics, epistemology, logic, etc. as distinct from the natural sciences'—the sense we are in danger of reading into it when old writers actually mean by it just science. *Fellow* (*d.s.*) would be '*fellow* used as a contemptuous vocative'.

When the *dangerous sense* is a sense which did not exist at all in the age when our author wrote, it is less dangerous. Moderate, and moderately increasing, scholarship will guard us against it. But often the situation is more delicate. What is now the *dangerous sense* may have existed then but it may not yet have been at all dominant.

It may possibly be the sense the old author really intended, but this is not nearly so probable as our own usage leads us to suppose. Our task is not the comparatively simple one of excluding an unqualified candidate; we have to conquer our undue predilection for one of those who are qualified.

IV. THE WORD'S MEANING AND THE SPEAKER'S MEANING

I use *speaker* throughout to cover *writer* as well.

The distinction between what a word means and what a speaker means by a word appears in its crudest form, of course, when a foreigner or imperfectly educated native is actually mistaken as to standard usage and commits a malapropism; using *deprecate*, say, to mean 'depreciate', or *disinterested* to mean 'bored', or *scarify* to mean 'scare'. But this is not what I have in mind. Speaker's meaning and word's meaning may be distinguishable where there is no lexical mistake involved.

'When I spoke of supper after the theatre, I meant by *supper* a biscuit and a cup of cocoa. But my friend meant by *supper* something like a cold bird and a bottle of wine.' In this situation both parties might well have agreed on the lexical (or 'dictionary') meaning of supper; perhaps 'a supernumerary meal which, if taken at all, is the last meal before bed'. In another way they 'meant' different things by it. The use of the verb *mean* both for the word's force and for the speaker's intention can doubtless be criticised, and distinctions could be drawn. But I am not here embarking on 'the meaning of meaning' nor high linguistics. That will not be necessary. To use *mean* thus

14

without further distinction is good English and will serve our turn.

For there is only one reason why the difference between the speaker's and the word's meaning concerns us. It is this. If some speaker's meaning becomes very common it will in the end establish itself as one of the word's meanings; this is one of the ways in which semantic ramification comes about.

For thousands of Englishmen today the word *furniture* has only one sense—a (not very easily definable) class of domestic movables. And doubtless many people, if they should read Berkeley's 'all the choir of heaven and furniture of earth', would take this use of *furniture* to be a metaphorical application of the sense they know—that which is to earth as tables and chairs and so forth are to a house. Even those who know the larger meaning of the word (whatever 'furnishes' in the sense of stocking, equipping, or replenishing) would certainly admit 'domestic movables' as one of its senses. It would in fact, by my system, be *furniture* (*d.s.*). But it must have become one of the word's meanings by being a very common speaker's meaning. Men who said 'my furniture' were often in fact, within that context, referring to their domestic movables. The word did not yet mean that; *they* meant it. When I say 'Take away this rubbish' I usually 'mean' these piles of old newspapers, magazines, and Christmas cards. That is not what the word *rubbish* means. But if a sufficiently large number of people shared my distaste for that sort of litter, and applied the word *rubbish* to it often enough, the word might come to have this as one of its senses. So with *furniture*, which, from being a speaker's meaning, has established itself so firmly as one of the word's meanings that it has ousted all the others in popular speech.

Estate is acquiring the dominant sense 'building estate' in our own time by just the same process. *Morality* and *immorality* have in the same way come to mean 'chastity' and 'lechery'. These are the forms of virtue and vice which both the prudish and the prurient most want to talk about. And since most of us have a dash of prudery or prurience and many among us of both, we may say simply 'which most people most want to talk about'. The speaker's meaning of 'all that immorality' was so often 'all that lechery' that lechery becomes one of the word's meanings; indeed, outside highly educated circles, its only meaning.

This is one of the most troublesome phenomena for the historian of a word. If you want to know when 'domestic movables' became one of the meanings (word's meanings) of *furniture*, it is no good just finding the earliest example where the things referred to as *furniture* in that context obviously were *in fact* domestic movables. The usage might record merely a speaker's meaning. You cannot infer a 'word's meaning' any more than you can infer from my most habitual use of *rubbish* that *rubbish* (lexically) had 'old newspapers etc.' as one of its senses in 1958. An old writer may use the word *gentle* of conduct which was clearly in fact what we call gentle (mild, soft, not severe); or may use *wit* to describe what was clearly in fact *wit* (*d.s.*); or *cattle* referring to what we call 'cattle'. But none of these prove the existence of the modern word's meaning at that date. They might all be speaker's meanings.

V. TACTICAL DEFINITIONS

Most of us who are interested in such things soon learn that if you want to discover how a man pronounces a word it is no use asking him. Many people will produce in reply the pronunciation which their snobbery or anti-snobbery makes them think the most desirable. Honest and self-critical people will often be reduced to saying, 'Well, now you ask me, I don't really know'. Anyway, with the best will in the world, it is extraordinarily difficult to sound a word—thus produced cold and without context for inspection—exactly as one would sound it in real conversation. The proper method is quite different. You must stealthily guide the talk into subjects which will force him to use the word you are chasing. You will then hear his real pronunciation; the one he uses when he is off his guard, the one he doesn't know he uses.

It is with meanings something the same. In determining what a word meant at any period in the past we may get some help from the dictionaries of that period; especially from bi-lingual dictionaries. These are the most trust-worthy because their purpose was usually humble and practical; the writer really wants to give you the nearest English equivalent of the Latin or Italian word. A purely English dictionary is more likely to be influenced by the lexicographer's ideas of how words ought to be used; therefore worse evidence of how they actually were used.

But when we leave the dictionaries we must view all definitions with grave distrust. It is the greatest simplicity in the world to suppose that when, say, Dryden defines *wit* or Arnold defines *poetry*, we can use their definition as evidence of what the word really meant when they wrote. The fact that they define it at all is itself a ground for scepticism. Unless we are writing a dictionary, or a text-book of some technical subject, we define our words only because we are in some measure departing from their real current sense. Otherwise there would be no purpose in doing so. This is especially true of negative definitions. Statements that honour, or freedom, or humour, or wealth, 'does not mean' this or that are proof that it was beginning to mean, or even had long meant, precisely this or that. We tell our pupils that *deprecate* does not mean *depreciate* or that *immorality* does not mean simply *lechery* because these words are beginning to mean just those things. We are in fact resisting the growth of a new sense. We may be quite right to do so, for it may be one that will make English a less useful means of communication. But we should not be resisting it unless it had already appeared. We do not warn our pupils that *coalbox* does not mean a hippopotamus.

The chapter devoted to the word *wit* will illustrate this. We shall find old critics giving definitions of it which are contradicted not only by other evidence but out of the critics' own mouths. Off their guard they can be caught using it in the very sense their definition was contrived to exclude. A student who should read the critical debate of the seventeenth century on wit under the impression that what the critics say they mean by *wit* is always, or often, what they really mean by *wit* would end in total bewilderment. He must understand that such definitions are purely tactical. They are attempts to appropriate for one side, and to deny to the other, a potent word. You can see the same 'war of positions' going on today. A certain type of writer begins 'The essence of poetry is' or 'All vulgarity may be defined as', and then produces a definition which no one ever thought of since the world began, which conforms to no one's actual usage, and which he himself will probably have forgotten by the end of the month. The phenomenon ceases to be puzzling only when we realise that it is a tactical definition. The pretty word has to be narrowed *ad hoc* so as to exclude something he dislikes. The ugly word has to be extended *ad hoc*, or more probably *ad hunc*, so as to bespatter some enemy. Nineteenth-century definitions of the word *gentleman* are also tactical.

I do not of course say (for I don't know) that such definitions cannot have uses of their own. But that of giving information about the actual meaning of a word is not one of them.

VI. THE METHODOLOGICAL IDIOM

Suppose that a conversation which we overhear contains the remark 'I'm afraid Jones's psychology will be his undoing'. Most of us, I suppose, would take this to mean that the state of his *psyche* will endanger his success and happiness. But suppose we then discover that the conversation is between two examiners; that Jones is a candidate in the examination; and that psychology is one of the three subjects in which he is being examined. The remark might now bear a different meaning—that Jones, having done fairly well on the other two subjects, had ruined his chances of the prize by his bad work on psychology. In other words, *psychology* is the name both of a science and of the things (or even one specimen of the things) which that science studies.

This transference I call the methodological idiom. It may produce ambiguity: 'Freud's psychology' might mean either a subject of which we have all heard much or one which, some would say, has been examined too little. But 'my anatomy' would almost certainly mean those facts about me which an anatomist would speak of as an expert, rather than my theories or proficiency in his science. It would be difficult to explain the word *physical* if one ignored the methodological idiom. When Milton says in *The Reason of Church Government*[1] that the Psalms are better than Pindar and Callimachus 'not in their divine argument alone but in the very critical art of composition', *critical art* must surely, by this idiom, mean the art that critics expound; those who practice it are the poets. The curious expression 'a scientific fact' may originally have meant a fact that is literally scientific or 'science-making'—a key fact whose discovery makes possible a wide range of further discoveries. But most modern users, I believe, mean merely 'a fact of the sort that scientists know about'. The methodological idiom, applied to *history*, has produced some confusion. It is

[1] Preface to Book II.

often hard to be sure whether the word means the past events themselves as they really were or the study that tries to discover and understand them.

VII. MORALISATION OF STATUS-WORDS

Words which originally referred to a person's rank—to legal, social, or economic status and the qualifications of birth which have often been attached to these—have a tendency to become words which assign a type of character and behaviour. Those implying superior status can become terms of praise; those implying inferior status, terms of disapproval. *Chivalrous, courteous, frank, generous, gentle, liberal*, and *noble* are examples of the first; *ignoble, villain*, and *vulgar*, of the second.

Sometimes there are complexities. All my life the epithet *bourgeois* has been, in many contexts, a term of contempt, but not for the same reason. When I was a boy —a *bourgeois* boy—it was applied to my social class by the class above it; *bourgeois* meant 'not aristocratic, therefore vulgar'. When I was in my twenties this changed. My class was now vilified by the class below it; *bourgeois* began to mean 'not proletarian, therefore parasitic, reactionary'. Thus it has always been a reproach to assign a man to that class which has provided the world with nearly all its divines, poets, philosophers, scientists, musicians, painters, doctors, architects, and administrators. When the *bourgeoisie* is despised for not being proletarian we get an exception to the general principle stated above. The name of the higher status implies the worse character and behaviour. This I take to be the peculiar, and transi-

tory, result of a revolutionary situation. The earlier usage
—*bourgeois* as 'not aristocratic'—is the normal linguistic
phenomenon.

It will be diagnosed by many as a symptom of the inveterate snobbery of the human race; and certainly the
implications of language are hardly ever egalitarian. But
that is not the whole story. Two other factors come in.
One is optimism; men's belief, or at least hope, that their
social betters will be personally better as well. The other is
far more important. A word like *nobility* begins to take
on its social-ethical meaning when it refers not simply to
a man's status but to the manners and character which are
thought to be appropriate to that status. But the mind
cannot long consider those manners and that character
without being forced on the reflection that they are sometimes lacking in those who are noble by status and sometimes present in those who are not. Thus from the very
first the social-ethical meaning, merely by existing, is
bound to separate itself from the status-meaning. Accordingly, from Boethius down, it becomes a common-
place of European literature that the true nobility is
within, that *villanie*, not status, makes the villain, that
there are 'ungentle gentles' and that 'gentle is as gentle
does'. The linguistic phenomenon we are considering is
therefore quite as much an escape from, as an assertion of,
that pride above and servility below which, in my
opinion, should be called snobbery. The behaviour
ideally, or optimistically, attributed to an aristocracy
provides a paradigm. It becomes obvious that, as regards
many aristocrats, this is an unrealised ideal. But the

paradigm remains; anyone, even the bad aristocrat himself, may attempt to conform to it. A new ethical idea has
come into power.

I think its power has been greatest at that frontier where
the aristocrats and the middle class meet. The court takes
from the class below it talented individuals—like Chaucer,
say—as its entertainers and assistants. We ordinarily think
of Chaucer learning his courtesy at court. And no doubt
he did; its manners were more graceful than those of his
own family. But can we doubt that he also taught
courtesy there? By expecting to find realised at court the
paradigm of courtesy and nobility, by writing his poetry
on the assumption that it was realised, such a man offers a
critique—and an unconscious critique—of the court's
actual *ethos*, which no one can resent. It is not flattery, but
it flatters. As they say a woman becomes more beautiful
when she is loved, a nobility by status will become more
'noble' under such treatment. Thus the Horaces, Chaucers,
Racines, or Spensers substantially ennoble their patrons.
But also, through them, many graces pass down from the
aristocracy into the middle class. This two-way traffic
generates a culture-group comprising the choicest members of two groups that differ in status. If this is snobbery,
we must reckon snobbery among the greatest nurseries of
civilisation. Without it, would there ever have been anything but wealth and power above and sycophancy or
envy below?

2

NATURE

[WITH *PHUSIS, KIND, PHYSICAL* ETC.]

In this chapter we shall have to consider Greek *phusis*, Latin *natura* (with its derivatives), and English *kind*. Each of the three has a great number of senses, and two of these senses are common to all of them. One appears to have been reached independently by all three words. The other was at first peculiar to *phusis* and was thence transferred to *natura*, and through *natura* to *kind*. Thus it is *phusis* that complicates the whole story, and that story will therefore be most easily told if, in defiance of chronology, we begin with some account of the Latin and English words in their un-hellenised condition, and only after that turn to the Greek.

I. 'NATURA'

By far the commonest native meaning of *natura* is something like sort, kind, quality, or character. When you ask, in our modern idiom, what something 'is like', you are asking for its *natura*. When you want to tell a man the *natura* of anything you describe the thing. In nineteenth-century English the word 'description' itself ('I do not associate with persons of that description') is often an exact synonym for *natura*. Caesar sent scouts to find out *qualis esset natura montis*, what the hill was like, what sort of a hill it was.[1] Quintilian speaks of a man *ingenii naturâ*

---

[1] *De Bello Gallico* I, 21.

24

praestantem (XII, 1), outstanding by the quality of his mind. Cicero's title *De Natura Deorum* could be translated 'What the gods are like'.

It will be noticed that whereas Caesar wanted to know the (doubtless unique) character of a particular hill, Cicero wrote about the common character of all gods, and Horace[1] can speak of *humana natura*, the character common to all men. There is a logical distinction here, but linguistically the two usages are the same. A class or species has a *natura*, and so has a particular or an individual.

It is not always possible, or necessary, to decide whether the idea of the species or that of the particular is uppermost. Cicero says that '*omnis natura* strives to preserve itself'.[2] It makes little difference whether we render *omnis natura* 'every class or species' or 'every kind (of thing)', hence 'a thing of whatever kind', and hence almost 'everything'.

Those who wish to go further back will notice that *natura* shares a common base with *nasci* (to be born); with the noun *natus* (birth); with *natio* (not only a race or nation but the name of the birth-goddess); or even that *natura* itself can mean the sexual organs—a sense formerly born by English *nature*, but apparently restricted to the female. It is risky to try to build precise semantic bridges, but there is obviously some idea of a thing's *natura* as its original or 'innate' character.

If we look forward, the road is clear. This sense of *natura*, though soon to be threatened by vast semantic growths of another origin, has shown astonishing persis-

---

[1] *Ars Poetica*, 353. [2] *De Finibus* IV, 7.

tence and is still as current a sense as any other for English *nature*. Every day we speak about 'the nature of the case' (or of the soil, the animal, the problem).

II. 'KIND'

From the earliest period of our language this has been both a noun (Anglo-Saxon *gecynd* and *cynd*) and an adjective (*gecynde* and *cynde*).

The meanings of the noun are very close to those of *natura*. The Anglo-Saxon word can mean what its modern descendant means, a 'kind' or sort. Thus *wæstma gecynde* are 'kinds' of fruit, or the rods which had miraculously been turned into gold in Ælfric's homily on the *Assumption of St John* can be presently turned back to their former *gecynde*. The meaning 'species', though now archaic, is still familiar to readers of A.V.: 'every winged fowl after his kind'.[1]

The *gecyndlimu* or 'kind-limbs' are certainly the genitals. When the author of the Anglo-Saxon *Phoenix* says (l. 355) that God only knows that bird's *gecynde* he certainly means its sex. But whether this is the author's meaning or the word's meaning may be doubted. He may use *gecynde* for 'sex' only because sex is a kind of kind, nameless and definable only by the context; just as Ælfric in his *Grammar* uses it for 'gender' when he glosses *neutrum* as 'neither *cynd*'. We easily forget how peculiar Latin is in having a special name for this kind of kind; Greek has to make do with *genos*, and German with *Geschlecht*.

Kind also means 'progeny', 'offspring'. In *Piers Plow-*

[1] Gen. i. 21.

man the beasts all 'follow reason', show moderation, 'in etying, in drynking, in gendrynge of kynde',[1] and there is a curse on all married couples who produce no *kynde*.[2] Closely linked to this is the larger sense of 'family' or 'stock'; a whole kindred is a *kind*, as when Jacob in the Middle English *Genesis and Exodus* left Canaan with many a man of his *kinde* (ll. 239 f.). 'Gentle kind' and 'noble stock' are almost certainly a doublet of synonyms (like the Prayer Book's 'acknowledge and confess') when Shakespeare writes 'came of a gentle kind and noble stock'.[3]

Thus the noun, though not historically connected with *natura* (unless you go back very far indeed), has a tolerably similar semantic area and presents no very serious difficulties. The adjective (*gecynde, cynde, cyndelic, kind* and *kindly*) has a more complicated repertory of meanings. It is not possible to reconstruct the bridges between them, still less to be sure in which direction the traffic crossed them. Indeed 'bridges' are probably too mechanical an image and the mutual influences between meaning and meaning are as subtle and reciprocal as those between a group of friends.

1. The adjective means 'hereditary'—the hereditary being, of course, what comes to one in virtue of one's birth or family (or *kind*). Thus we are told in *Beowulf* (l. 2197) that the hero and Hygelac both had *gecynde* land, hereditary estates, in their native country. Similarly, a *kind* or *kindly* lord is one who inherits his lordship. In the Anglo-Saxon *Metres of Boethius* the Goths are said to have had two *gecynde* kings.[4] In Malory Arthur tells Launcelot

[1] C. XIV, 144.   [2] C. XIX, 223.   [3] *Pericles* v, i, 68.
[4] *Alfred's Boethius*, ed. W. J. Sedgefield (1899), p. 151.

and Bors to go and look after their dead fathers' lands 'and cause youre lyege men to know you as for their kynde lord'.[1] Presumably by an extension from this, any thoroughly legitimate lord, as distinct from a conqueror or usurper, may be 'kindly'. 'The Red City and all that be therein will take you for their kindly lord.'[2]

It is interesting to notice that the derivatives, both French and English, of Latin *naturalis* develop the same sense. In Villehardouin's *Conqueste de Constantinople* the crusaders present Alexius to the Byzantines as *vostre seignor naturel*; in Sidney we find 'your naturall prince';[3] and in Shakespeare 'his natural king'.[4] It is most improbable that *naturalis* could have reached this sense by a native Latin development. But those who knew the noun *kind*, or its Frankish equivalent, as their word for Latin *natura*, might come, when they were writing Latin, to think that *naturalis* would do for the adjective *kind*.

2. Any behaviour or state which shows a thing's, or a person's, kind or nature—which is characteristic of it, typical, normal, and therefore to be expected—may be called 'kind'. We are told that on a particular occasion Beowulf behaved with valour, as was *gecynde* to him (l. 2696)—as was 'just like him'. Malory leaves two lovers in a bed 'clipping and kissing as was kindly thing'— as of course they would.[5] And here again the sense of the Latin derivative may have been influenced by that of the Germanic word. *Naturaliter* did not mean 'of course', as

---

[1] Vinaver, p. 245, l. 17. Not in Caxton.
[2] Vinaver, p. 714, l. 5. Not in Caxton.
[3] *Arcadia* II, xxvi, 4. [4] *Hen. VI*, Pt 3, I, i, 82.
[5] XI, viii. Vinaver, pp. 804–5.

'naturally' and *naturellement* often do. This sense is so strangely remote from other senses of 'naturally' that we can say 'As my hostess had cooked it herself, I *naturally pretended* to like it'. But it becomes easy enough when the original equivalence of *gecynd* and *natura* has worked for centuries towards the possible infection of almost any sense of one by almost any sense of the other.

From the idea of the characteristic or normal to that of the proper, the fitting, the desirable, is an easy transition. Indeed the sense-development of the word *proper* itself, from that which belongs to a thing or makes part of its definition to that which ought to be found in it, is a striking instance. When Philautus says 'so unkinde a yeare it hath beene...that we felt the heate of the Summer before we coulde discerne the temperature of the Spring',[1] 'unusual' would cover all he need mean by *unkinde*, though one may suspect that some complaint of unfitness or unsuitability goes with it. When Criseyde asks how any plant or living creature can last without 'his kinde noriture',[2] it is impossible to draw any distinction between an organism's characteristic or normal, and its suitable or appropriate, food. But the value judgement is clear, and the sense 'fitting' or 'proper' is certain when Malory, enumerating the knights who tried to heal Sir Urre, says 'we must begin at King Arthur, as is kindly to begin at him that was the most man of worship'.[3]

3. Sometimes the adjective has a range of meaning

---

[1] *Euphues and his England*, ed. Arber (1919), p. 465.
[2] Chaucer, *Troilus and Crysyde*, IV, 768.
[3] XIX, x. Vinaver, p. 1147, l. 3, *was* for *is*.

very like that of *pius* in classical Latin; somewhere between 'dutiful' and 'affectionate'. The man who is *pius* or 'kind' (in this sense) is one who does not good offices in general, but good offices to which close kinship or some other personal relationship binds him. When Sidney speaks of 'the Paphlagonian unkinde king and his kind son'[1] he means that the father was a very bad (unfatherly) father and the son a very good (filial) son. Here again we shall find the derivative of *natura* taking on the sense of the Germanic words, so that *unnatural* and *natural* mean 'lacking (or having) due family affection', and *nature* itself can mean *pietas*. Both usages come together when William Bulleyn writes 'Parents are more natural to their children then children to their fathers and mothers. Nature doth descend but not ascend.'[2] The Latin and English words are used as a doublet by Shakespeare: 'A brother in his love towards her ever most kind and natural.'[3] But the family (or *kind*), though the usual, is not the only ground of the special obligation which 'kindness' fulfils. Ingratitude is also 'unkindness'. Sloth, in *Piers Plowman*, confesses he is 'unkynde ageyns courtesye';[4] do him a good turn and he will not respond.

4. The next meaning in our catalogue is closely parallel to that of Latin *generosus*. If *genus* is a stock or lineage, *generosus* ought in logic to mean 'pertaining to, or having, a lineage'. But in that sense it would be a useless word and to call a man *generosus* would be to say nothing; for every

---

[1] *Arcadia* II, 10, Rubric.
[2] *Dialogue Against the Fever Pestilence* (1564).
[3] *Measure for Measure* III, i, 225.   [4] C. VIII, 43.

man has a lineage of some sort. In fact, *generosus* means well-born, noble, having a good lineage. Similarly when the Germans call a man *geboren* they mean *hoch-geboren*, well or nobly born. In just the same way the adjective *kind* means not 'having a family or kind' but 'noble'. In all three languages one can imagine different routes by which this sense would be reached. When a man advertises his shop as 'the shop for quality', he ignores the fact that badness is just as much a quality as goodness; by 'quality' he means 'good quality'. By a similar ellipsis 'a man of family' means, or used to mean, 'a man of good family'. That is one way in which *generosus* and *kind* could come to mean not merely 'familial' but 'of a good (noble) family'. Or it might be that certain people were deemed, by earlier societies, to have 'no family' in a far more nearly literal sense. The slave, the beggar, the stranger belong to none of the groups which we have been taught, in this settlement, to call families. No doubt (if you come to think of it) they must, in physical fact, have had parents and even grandparents. But not ones we know. They may not even know them themselves. If you ask of which family they come—are they Erlings or Birmings or Wolfings?—the answer is 'none'. They are outside the organisation we know, as animals are outside it.

By whatever process, *kind*, then, comes to mean 'noble' or 'gentle': thus in *Genesis and Exodus* (l. 1452) we have 'begotten of kinde blood'. As we should expect —did not our ancestors speak of 'noble' and 'base' metals?—this can be extended beyond the human sphere, so that one Hales (*c.* 1656) talks of grafting 'apples and kind fruit upon thorns'. It is possibly along this branch of meaning that we reach Cleopatra's 'kindly creatures, turn all to serpents'[1]—let all the nobler or gentler creatures turn into those we most abhor. The passage in Malory where Percivale helps a lion in its fight against a snake because it is 'the more naturall beast of the two' is curious.[2] If 'more naturall' means nobler, superior in the supposed social hierarchy of beasts, this will be another instance of the Latin derivative's semantic infection by the corresponding Germanic word.

Instances of the purely social meaning for *kinde* are not plentiful. More often (like 'noble' itself) it has a vaguely eulogistic sense. Hence 'kind jeweler' in *Pearl* (l. 276), or 'kinde caroles' in *Gawain* (l. 473).

5. The meanings 'suitable', *pius*, and 'noble'—and especially the last, as the parallel development of *gentle* shows—may all have played a part in producing that of 'exorable, compassionate, beneficent—the opposite of cruel'. 'Each Christian man be kinde to other', says Langland,[3] meaning, I think, exactly what we should mean now. This is the *dangerous sense* of the word *kind*. We may sometimes read it into an old text where it was not intended. In Chaucer's 'He was a gentil harlot and a kinde'[4] the modern meaning for both adjectives is probable, but not, I think, certain. In Herbert's 'I the unkinde, ungratefull' (from *Love*) the modern meaning would be disastrous; the idea of general beneficence from man to God borders on the absurd. Herbert is classing himself

---

[1] *Antony and Cleopatra* II, v, 78. [2] XIV, vi. Vinaver, p. 912, l. 25.
[3] A. XI, 243. [4] *Canterbury Tales*, A. 647.

with 'unkind mothers' and 'unnatural children' as one who, with gross insensibility, makes no response to the arch-natural appeal of the tenderest and closest personal relation that can be imagined; one who is loved in vain.

The peculiar erotic use of the word *kind* is not a special sense but a special application of the sense 'beneficent or exorable'—especially the latter. The woman who yields to your suit is exorable, therefore *kind*. Euphemism and gallantry, not always without a touch of irony, probably lie behind this. It must not be hinted that the lady has any passions or senses, and so her favours must be attributed as in the medieval tradition, to mercy, *pite*, or *ore*. Hence Collins writes

> fair Circassia where, to love inclin'd,
> Each swain was bless'd for every maid was kind.[1]

Elsewhere the euphemism almost ceases to be a euphemism and *kindness* can become a name for (a woman's) violent sexual passion; so that Dryden, in a startling phrase, speaks of Roman ladies whispering Greek endearments to their lovers 'in the fury of their kindness'.[2]

III. PHUSIS

(G)*nasci* and *kind* have a common root, if you go far enough back. *Phusis* has quite a different origin. Its representatives, or what seem to be its representatives, in various Indo-Germanic languages suggest two main branches of meaning; the one, something like 'inhabit,

---

[1] *Persian Eclogues* IV, I.
[2] *Dramatic Poesy. Essays*, ed. Ker, vol. I, p. 54.

live (at), dwell, remain, be' (at a place or in a condition); the other, 'to grow (transitively, as one "grows" cucumbers or a beard, and intransitively as beards and cucumbers grow), to become'. The latter branch is well represented by the Greek verb *phuein*. Dionysus grows (*phuei*) the vine for mortals;[1] a father begets (*phuei*) a son;[2] 'not to have been born (*phunai*) has no fellow', says Sophocles.[3]

The noun *phusis* can hardly mean anything except 'beginning, coming-to-be' when Empedocles says 'there is neither a *phusis* nor an end of all mortal things'.[4] On the other hand, it much more often means, like *natura* or *kind*, sort or character or 'description'. 'A horrid *phusis* of mind',[5] 'the *phusis* of the Egyptian country',[6] 'the philosophic *phusis*',[7] are typical. The connection between this and the meaning of the verb *phuein* is not obvious, though as usual 'bridges' can be devised. Aristotle is trying his hand at one in his famous definition; 'whatever each thing is like (*hoion hekaston esti*) when its process of coming-to-be is complete, that we call the *phusis* of each thing'.[8] On this view a thing's *phusis* would be what it *grows* into at maturity.[9] This explanation does not seem to me at all improbable, but Aristotle's statement is no evidence for it, and Sir David Ross thinks it philologically wrong. Like all philosophers, Aristotle gives words the definitions which will be most useful for his own purpose

[1] Euripides, *Bacchae*, 651.
[2] Euripides, *Helena*, 87.
[3] *Oed. Col.* 1222.
[4] *Fragment* 8.
[5] Euripides, *Medea*, 103.
[6] Herodotus II, 5.
[7] Plato, *Republic*, 410 e.
[8] *Politics*, 1252 b.
[9] Cf. *Metaphysics*, 1014 b.

and the history of his own language is one of the few
subjects in which he was not a distinguished pioneer.

But already, before Aristotle wrote, *phusis* had taken
on, in addition to the meaning 'sort', a new and quite
astonishing sense. The pre-Socratic Greek philosophers
had had the idea of taking all the things they knew or
believed in—gods, men, animals, plants, minerals, what
you will—and impounding them under a single name; in
fact, of regarding Everything as a thing, turning this
amorphous and heterogeneous collection into an object
or pseudo-object. And for some reason the name they
chose for it was *phusis*. Thus in the late sixth or early
fifth century we have the great philosophical poem of
Parmenides, whose title is everywhere given as *About
Phusis*. In the fifth century we have that of Empedocles
About the Phusis tôn ontôn (the *Phusis* of the things that
are).

Why they chose the name *phusis* is a question to which
I can give no confident answer.

We have already noticed that in one of the fragments of
Empedocles the word appears to mean 'a beginning'.
This at first sounds hopeful; a work on 'everything' might
possibly be entitled 'About the Beginning' or 'About
Becoming'. But not, unfortunately, a work of Empedocles. For in that very fragment he is denying that there
are any beginnings, and we know that his whole system
excluded them. Growth and change, and every sort of
becoming, he regarded as an illusion. Whatever others
might do, he of all men could not write a poem about
beginning.

Another hypothesis would be that *phusis* sometimes meant for him 'being'. We have seen that words from the same root can mean something like that in other Indo-Germanic languages. And from what we know about the behaviour of language in general we cannot deny the possibility that this sense, protected from the others by the insulating power of the context, might have occurred, and even lasted for centuries, in Greek. The real difficulty is that it has left no trace. We are inventing, to explain one difficulty, a usage for which we have not a shred of evidence.

A third hypothesis would begin from noticing that Parmenides' title alone is troublesome. We could explain the Empedoclean 'About the *phusis* of the things that are' and the Lucretian *De Rerum Natura*. Both could mean 'What things are like', and both would be simply two more instances of *phusis* and *natura* in the sense 'character, sort'. If we then assumed that *phusis* in the title of Parmenides' poem had originally been followed by a genitive (of things, of all things, of all), the story would become perfectly clear. Men begin by asking what this or that thing is like, asking for its *phusis*. They then get the idea of asking what 'everything' or 'the whole show' is like. The answer will give the *phusis* of everything. By an ellipse, the qualifying genitive then comes to be omitted, and the word which originally meant 'sort', in certain contexts, and protected by those contexts, comes to mean 'everything' or the universe. All this, I believe, could have happened; I am not claiming to know that it did.

However it came about, the amazing leap was made.

A comparatively small number of speculative Greeks invented *Nature*—Nature with a capital, *nature* (*d.s.*) or *nature* in the dangerous sense, for of all the senses of all the words treated in these pages this is surely the most dangerous, the one we are readiest to intrude where it is not required. From *phusis* this meaning passed to *natura* and from *natura* to *kind*. All three become names for what in China (I am told) is called 'the ten thousand things'.

Linguistically *nature* (*d.s.*) is more important for the slightly different senses which it led into than for any great use which was made of it in its purity. *Nature* (*d.s.*), if taken strictly, has no opposite. When we say that any particular thing is part of *nature* (*d.s.*), we know no more about it than before. 'Everything' is a subject on which there is not much to be said. Perhaps the chief use of *nature* (*d.s.*) in its purity is as the grammatical subject for expressions of optimism or pessimism: it is in that way rather like the word *life*.

But when *nature* (*d.s.*) loses its purity, when it is used in a curtailed or 'demoted' sense, it becomes important.

Parmenides and Empedocles had thought that they were giving, in principle, an account of everything. Later thinkers denied this; not in the sense that they wanted to add particular items here and there, but in the sense that they believed in realities of a quite different order from any that their predecessors took account of. They expressed this not in the form '*phusis* contains more than our ancestors supposed', but in the form (explicitly or implicitly), 'there is something else besides *phusis*'. The moment you say this, *phusis* is being used in what I call its demoted sense. For it had meant 'everything' and you are now saying there is something in addition to it. You are in fact using *phusis* to mean 'all the sort of things which our predecessors believed to be the only things'. You are also executing a movement of thought which would have been very much more difficult if those predecessors had not already impounded all those things in a single noun and, in fact, made the mere aggregate into what seemed to be an object with a determinate character of its own. Once that had been done it was possible, and convenient, to use the word *phusis* for that object, now no longer equated with everything. The 'demoted *d.s.*' presupposes and profits by, the pure *d.s.* By (so to speak) inventing Nature the old thinkers had made possible, or at least facilitated, the question whether there is anything else.

There were three principal movements towards demotion.

1. *The Platonic.* In Platonism, as everyone knows, the whole perceptible universe in space and time is an imitation, and product, of something different: the imperceptible, timeless, archetypal forms. This product or imitation, since it contains all the things which the older writers include in *phusis*, easily comes to be itself called *phusis*; as when Plotinus says that the arts imitate, not sensible objects, but those principles (*logoi*) from which *phusis* itself proceeds.[1] It is a demoted *phusis* because, far from being all that is, it is far less real and valuable than the realm of forms.

[1] *Enneads* v, viii, 1; some editions xxviii, 1.

2. *The Aristotelian.* Aristotle criticised thinkers like Parmenides because 'they never conceived of anything other than the substance of things perceptible by the senses'.[1] *Phusis* he defines as that which has in itself a principle of change. It is the subject-matter of natural (*phusike*) philosophy. (This is illuminating. We are getting to the age of universities and *phusis* (*d.s.*) *demoted* can be defined as the 'subject' of a particular discipline. Soon, in a new sense, everyone will 'know what *phusis* is': it is what so-and-so lectures on. The methodological idiom thus gets to work.) But there are two things outside *phusis.* First, things which are unchangeable, but cannot exist 'on their own'. These are the subject-matter of mathematics. Secondly, there is one thing which is unchangeable and does exist on its own. This is God, the unmoved mover; and he is studied by a third discipline.[2] On him 'the sky and all *phusis* depend';[3] words reproduced by Dante in *Paradiso* XXVIII, 41.

3. *The Christian.* Christianity involves a God as transcendent as Aristotle's, but adds (this was what it inherited from Judaism and could also have inherited from Plato's *Timaeus*) the conception that this God is the Creator of *phusis. Nature* (*d.s.*) *demoted* is now both distinct from God and also related to him as artifact to artist, or as servant to master; so that God in Tasso has *natura* under his feet.[4]

In the Middle Ages a still further demotion or restriction occurred, by which *nature* no longer covered the

---

[1] *De Caelo* III, 278 b.
[2] *Metaphysics*, 1064 a. Everyman trans. p. 156.
[3] *Ibid.* 1072 b. Trans. p. 346.   [4] *Gerusalemme* IX, 56.

whole even of the created universe. *Nature's* realm was supposed to extend only as far upwards as the orbit of the moon.[1] That may lend an unsuspected precision to the words which Chaucer puts into the mouth of *nature* personified.

> Eche thing in my cure is
> *Under the Mone* that mai waxe and wane.[2]

Childish as this particular demotion may sound, it goes back to a respectable division between the sublunary and the translunary which Aristotle made in order to cover what observation seemed, in his time, to show.[3] Even in the passage already quoted, it will be remembered, not only *phusis* but 'the sky and *phusis*' hung upon God.[4]

When we emphasise the idea that *nature* is a divine artifact, we get yet another contrast. Pagan myths (you will find them in the first book of Ovid's *Metamorphoses*) and *Genesis* seemed to agree that matter first existed in a state of disorder (*tohu-bohu* or chaos) and was afterwards ordered and worked up into a *kosmos* (*kosmein*, to arrange, organise, embellish, whence also *cosmetics*). The cosmos can then be called *nature* and contrasted with the preceding —and perhaps subsequent—disorder. Hence Milton describes chaos as 'the womb of Nature and perhaps her grave'.[5]

But besides all these demotions there was also apotheosis. This would perhaps have been hardly possible before *nature* (*d.s.*) had been named, and seems wholly

---

[1] See Deguileville, *Pilgrimage*, trans. Lydgate, 3415.
[2] *Phisicien's Tale*, C. 22.   [3] *De Mundo*, 392 a.
[4] *Metaphysics*, 1072 b.   [5] *Paradise Lost* II, 911.

foreign to the spirit of the earliest Greek mythology.[1]
But once you can talk about *nature* (*d.s.*) you can deify it
—or 'her'. Hence the sense which I shall call *Great
Mother Nature*; *nature* used to mean not simply all the
things there are, as an aggregate or even a system, but
rather some force or mind or *élan* supposed to be immanent in them. It is of course often impossible to be
sure in a given instance whether the sense Great Mother
Nature implied genuine personalisation (a deity believed
in) or merely personification as a rhetorical figure. When
Cicero says that Cleanthes gave the name of God to the
mind and spirit of all *natura*[2] it is almost certainly the
former. But when he says 'What workman save *Natura*
could have attained such skill?'[3] it might be not much
more than a figure. When Marcus Aurelius, or any sound
Stoic, calls *Phusis* 'the eldest of deities' (IX, I), I think this
is the language of actual religion; about the *natura* who
appears in Statius' *Thebaid* I am in doubt. But the *kinde*[4]
or *natura* and *physis*[5] or *nature*,[6] the 'vicaire of the almightie Lorde',[7] who so dominates medieval poetry, is
a personification, though a very grave and active one.

Great Mother Nature has proved a most potent sense
down to the present day. It is 'she' who does nothing by
leaps, abhors a vacuum, is *die gute Mutter*, is red in tooth
and claw, 'never did betray the heart that loved her',

---

[1] The gods of mythology, who had parents and a history and known
birthplaces, were of course items in *nature* (*d.s.*).
[2] *De Natura Deorum* I, 14.   [3] *Ibid.* II, 57.
[4] Langland, C. XXIII, 80.
[5] Bernardus Silvester, Alanus ab Insulis.   [6] *Romance of the Rose.*
[7] Chaucer, *Parlement*, 379.

eliminates the unfit, surges to ever higher and higher forms of life, decrees, purposes, warns, punishes and consoles. Even now I am not sure that this meaning is always used purely as a figure, to say what would equally make sense without it. The test is to remove the figure and see how much sense remains. Of all the pantheon Great Mother Nature has, at any rate, been the hardest to kill.

IV. 'NATURE' AND ITS OPPOSITES

The sense we have just been considering might seem so overwhelming that, once reached, it would dominate, or perhaps devour, all other senses of the word. But we daily prove that this is not so by speaking of 'the nature of the case' or 'a good-natured man' when there is before our mind no idea of *nature* (*d.s.*), strict or demoted, personified or literal. For the hierarchy of meanings is not like the hierarchy of things. That sense of the word which refers to the most ancient thing need not be the most ancient sense; that which refers to an all-embracing thing need not be the all-embracing sense. The thing we mean by *nature* (*d.s.*) may be the trunk on which we all grow; the sense *nature* (*d.s.*) is by no means the semantic trunk on which all the meanings grow. It is itself only one of the branches. Hence we shall go widely astray if we assume that whenever authors use the word *nature* they must be thinking of *nature* (*d.s.*). Especially, we shall go astray if we think that all uses of the word *nature* which carry approval indicate an optimistic, and all disapproving usages a pessimistic, view of *nature* (*d.s.*). These usages may have a different source and need imply no view of *nature* (*d.s.*) at all. Of course the hovering presence of *nature* (*d.s.*) in the background often moulds the rhetorical form, and sometimes even modifies the thought when the author is saying things which (fundamentally) require different senses.

The best clue is to ask oneself in each instance, what is the implied opposite to *nature*, and a list of such opposites will now occupy us for some pages. Their very existence proves how little the sense *nature* (*d.s.*) (which has no opposite) is involved.

V. 'NATURAL AND UNNATURAL'

There are two chief branches.

1. Since *natural* can mean 'having due affection', or *pius*, *unnatural* (as already noticed) of course means the reverse. Thus old Hamlet's ghost says that, while all murder is 'most foul', his own murder was 'strange and unnatural', because it was fratricidal.

2. Anything which has changed from its sort or kind (*nature*) may be described as *unnatural*, provided that the change is one the speaker deplores. Behaviour is *unnatural* or 'affected', not simply when it is held to be a departure from that which a man's *nature* would lead to of itself, but when it is a departure for the worse. When the timid man forces himself to be brave, or the choleric man to be just, he is not called *unnatural*. '*Unnatural* vices' are so called because the appetite has exchanged its characteristic and supposedly original bent, its *phusis*, for one which most men think worse. (Perpetual continence, though equally a departure from the *phusis*, would be, and is,

called *unnatural* only by those who disapprove of it.) It is just possible that the Great Mother Nature meaning has had an influence here, for in medieval personifications of her she is very apt to talk about fertility, and the 'plaint' which she makes in Alanus ab Insulis' *De Planctu Naturae* is one against homosexuality. But I do not think this at all probable.

Why *unnatural* should always (as *unearthly* is not) be a term of reprobation is not easy to understand. The strongly pejorative force of its first usage (lacking in due affection) may have something to do with it.

It is sufficiently obvious that neither sense is derived from *nature* (*d.s.*) which of course includes fratricide and perversion as it includes everything else.

VI. THE 'NATURAL' AND THE INTERFERED WITH

A beautifully pure example of this sense occurs in Chaucer. Medieval astronomers believed that the lower heavenly spheres had an inherent impulse to move from west to east, but that the *Primum Mobile*, moving from east to west, forced them backwards in that direction. Chaucer complains that the 'firste moeving cruel firmament' thus forces westward all those things 'that naturelly wolde holde another way'.[1] Now of course both movements are equally within *nature* (*d.s.*). But Chaucer is not thinking of *nature* (*d.s.*). Nor are we while we read his line. His usage is still so familiar and intelligible that we all know at once, without having to think about it, what he means by 'would *naturally*'; he means 'would spontaneously, of their own accord, if they were let alone'.

[1] *Man of Law's Tale*, B. 298.

Similarly, we feel no difficulty when Aristotle says 'We must study what is *natural* (*phusei*) in specimens which are *in their natural condition* (*kata phusin*), not in those which have been damaged'.[1]

This, as it is one of the oldest, is one of the hardiest senses of *nature* or *natural*. The nature of anything, its original, innate character, its spontaneous behaviour, can be contrasted with what it is made to be or do by some external agency. A yew-tree is *natural* before the topiarist has carved it; water in a fountain is forced upwards against its *nature*; raw vegetables are *au naturel*. The *natural* here is the Given.

This distinction between the uninterfered with and the interfered with will not probably recommend itself to philosophers. It may be held to enshrine a very primitive, an almost magical or animistic, conception of causality. For of course in the real world everything is continuously 'interfered with' by everything else; total mutual interference (Kant's 'thorough-going reciprocity') is of the essence of *nature* (*d.s.*). What keeps the contrast alive, however, is the daily experience of men as practical, not speculative, beings. The antithesis between unreclaimed land and the cleared, drained, fenced, ploughed, sown, and weeded field—between the unbroken and the broken horse—between the fish as caught and the fish opened, cleaned, and fried—is forced upon us every day. That is why *nature* as 'the given', the thing we start from, the thing we have not yet 'done anything about', is such a persistent sense. *We* here, of course, means man. If ants

[1] *Politics*, 1254 a.

45

had a language they would, no doubt, call their anthill an artifact and describe the brick wall in its neighbourhood as a *natural* object. *Nature* in fact would be for them all that was not 'ant-made'. Just so, for us, *nature* is all that is not man-made; the *natural* state of anything is its state when not modified by man. This is one source of the antithesis (philosophically so scandalous) between *nature* and Man. We as agents, as interferers, inevitably stand over against all the other things; they are all raw material to be exploited or difficulties to be overcome. This is also a fruitful source of favourable and unfavourable overtones. When we deplore the human interferences, then the *nature* which they have altered is of course the unspoiled, the uncorrupted; when we approve them, it is the raw, the unimproved, the savage.

Inevitably this contrast is represented in all the languages we have had to consider. Things may be in a satisfactory condition either by *nature* (*phusei*) or by art (*techne*), in Plato.[1] A death which occurs of itself, without external violence, is a *natural* (*kata phusin*) death. The peasant to whom Electra had been, outrageously, married, abstained from her bed for various reasons, one being that he *was naturally* (*ephu*) chaste; not through fear, nor by painful efforts of resolution—he was 'that sort of man'.[2] Quintilian says that in oratory *natura* can do much without training but training can do little without *natura* (II, xix). The *nature* in question is of course the 'given' capacity in the pupil, what the teacher finds to work upon. Addison speaks of 'the rustic part of the species who on all occasions

[1] *Republic*, 381 a.   [2] Euripides, *Electra*, 261.

acted bluntly and *naturally*:[1] no efforts of their own had modified their given behaviour (given by temperament, environment, and the passions) in the direction either of refinement or affectation.

This contrast easily accommodates, without substantial change of what is being said, allusions to Great Mother Nature; as in Milton's description of the paradisal flowers

> which not nice Art
> In Beds and curious knots, but nature boon
> Pour forth profuse[2]

Sometimes it is difficult to say whether Great Mother Nature, even rhetorically, is intended or not. Sannazaro, in the Proem to his *Arcadia*, prefers to the products of the gardener's art the trees on the rude mountains 'brought forth by *nature*' (*de la natura produtti*). Is *natura* here intended to arouse the image of the Great Mother, or does it only mean *naturally*? Seneca says 'for *natura* does not give virtue; it is an art to become good'.[3] It might mean simply 'We are not born with all the virtues, they don't come of their own accord. We have to work at them.' On the other hand, he was a Stoic and Great Mother Nature was very often in his mind. It is of course very possible that neither he nor Sannazaro could have answered the question or had ever raised it.

VII. THE 'NATURAL' AS AN ELEMENT IN MAN

I divide this class into three sub-classes and must give warning that I am in some doubt about all of them except

---

[1] *Spectator*, 119.   [2] *Paradise Lost* IV, 241.   [3] *Epistles* XC, 44.

the first. The second I am not sure that I have understood; the third, for a reason which will appear, is bound to have an uncertain fringe. I think it better to give the reader even a dubious classification (which he can then pull to pieces for himself) than a jungle of *miscellanea* at the end.

1. Speaking of worldly goods Boethius says that *natura* is content with few of them.[1] Alfred, correctly, translates 'in very little of them *kind* (*gecynd*) has enough'. Spenser, probably with the Boethian passage in mind, remarks 'with how small allowance Untroubled Nature doth herself suffice'.[2] When Adam and Eve and the Archangel dined together they ate what 'sufficed, not burdened nature'.[3] The implied contrast in all these is between what the *nature* of man wants—what a man wants simply in virtue of being the *kind* of organism he is—and what this or that man learns to want by being luxurious, fanciful, or fashionable. This would be an application of the more general contrast of *nature* as the given against the interfered with. Our 'built in' appetites are interfered with by our individual ways of life.

2. But what are we to make of the following usages? A *natural* is an idiot or imbecile. 'Love is like a great natural that runs lolling up and down to hide his bauble in a hole.'[4] Again, the unconscious vital powers in a man's body can be *nature*. 'Ther nature wol not wirche', says Chaucer of the dying Arcite, 'Far-wel Physik! Go bear the man to chirche'.[5] Most startling of all, Dryden's

---

[1] *Consolation* ii, Pr. v. [2] *Faerie Queene*, ii, vii, 15.
[3] *P.L.* v, 451. [4] *Romeo and Juliet* ii, iv, 92.
[5] *Knight's Tale*, A. 2759.

Abdalla says 'Reason's a staff for age when nature's gone'.[1]
We could, at a pinch, get rid of the Chaucerian passage.
Nature in it might be Great Mother Nature refusing to
work in one man's body. The two other specimens are
alike in suggesting a contrast between *nature* and reason.
The idiot is a *natural* for lacking it, and Abdalla will not
use it as long as he has *nature* instead. Now, since the
nature of man was defined as 'rational animal', it seems
very odd that the absence, or opposite, of reason in him
should be *natural*.

The explanation I would suggest is as follows. We have
already seen how the contrast between *nature* and man
arises from our practical life. But it was also reinforced
from another direction. Man is represented both in the
Timaeus and in *Genesis* as the subject of a separate and
special creation; as something added, by a fresh act of God,
to the rest of *nature* (*d.s.*) *demoted*. (In Bernardus and in
the *Anticlaudian* of Alanus the creation of man becomes
even more special and more separate.) And of course
'the rest of *Nature*' could easily, in opposition to Man, be
called simply *nature*. It could therefore be felt that what
man shares with (the rest of) *nature*, what he has only
because he is a creature and not because he is a special
creature, is *natural* in contradistinction to his specific,
specially created, differentia. Thus, paradoxically but not
unintelligibly, man could be most *natural* (most united
with the rest of *nature*) in those states and activities which
are least rational. And we may perhaps add to this that
the specifically human, the exercise and domination of

[1] *Conquest of Granada*, Pt. I, II, i.

reason, is achieved in each man only by effort. The state of a man before reason has developed in him, or while reason is in abeyance, may therefore be *natural* also in the sense of being 'given'—being what happens if nothing is done about it. The idiot has only remained in the state of irrationality in which we all began. Abdalla identifies *nature* either with passion itself or with the dominance of passion because passion both arises and rules us unless we 'interfere' with ourselves.

Along these lines the word *nature* could reach the sense 'that in man which is not specifically human, that which he shares with the animals'. Hence such euphemisms as 'a call of *nature*'. Hence, as perhaps in the Chaucerian passage, the unconscious processes (digestion, circulation etc.) could be *nature*.

3. Here I feel pretty confident that the class I am discussing is a real class; but one older meaning of *nature* makes it doubtful whether certain instances fall within it or not. We have seen that *nature* can mean 'due affection' or *pietas*. Thus there are two possible ways of taking the ghost's words to Hamlet 'If thou hast nature in thee, bear it not' (I, v, 81), and Prospero's 'You, brother mine that entertained ambition, expelled remorse and nature' (v, i, 75). The ghost might mean 'if you have any filial feelings'; Prospero might mean 'You expelled all the feelings of a brother'. But equally the ghost might mean 'If you still retain the *nature* of a man, if you have not departed from the human *phusis*'. And Prospero might mean 'You drove out the given *nature* of humanity, voluntarily depraved yourself from your kind.' I suspect the first explanation

is the more likely for these passages. (Both senses might of course be present, or the distinction might never have been consciously before Shakespeare's mind.) But the second seems more probable when Lady Macbeth prays that 'no compunctious visitings of nature' may shake her fell purpose (I, v, 45). She might possibly be praying that the 'due affection' and loyalty which she owes to Duncan as king, guest, kinsman, and benefactor, should not visit her with compunction. But, taken in connection with 'unsex me here', *nature* seems more likely to mean 'my original *datum* of human *nature*'. She is deliberately casting out, and forbidding to return, her womanhood, her humanity, her reason (as our ancestors understood the word *reason*).

Nature here appears as good because the creature is departing from its *phusis* for something worse. This has nothing to do with an optimistic view of human *nature* in general, much less of *nature* (*d.s.*). We can interfere with our given *nature* either to mend or to mar it; we can climb above it or sink below it. Thus in a man who is depraving himself his *nature* will be the only trace of good still left in him (his form has not yet lost *all* her original brightness). Later, it will be the good he has finally lost. But when a man is growing better, rising above or (as we say) 'conquering' his original psychological *datum*, *nature* will be relatively bad—the element in him still unconquered or uncorrected. Banquo is a good man, but he has to pray 'Merciful powers, Restrain in me the cursed thoughts that nature gives way to in repose' (II, i, 7). The original human *datum* in him is not yet so conquered that

it cannot raise its head in his dreams.[1] Thus Johnson can
say 'We are all envious naturally but by checking envy we
get the better of it.[2] Pope's usage is more complex—a
good subject for Professor Empson—when he makes
Eloisa say

> Then Conscience sleeps and, leaving Nature free,
> All my loose soul unbounded leaps to thee.[3]

From the point of view of her pious resolutions *nature*
here is the given which ought to be conquered and whose
persistence is therefore bad. But she probably also pleads
by implication that her passion for Abelard is after all
natural and therefore excusable (a usage we must return
to); *natural* as ordinary, to be expected, and also perhaps
as something authoritatively sanctioned or irresistibly
imposed by Great Mother Nature. The idea that sexual
desire is *natural* because it is not specifically human may
also come in.

My examples so far have all been ethical, the *natural*
element in a man appearing as something morally better
or worse than what he may make of it. But it can be contrasted as 'given' with things which are not, in the context,
regarded as obligatory or culpable. An example (despite
the borrowing of a religious term in it) is Coleridge's

> And happly by abstruse research to steal
> From my own nature all the natural man.[4]

Coleridge was determining, like Lady Macbeth, to depart
from his *phusis*, but not (on most views) to deprave it.

---

[1] This degree of psycho-analysis is as old as Plato's *Republic*, 571 a–
572 d.
[2] Boswell, 12 April 1778.   [3] Line 227.   [4] *Dejection*, VI.

We get the same non-moral contrast, complicated by Great Mother Nature, in this from *Tristram Shandy* (v, iii): 'When Tully was bereft of his daughter at first he listened to the voice of nature and modulated his own unto it...O my Tullia, my daughter, my child...But as soon as he began to look into the stores of philosophy and consider how many excellent things might be said upon the occasion...no body on earth can conceive, says the great orator, how joyful it made me.' 'Voice' here brings in the personification; but substantially the contrast is between the given—what Cicero, what anyone, would spontaneously feel—and what philosophy and rhetoric (conceived by Sterne as affectations) could make out of it.

VIII. 'NATURE' AND GRACE

Banquo's evening prayer brought us already to the frontier of this class. Human *nature* (man as he is of himself) can be contrasted not only, as above, with man as he can become by moral effort but with man as he can be refashioned by divine grace. The antithesis is now not merely moral. 'The loss of my husband', says Christiana, 'came into my mind, at which I was heartily grieved; but all that was but natural affection'.[1] What is here depreciated or discounted as 'but natural' is nothing depraved or sub-human; on the contrary, it is something, on its own level and in its own mode, lawful, commanded, entirely good. But it involves none of the new motives, the new perspective, the revaluation of all things, which, on the Christian view go with conversion. It does not

[1] *Pilgrim's Progress*, Pt 2.

(in most theologies) need to be repented of; but neither does it indicate 'the New Man'. It is therefore merely *nature*, not grace—or not of faith, or not spiritual. Often, of course, this contrast is merely implicit:

> see, sons, what things you are!
> How quickly nature falls into revolt
> When gold becomes her object![1]

The choice of the word *nature*, in the context, would in Shakespeare's time have made the theological implication clear. *Nature* means 'we human beings in our natural condition', that is, unless or until touched by grace. This is what '*Nature*' means as the title of one of Herbert's poems. It is about the element of untransformed, ungraced human nature in the poet—his Old Man, Old Adam, his *vetustas*, full of rebellion and venom, untamed, precarious, and perishing. The classic place for this contrast is the *Imitation* (III, liv): 'Diligently watch the motions of nature and of grace...nature is subtle and always has self for end...grace walks in sincerity and does all for God.' In the next chapter the author adds a linguistic note: 'for nature is fallen and so the very word *nature* (though she was created good and right) now means the weakness of fallen nature.'

IX. NATURE AND THE MIMETIC ARTS

The contrasts we have hitherto been considering are all really variations upon a single contrast; that of *nature* as the given or uninterfered with, over against what has

---

[1] *Hen. IV*, Pt 2, IV, v, 65.

been, for better or worse, made of it. We now come to a different contrast; the *nature* of a thing as its real character, over against what it is thought to be or represented as being or treated as if it were.

Thus poets and painters are said to be imitating *nature*. *Nature* in this context primarily means the real character (the *phusis* or what-sortedness) of the things they are representing. When the horses in your picture are like real horses or the lovers in your comedy behave like real lovers, then of course your work is 'true to nature' or 'natural'. And just as we call the painted shapes 'horses' and the dramatic personages 'lovers', so the correct depiction of them in the mimetic work can itself be called *nature*. Thus Pope can speak of a work 'Where nature moves and rapture warms the mind';[1] or Johnson can complain 'In this poem there is no nature for there is no truth.'[2]

A full account of *nature* as a term in neo-classical criticism would require a whole book and will not, of course, be attempted here. But two points must be made.

1. Some of those who were neo-classical critics held optimistic views about *nature* (*d.s.*) and willingly used the figure of Great Mother Nature. But their frequent eulogies on *nature* in works of art are not necessarily connected with this. They may be emotionally tinged by it, or the writers themselves may sometimes be confused. But in logic, if your theory of art is mimetic, then of course you must praise artists for 'following' *nature* and blame them for departing from it—must praise *nature* in a work of art and censure the absence of *nature*—whatever

[1] *Essay on Criticism*, 236.   [2] *Life of Milton*.

you think about *nature* (d.s.). An imitation must be judged by its resemblance to the model.

2. We have already learned from Aristotle that the *phusis* of anything is 'what it is like when its process of coming to be is complete'.[1] We have learned also from Aristotle, that we must 'study what is natural from specimens which are in their natural condition, not from damaged ones'.[2] An immature or deformed specimen does not display its *phusis* accurately. Now if you once get (from Aristotle's *Poetics* and Horace's *De Arte*) the theory that art imitates the general, not the individual, that the *nature* to be imitated is really the *natures* of whole classes (horses, lovers), then the same principles apply to art as to biology. This doctrine of generality was of course widely held in the neo-classical period; 'nothing can please many and please long' except by 'just representations of general nature'.[3] It would have been clearer[4] if he had said 'general natures'. Obviously you can depict the general *nature* of a class only by displaying it in a fully developed, normal, undeformed specimen. The general *nature* of feet is not revealed by a drawing, however accurate, of a club foot (though of course club feet are an item in *nature* (d.s.)). The general nature of pedlars is not revealed by Wordsworth's portrait of the Wanderer in

---

[1] *Politics*, 1252 b.   [2] *Ibid.* 1254 a.
[3] Johnson's *Preface to Shakespeare*.
[4] Clearer for an understanding of the theory as usually held. Johnson has his own modification of it. Where others wanted the generality *King* or *Senator* to show through the individual Claudius or Menenius he wanted the universal *Man* to show through the generality *King* or *Senator*.

The Excursion (though of course it is not strictly impossible that *nature* (*d.s.*) should once have included an individual pedlar who was just like him).

This view explains some otherwise unintelligible statements by Thomas Rymer. 'Nature knows nothing in the manners which so properly distinguishes woman as doth her modesty'.[1] This does not mean that Rymer is so simple as to deny the existence of immodest women. He knows perfectly well that *nature* (*d.s.*) includes immodest women, as it includes bearded women, hunchbacks and homosexuals. But they are not specimens in which we can observe general female *nature*. He makes this quite clear by adding 'if a woman has got any accidental historical impudence' (i.e. immodesty, *impudicitia*) 'she must no longer stalk in Tragedy…but must rub off and pack down with the carriers into the *Provence* of Comedy'.[2] She is proper in comedy (no doubt) because its corrective function is precisely to pillory aberrations from (general) *nature*. But female 'impudence' is no matter for serious poetry because, though it certainly occurs in *nature* (*d.s.*), when it does so it is merely 'accidental' (in the logical sense) and 'historical'. That is, it merely records the particular, which, as Aristotle had taught, is the function of history, not of tragedy.[3] It is in the light of this that we must understand his notorious remark about Iago. He condemns Iago for being an 'insinuating rascal' instead of a 'plain-dealing souldier'—'a character constantly worn

---

[1] *Tragedies of the Last Age.* Spingarn, *Critical Essays of the XVIIth Century*, vol. II, p. 193.
[2] *Ibid.* p. 194.   [3] *Poetics*, 1451 a–b.

by them for thousands of years in the World'.[1] Rymer is not in the least denying that such a soldier as Iago could exist; the point is that, if he did, he would be a mere historical accident, not instructive as to the general *nature* of soldiers, and therefore improper in tragedy.

It will be seen that this demand for the typical easily merges into a demand for the perfect. The quest for the wholly normal cabbage—as we significantly say 'the perfect specimen'—would involve the rejection of every cabbage which had suffered from such historical accidents as bad soil, unequal sun (and therefore different growth) on this side and that, too much or too little rain, and so on. In the end you would be looking for the ideal cabbage. This development, I suspect, is more easily seen in the criticism of painting. But Rymer is moving in that direction when he says that 'no shadow of sense can be pretended for bringing any wicked persons on the stage'.[2] I fear he was encouraged by Aristotle's strange maxim that the characters in a tragedy should, before everything else, be 'good'.[3]

X. BY 'NATURE' OR BY LAW

Here, as in the preceding contrast, *nature* is the actual. What a thing is in its own *nature* and therefore really is, is set against what law (or custom, or convention) treats it as being. The claims made by women when the suffragist movement began, or by native Africans in parts of Africa, could in traditional language have taken the form

---

[1] *Short View of Tragedy, ibid.* p. 224.
[2] *Ibid.* p. 197.   [3] *Poetics,* 1454 a.

'Our inferiority to you (men or whites) is legal or conventional, not *natural*'. A good example is the discussion
on slavery in the first book of Aristotle's *Politics*. Aristotle
thought that some men were specially qualified by their
character to be slaves and others to be masters. The one
sort were therefore *natural* slaves, the other *natural*
masters. But of course the actual working of the slave
trade, which gets its livestock by kidnapping, purchase,
or capture in war, did not at all insure that only the
natural slaves were enslaved. (He oddly ignores the
equally obvious truth that those who own slaves will
often not be *natural* masters.) We must therefore distinguish the *natural* from the *legal* slave: him who ought to
be, who is fit only to be, a slave, from him who is a slave
in the eyes of the law.

Again, it must have been a primeval question whether
what your father, or teacher, or king, or the laws of your
country declared to be just or right was 'really' just or
right. Linguistic analysts may (and what a comfort that
will be to all governments!) succeed in convincing the
world that the expression 'really right' is meaningless;
but for millennia it was accepted as full of meaning. The
idea of the 'really right', as against the law of the political
ruler, is expressed in its purity by Sophocles through the
mouth of Antigone: 'I did not think your proclamation
of such force that you, a man, destined to die, should
override the laws of the gods, unwritten and unvarying.
For those are not of yesterday nor of today, but everlasting. No one knows when they began.'[1]

[1] *Antigone*, 453.

In plain prose the antithesis takes the following form. Someone in Plato's *Gorgias* (482ᵉ) speaks of things 'which are laudable (*kala*) not by *phusis* but by law or convention (*nomô*)'. Or Cicero says 'If, as it is *naturally* (*naturâ*), so it were in men's thoughts, and each regarded nothing human as alien from him'.[1] Plato's *phusis* could here be rendered 'really': Cicero's *natura* 'in reality'. But such thoughts lead to a new usage which has, historically, been more important even than the conception of *nature* (*d.s.*). We can see it beginning in another passage from the *Gorgias*: 'They do these things according to the *phusis* of justice and, by heaven, according to the law of *phusis*, though perhaps not according to the law we men lay down' (483ᵉ).

Notice, first, that an abstract like Justice (at least, it is an abstract for modern thought) can now have its *phusis*. This I take to be a consequence of asking whether the state's 'justice' is *real* justice or not. For this seems to imply that the question 'What's justice like—really like?' is significant; and what would you then be asking about if not about the real *phusis* of justice?

Secondly, we now have the conception 'law of *phusis*'. I am not at all sure what Plato meant by this second *phusis*; but it would seem at least to mean 'reality'. The law of reality would be the real law. But is he also bringing in something of *nature* (*d.s.*) or of Great Mother Nature? (His own particular demotion of *nature* (*d.s.*) is not relevant at this point.)

However that may be, the way is now open to the gigantic antithesis (ancient, medieval, and early modern)

[1] *Laws*, I, xii.

between *natural* and *civil* law; the unchangeable and universal law of *nature* and the varying law of this or that state. But the ambiguity of the word *nature* allowed men to use this antithesis for the expression of very different political philosophies.

On the one hand, if *nature* is thought of mainly as the real (opposed to convention and legal fiction) and the laws of *nature* as those which enjoin what is really good and forbid what is really bad (as opposed to the pseudo-duties which bad governments praise and reward or the real virtues which they forbid and punish), then of course 'the law of *nature*' is conceived as an absolute moral standard against which the laws of all nations must be judged and to which they ought to conform. It will be in fact the sort of thing Antigone was talking about. Great Mother Nature may well come in at this point but she will be either, for Stoics, a deified Mother Nature, or, for Christians, a Mother Nature who is the 'vicaire of the almightie lord', inscribing her laws, which she learned from God, on the human heart. This is the conception of *natural* Law that underlies the work of Thomas Aquinas, Hooker and Grotius.

On the other hand *nature* may mean *nature* (*d.s.*), and even with a special emphasis on the non-human parts of it (the obstinate contrast of Nature and man helps here) or, within man, on those motives and modes of behaviour which are least specifically human. The 'laws of *Nature*' on this view are inferred from the way in which non-human agents always behave, and human agents behave until they are trained not to. Thus what Aquinas or

Hooker would call 'the law of *Nature*' now becomes in its turn the convention; it is something artificially imposed, in opposition to the true law of *nature*, the way we all spontaneously behave if we dare (or don't interfere with ourselves), the way all the other creatures behave, the way that comes 'naturally' to us. The prime law of *nature*, thus conceived, is self-preservation and self-aggrandisement, pursued by whatever trickeries or cruelties may prove to be advisable. This is Hobbes's *Natural Law*.

XI. THE STATE OF 'NATURE' AND THE CIVIL STATE

On either of these views civil law is man-made and *natural* law is not. The one is a contrivance, the other a given; so that this contrast, though it seems to begin in that of real and conventional, slides back into the more familiar one of the raw (or unspoiled) and the improved (or sophisticated). That was perhaps why nearly all political thinkers except Aristotle assumed that men had once lived without social organisation and obeyed no laws except those (whatever those were) of *nature*. That pre-civil condition was described as *nature* or 'the state of *nature*'. This too, of course, might be conceived in opposite ways. It might be a primeval innocence from which our transition to the civil state was a fall. 'The first of mortals and their children followed nature, uncorrupted, and enjoyed the nature of things in common', says Seneca.[1] The 'nature of things' which they enjoyed is

[1] Epistle xc, 4, 38.

nature (*d.s.*). The *nature* they followed is primarily their own, still unspoiled, *phusis*. But they enjoyed 'the *nature* of things in common' because civil government and private property had not yet been contrived—not while they were in the state of *nature*. So Pope:

> Nor think in Nature's state they blindly trod;
> The state of Nature was the reign of God.[1]

On the other hand it could be conceived of as the state of savagery to escape from which we had contrived the civil state, finding that in the state of *nature* man's life was, as Hobbes said, 'solitary, poor, nasty, brutish, and short'.[2]

The state of *nature* which (it was thought) had preceded civil society, and would return if civil society were abolished, still in a sense underlies it. Government is supposed to do for us certain things we should have done for ourselves in the state of *nature*; it can be maintained that where it fails to do any of them we are, as regards those things, still in the state of *nature* and may act accordingly. Johnson says that a man whose father's murderer, by a peculiarity of Scotch Law, has escaped hanging, might reasonably say 'I am among barbarians who refuse to do justice. I am therefore in a state of nature and consequently...I will stab the murderer of my father.'[3]

It should be noticed that the expression 'state of *nature*' is sometimes borrowed from its proper political context and given a meaning which really attaches it to our

---

[1] *Essay on Man* III, 147.   [2] *Leviathan*, 13.
[3] Boswell, *Hebrides*, 22 August 1773.

section VI. It may be used to mean not the pre-civil but the pre-civilised; the condition of man, not without government, but without arts, inventions, learning, and luxury. Thus in another part of his *Hebrides* Boswell records 'our satisfaction at finding ourselves again in a comfortable carriage was very great. We laughed at those who attempted to persuade us of the superior advantages of a state of nature.'[1] The 'state of nature' here means ponies and mountain tracks as against carriages and metalled roads. He even uses *nature* by itself in what I take to be the same sense when he speaks of wishing 'to live three years in Otaheite and be satisfied what pure nature can do for man'.[2]

XII. 'NATURAL' AND 'SUPERNATURAL'

1. In its strict theological sense this distinction presents little difficulty. When any agent is empowered by God to do that of which its own *kind* or *nature* would never have made it capable, it is said to act *super-naturally*, above its *nature*. The story in which Balaam's ass speaks is a story of the *supernatural* because speech is not a characteristic of asinine *nature*. When Isaiah saw the seraphim he saw *supernaturally* because human eyes are not by their own *nature* qualified to see such things. Of course examples of the *supernatural* need not be, like these, spectacular. Whatever a man is enabled to receive or do by divine grace, and not by the exercise of his own *nature*, is *supernatural*. Hence 'ioy, peace and delight' (of a certain sort) can be described by Hooker as 'super-

[1] *Hebrides*, 27 October 1773. [2] *Life*. Just before 29 April 1776.

naturall passions' (I, xi, 3). If this were the only sense the word bore, I should of course have mentioned it above when we were dealing with *nature* and *grace*. Unfortunately it has others.

2. We have already noticed that Aristotle speaks about things being 'in their natural condition': i.e. not damaged, or otherwise interfered with. But things can be changed from this *natural* condition: changed, in that sense, from their *nature*. A farmer can give a pig a degree of fatness which its *nature*, unaided, would never have achieved. It would then be fat 'above (its) *nature*'. Illness can raise a man's temperature higher than in his *natural* (normal, unimpaired) condition it would rise. To call him then *supernaturally* hot would now be startling, but the word could once, and quite intelligibly, be so used. Elyot says 'Unnaturall or supernaturall heate destroyeth appetite'.[1] In *The Flower and the Leaf* (l. 413) 'Unkindly hete' means, with some hyperbole, feverishness, pathological heat.

3. But neither of these senses is very close to that which *supernatural* bears in modern, untheological English. Why is a ghost called *supernatural*? Certainly not because it stands outside *nature* (*d.s.*). The proper word for 'outside *nature* (*d.s.*)' is 'non-existent'. But that cannot be what *supernatural* means, for it would be used of ghosts equally by those who believe and those who disbelieve in them. Nor does anyone call phlogiston *supernatural*. You could of course make 'demotions' of *nature* (*d.s.*) which would exclude the ghost, but they would have to be artificially contrived for that express purpose. The Platonic one

[1] *Castle of Health.*

would not do, for ghosts, being particulars, could not be in the realm of forms; nor the Aristotelian, for ghosts are not God, nor are they mathematical concepts; nor the Christian, for they are creatures. It is indeed doubtful whether the modern usage arises from *nature* (*d.s.*).

Macbeth calls the witches' prophesying a 'supernatural soliciting' (I, iii, 130). Witchcraft and magic are at first *supernatural*, I think, in a sense close to the theological. By the aid of spirits the magician does that which his own *nature* could not have done, or makes other objects do to each other what their *natures* were not capable of. It is not the spirits by whose aid he works that are *supernatural* but the operations performed. Again, when a prophet sees angels his experience is *supernatural*, in the sense already explained. It is equally so when he foresees the future. To call the angels themselves *supernatural* is, at first sight, no less odd than if we called the future *supernatural*. But certainly modern usage allows us to speak of 'supernatural beings'. It is a usage philosophically scandalous. If demons and fairies do not exist, it is not clear why they should be called *supernatural* any more than the books that no one ever wrote. If they exist, no doubt they have their own *natures* and act according to them.

Several causes probably contributed to this sense. Whatever such creatures might be in themselves, our encounters with them are certainly not *natural* in the sense of being ordinary or 'things of course'. It may even be supposed that when we see them we are acting above our *nature*. If on these two grounds the experience were vaguely felt to be *supernatural*, the adjective might then be transferred to the things experienced. (It is of course linguistically irrelevant whether the experience is regarded as veridical or hallucinatory.) Again, such creatures are not part of the subject matter of 'natural philosophy'; if real, they fall under pneumatology, and, if unreal, under morbid psychology. Thus the methodological idiom can separate them from nature. But thirdly (and I suspect this might be most potent of all), the beings which popular speech calls supernatural, long before that adjective was applied to them, were already bound together in popular thought by a common emotion. Some of them are holy, some numinous, some eerie, some horrible; all, one way or another, uncanny, mysterious, odd, 'rum'. When the learned term supernatural enters the common speech, it finds this far older, emotional classification ready for it, and already in want of a name. I think the learned word, on the strength of a very superficial relation of meaning to the thing the plain man had in mind, was simply snatched at and pummelled into the required semantic shape, like an old hat. Just so the people have snatched at once learned words like sadist, inferiority-complex, romantic, or exotic, and forced them into the meanings they chose.

The process is apt to shock highly educated people, but it does not always serve the ends of language (communication) so ill as we might expect. Supernatural in this modern and, if you like, degraded sense, does its work quite efficiently. Anthropologists find it convenient to talk of 'supernatural beings' and everyone understands them; and if our friend says, 'I can't stand stories about the supernatural', we know, for all ordinary purposes, what books not to lend him. A general term whose particulars are bound together only by an emotion may be quite a practicable word provided that the emotion is well known and tolerably distinct.

4. Finally we have once (in Golding) 'the supernaturalls of Aristotle', meaning his *Metaphysics*. That leads to my next.

XIII. PHYSICAL AND METAPHYSICAL

Aristotle's works were usually arranged in the following order: 1. The *Organon* (tool) or works on logic. 2. The scientific works or *phusika*. 3. A book or books on God, Unity, Being, Cause, and Potentiality. 4. Works on human activities (*Ethics, Politics, Rhetoric, Poetics*). As it was not very easy to find a name for the things in the third section, they were named simply from their position and called 'the things after the *phusika*' (*ta meta ta phusika*). When these 'things' came (no doubt wrongly) to be regarded as one book, this book was called 'the *Metaphysics*'.

It would be easy to make an ironic point by saying that the word *metaphysical*, for all its grandiose suggestions, thus has no higher origin than a librarian's practical device for indicating a subdivision of the Aristotelian corpus which nobody could find a name for. But the name is not so unhappy and certainly not so foreign to Aristotle's thought as this sally would suggest. We have already seen that he believed in realities outside what he called *phusis* and made them the subject of disciplines distinct from *phusike* (or *natural* philosophy). If the names are superficial, the division they express is genuinely Aristotelian.

These names, and the academic arrangements which go with them, affect the semantic situation. Originally a thing was *phusikon* because you thought it belonged to, or was included in, *phusis*; your own definition of *phusis* would come into play. But once *phusike* (natural philosophy) as a subject, distinct from *mathematike* and *metaphusike*, exists, most people have a shorter way of deciding what is or is not *phusikon*. Any thing is *phusikon* if you meet it while doing your course in *phusike*. You need not ask what *phusis* itself is; you need only know whose lectures a thing comes in, in what year you read about it, finally for what examination it prepares you. Here, in fact, we have the Methodological Idiom at work.

Aristotle's division of studies, or divisions derived from it, lasted for centuries. Under it a man who is *phusikos* means, not a '*natural*' man but that particular kind of learned man who studies *phusike*. '*Savants (philosophi)*', says Isidore, 'are either *physici* or *ethici* or *logici*.'[1] The *physici* study *natures*—sort things out and tell you their *kinds*. But the part of their work which the public is most interested in is, of course, that which may relieve our pains or preserve our life. Hence the *physicus* or *physician* comes to mean primarily a doctor of medicine. The stuff he gives you becomes *physic* ('throw physic to the dogs', says Macbeth, v, iii, 47). The adjective *physical* comes to mean medicinal, or 'good for you'; so that Portia can say

> Is Brutus sick, and is it physical
> To walk unbraced and suck up the humours
> Of the dank morning?[2]

[1] *Etymologics* VIII, vi, 3. [2] *Julius Caesar* II, i, 261.

Metaphysical, as we should expect, comes to mean (in the popular sense) *supernatural*; either as 'pertaining to what things do when acting beyond their natures', or (more probably) 'studied by arts and sciences which go beyond those of the *physicus*'. Hence in Marlowe a magical ointment has been 'tempered by science meta-phisicall';[1] and witchcraft is for Lady Macbeth 'meta-physical aid' (I, v, 30).

Phusike (*natural* philosophy) had from its beginning been 'principally concerned with bodies', as Aristotle notes.[2] It was therefore to be expected that *physical*, by the methodological idiom, would sooner or later come to its modern sense of 'corporeal'. This tendency would be encouraged by the fact that, as special sciences which dealt with bodies from a special point of view (like chemistry) or with only some bodies (like botany) were quarried out of the once undifferentiated *phusike*, and were given their separate names, *phusike*, left like a sort of rump, became the name of that science which still dealt with bodies, or matter, as such. The plural form *physics* survives to remind us that it was once all 'the *phusika*', as *metaphysics* were once 'the things after the *phusika*'. A singular form, *metaphysic*, is now gaining ground, but *physics* will perhaps hardly drop its final -*s* until the meaning 'medicine' for the word *physic* has become more completely archaic.

'Corporeal' is a mildly dangerous sense of *physical*. When Baxter says 'common love to God and special saving love to God be both acts upon an object physically

[1] *Tamburlaine*, Pt 2, 3944.   [2] *De Coelo* III, 298 b.

the same',[1] *physically* means 'in its own nature'. When Hooker says that sacraments 'are not physical but moral instruments of salvation' (v, lvii, 4) I do not think he means 'corporeal' by *physical* any more than 'ethical' by 'moral'. He probably means 'Their efficacy is of the sort that would be studied by moral, not by *natural*, philosophy'.

XIV. THE 'NATURAL' AS THE EXCUSABLE

Coleridge once entitled a piece of verse 'Something childish but very natural'. In Rider Haggard's *She*, when the young native unwisely avows her passion for Leo in the presence of the Queen, Holly pleads 'Be pitiful...it is but Nature working' (ch. XVIII). 'It's only natural' is used daily in the same deprecatory way. One extenuates one's peccadillo as *natural*, I suspect, in more than one sense. It is *natural*, ordinary, a thing in the common course, I'm no worse than others. It is at least not *un-natural*, I have been foolish or faulty at least in human, not in bestial or diabolical, fashion. What I did was *natural*, spontaneous, I have not gone out of my way to invent new vices. Sometimes a higher plea, less of a defence than a counter-attack, is urged, as in Pope's

> Can sins of moment(s) claim the rod
>   Of everlasting fires,
> And that offend great Nature's God
>   Which Nature's self inspires?[2]

A medieval poet would have been surprised to find Great Mother Nature inspiring sins, for he would have supposed that her 'inspiration', so far as concerned man, lay in

[1] *Saints' Everlasting Rest* III, xi.   [2] *Universal Prayer.*

the *nature* (*animal rationale*) appointed by her for man. Pope is closer to Dryden's Abdalla; the 'voice' of *Nature* here is the less rational, less specifically human, element in us.

XV. 'NATURE' IN EIGHTEENTH- AND NINETEENTH-CENTURY POETRY

Nature (*d.s.*) and hardly even demoted, appears in Pope's couplet

> All are but parts of one stupendous whole
> Whose body Nature is and God the soul.[1]

When Thomson, on the other hand, describes the colour green as 'Nature's universal robe'[2] an enormous shrinkage has occurred. Most of *nature* (*d.s.*), as anyone can see on a fine night, is not green but black, and the better the visibility the blacker. Even terrestrial *nature* is by no means all green. Thomson is actually thinking of British landscapes when he says *Nature*.

Wordsworth's doctrine of *Nature* does not here concern us; his contrasts make it clear how he (and others, and presently thousands of others) used the word. In the *Prelude* Coleridge is congratulated on the fact that, though 'reared in the great city', he had 'long desired to serve in Nature's temple' (II, 452–63). *Nature*, in fact, or anyway her 'temple', excludes towns. 'Science' and 'arts' are contrasted with *Nature* in III, 371–78; books and *Nature* in v, 166–73; Man and *Nature* in IV, 352, and of course in the sub-title of Book VIII. Whatever his doctrine may have been, he does not in fact use *nature* in the *d.s.*; for *nature* (*d.s.*) of course includes towns, arts, sciences, books, and

[1] *Essay on Man* I, 267.   [2] *Seasons* I, 83.

72

men. The antithesis of *Nature* and man, and again of *nature* and the man-made, underlie his usages, and those of most '*nature* poets'.

For most purposes, then, *Nature* in them means the country as opposed to the town, though it may in particular passages be extended to cover the sun, moon, and stars. It may also, despite its frequent opposition to 'man', sometimes cover the rustic way of (human) life. It is the country conceived as something not 'man-made'; Cowper's (or Varro's)[1] maxim that God made the country and man made the town is always more or less present. That the landscape in most civilised countries is through and through modified by human skill and toil, or that the effect of most 'town-scapes' is enormously indebted to atmospheric conditions, is overlooked.

This does not at all mean that the poets are talking nonsense. They are expressing a way of looking at things which must arise when towns become very large and the urban way of life very different from the rural. When this happens most people (not all) feel a sense of relief and restoration on getting out into the country; it is a serious emotion and a recurrent one, a proper theme for high poetry. Philosophically, no doubt, it is superficial to say we have escaped from the works of man to those of *Nature* when in fact, smoking a man-made pipe and swinging a man-made stick, wearing our man-made boots and clothes, we pause on a man-made bridge to

[1] *Task* I, 749, *Rerum Rusticarum* III, i. '*Divina natura* gave the land (*agros*), but human art built cities'. Does *divina natura* mean 'the divine nature' (*to theion*, God) or the divine species (the gods) or *nature* (*d.s.*) (the goddess)? Or could Varro have told us?

look down on the banked, narrowed, and deepened river which man has made out of the original wide, shallow, and swampy mess, and across it, at a landscape which has only its larger geological features in common with that which would have existed if man had never interfered. But we are expressing something we really feel. The wider range of vision has something to do with it; we are seeing *more* of *nature* (in a good many senses) than we could in a street. Again, the *natural* forces which keep the buildings of a town together (all the stresses) are only inferred; the *natural* action of weather and vegetation is visible. And there are fewer men about; therefore, by one of our habitual contrasts, more *nature*. We also feel (most of us) that we are, for the moment, in conditions more suited to our own *nature*—to our lungs, nostrils, ears and eyes.

But I need not labour the point. Romantic *nature*, like the popular use of *supernatural*, is not an idle term because it seems at first to stand up badly to logical criticism. People know pretty well what they mean by it and sometimes use it to communicate what would not easily be communicable in other ways. To be sure, they may also use it to say vaguely and flatly (or even ridiculously) what might have been said precisely and freshly if they had had no such tool ready. I once saw a railway poster which advertised Kent as 'Nature's home'; and we have all heard of the lady who liked walking on a road 'untouched by the hand of man'.

3

SAD

[WITH *GRAVIS*]

I. 'GRAVIS' AND 'GRAVE'

THOUGH *sad* has never, to my knowledge, been influenced by Latin *gravis* and its English derivative *grave*, the likeness between their semantic histories makes it natural to begin this chapter with a glance at the latter.

As everyone knows *gravis* means 'heavy'. And because we do not like carrying or 'bearing' heavy objects, it also means 'grievous'. *O passi graviora*, says Aeneas, oh you who have suffered worse things than this![1] English *heavy* more often than English *grave* corresponds to this sense; as in Spenser's 'O heavie herse!'[2] It is true that we speak of 'grave danger' or 'a grave disaster', but this, I believe, brings in something of the next sense.

What is heavy is, in all physical operations, important. We cannot put it where we want it without effort, perhaps not even without planning; and, in return, wind or water or enemies cannot easily remove it. It will 'stay put'. It is, every way, something serious, something to be reckoned with. *Gravis* therefore also describes the sort of man who has to be reckoned with; the man whose action or opinion, as we significantly say, 'carries weight'. (Memories of muscular exertion turn up at every moment

[1] *Aeneid* I, 199.   [2] *Calendar, Nov.*, 60, 70 etc.

75

in this semantic area.) Lucretius, depreciating Heraclitus, says he has a higher reputation among those Greeks who are *inanes* than among those Greeks who are *gravis* and really want to know the truth. The contrast is between 'empty' and 'heavy' Greeks (an empty jug is lighter than a full one); between *dilettanti* or frivolous ones who make philosophy a hobby and those who are in earnest, serious —*solides* as the French say. This merges into the sense 'venerable, authoritative, or august'. Thus in Virgil: 'if the crowd catches sight of a man who is *gravis* by reason of his *pietas* and his good record'.[1]

This sense is pretty accurately reproduced by the English word when Othello says 'Most potent, grave, and reverend Seniors' (I, iii, 76) or Ariel salutes Prospero as 'grave Sir' (I, ii, 189). We are moving a little away from it when Milton says 'the men, though grave, eyed them'.[2] *Grave* here probably means something like 'serious-minded' with a more specifically religious and moral emphasis than the Lucretian, Virgilian, and Shakespearian uses would bear. And perhaps it already includes some reference to the externals of mien and deportment. It was certainly in this latter and more external sense that the word developed. Gulliver says the Brobdingnagian clothes 'are a very grave and decent habit' (ch. III). And everyone will remember the parish bull who was in reality 'no way equal to the department' but of whom Mr Shandy had a 'high opinion' because 'he went through the business with a grave face'.[3]

---

[1] *Aen.* I, 151.　　　　　　　　　　[2] *P.L.* XI, 585.
[3] *Tristram Shandy* IX, 33.

II. 'SAD': THE 'FULL'-SENSES

Anglo-Saxon *sæd* (plural *sade*) is brother to Old Norse *saddr* and cousin to Latin *satur*, and all three words have originally the same meaning: gorged, full (of food), replete. Thus in Psalm lxxviii. 30, where the Latin has *manducaverunt et saturati sunt nimis*, and Coverdale 'So they did eat and were well-filled', an Anglo-Saxon translator has 'They ate largely (*swiþe*) and became *sade*'. In Old Norse *saddr lifdaga* 'full of life-days' is equivalent to the biblical 'full of years'.

The distinction between having had enough and having had too much is, as we all know, a fine one. Our modern 'fed up' bears witness to it; also, though here litotes comes into it, the common use of 'I've had enough of your impudence' to mean 'I have had more than I want'. And to say of a man who wants to stop fighting 'He's had his bellyful', though a trifle archaic, would still be an intelligible taunt. *Saddr* and *sæd* both underwent this development. In the *Laxdale Saga* the cowman, flying from Hrapp's ghost (which he has met several times before) says 'I am *saddr* of wrestling with him' (ch. xxiv). 'I'm fed up with' or 'I've had enough of' would be equally accurate translations. A somewhat similar use occurs in Anglo-Saxon poetry. The Brunnanburh poem says of the battlefield 'there lay many a man, weary and *sæd* of war'—many a man who 'had his fill' of it in the sense that he was dead or dying.[1] There is no taunt here; only the wry and grim pity

[1] *Chronicle*, ann. 937, l. 20.

of the Old Germanic style. Wiglaf dashed water over Beowulf who was '*sæd* of battle', i.e. mortally wounded (l. 2722).

The sense 'over-full' or 'fed up' descended into Middle English. In the *Owl and Nightingale* the latter says that she does not sing all the year round because she does not want her audience to become *to sade*, too satiated (l. 452). Chaucer observes that inveterate alchemists can never 'wexen sadde', never grow tired of their delusive art (G. 877).

It is tempting to derive the modern sense of 'melancholy' (*sad* (*d.s.*)) directly and exclusively from the sense 'fed up', but this would be rash.

Now a man—or a thing—that is full is heavier than one that is empty. 'Heavy' therefore becomes one of the meanings of *sæd*. Gower says that the Earth 'is schape round, Substantial, strong, sad and sound' (VII, 225). So in Cotgrave's French Dictionary (1611) we find *Fromage de taulpe* defined as 'heavy or sad cheese'; and in many parts of the country till this day we call 'sad' a cake or loaf which has not risen. Where the English version of the *Romance of the Rose* speaks of 'sadde burdens' that make men's shoulders ache, one who did not know the history of the word would see a psychological epithet; in reality, *sadde* means just 'heavy'.[1]

Emptiness and hollowness, fulness and solidity, are closely related conceptions. We need therefore feel no surprise to find Wycliff saying 'the altar was not sad but hollow'.[2] But this opens the way to a much more im-

[1] Fragment C. 6907.   [2] On Exodus xxxviii. 7.

portant development. Sad becomes the equivalent of Latin *solidus* and, whether as the result of this equivalence or not, takes on many of the same meanings: firm (the opposite of flimsy), complete (not broken or interrupted), reliable, sound. Virgil describes the spear to which her father bound the infant Camilla as *solidum*;[1] Gavin Douglas renders it 'the schaft was sad and sound'—a collocation of adjectives we had in Gower a moment ago. In Malory *sadly* is used where we should use *soundly*: 'and there he found a bed and laid him therein and fell on sleep sadly'[2]—fell sound asleep. And when Chaucer says 'The messenger drank sadly ale and wyn' (B. 743) we could almost translate it 'drank solidly'—settled down, as the sequel shows (for he was soon 'sleeping like a pig'), to a solid, or uninterrupted, or sound, or heavy, or serious, evening's toping.

III. THE 'GRAVE'-SENSES

When *sad* has acquired the meaning 'firm' or 'sound' it will almost inevitably be applied to human character. Thus the person who 'like seasoned timber never gives' will be *sad*. We find the word applied to a good wife: 'o dere wyf...that were to me so sad and eek so trewe'.[3] *Sadness* is the proper virtue of mature or elderly people. Lydgate bids us 'In youth be lusty, sad when thou art olde'.[4] The virtue of *sadness* is hardly to be expected in youth, but sometimes we are pleasantly surprised to find

[1] *Aen.* XI, 553.   [2] VI, iv. Vinaver, p. 259, l. 27.
[3] *Manciple's Tale*, H. 275.
[4] R. Hope Robbins, *Secular Lyrics of the Fourteenth and Fifteenth Centuries*, no. 78, 63.

an old head on young shoulders. Thus we are told of Griselda

> though this mayde tendre wer of age,
> Yet in the brest of hir virginitie
> Ther was enclosed rype and sad corage.[1]

In the same tale the fickle rabble run with enthusiasm to welcome Walter's new wife because they are 'unsad and ever untrewe' (l. 995), unstable and faithless. The 'sadde folk' (l. 1002) who censure this new-fangleness are what a Roman would have called *graviores*; men of principle, not to be blown about by every gust of fashion.

It will be noticed—so deeply is thought in debt to the senses—that in all these instances *sad* has still so much attachment to the idea of weight, that the adjective 'light' could be its opposite. It returns also to the physical level by another route. Bodily acts, if firm and steady, can be *sad*: 'in goon the speres ful sadly in arest'.[2] They are firmly laid in the rest, in a manner which shows that the combatants mean business. And of course a face will be *sad* when its expression betokens *sadness* within. The narrator in *Pearl* had last seen his daughter as an infant; by a contrast of immense poetical power she comes before him in the trans-mortal country with 'semblant sad for doc other erle' (l. 211), with all the state and gravity of a great nobleman. So, later in the poem, the Elders before the Throne are 'sad of chere' (l. 887).

In both these passages any intrusion of *sad* (*d.s.*) (melancholy, dejected) would be ruinous. But in the *Clerk's Tale* (E. 693) it would make sheer nonsense. We

---

[1] E. 218.   [2] *Knight's Tale*, A. 2602.

are told that if Walter had not known, on other grounds, how dearly Griselda loved her children, he would have thought her cruel for wearing such a 'sad visage' when she submitted to the murder of her son. *Sad* here is, of course, composed, unmoved, the opposite of distraught. It is indeed used as a translation of *compositus* in Chaucer's Boethius.[1] Her heart was breaking but her face did not show it. This is perhaps the strongest instance I know of the context's insulating power. For that very sense of *sad* which would have made the passage idiotic already existed in Chaucer's time. Obviously, he has not the slightest fear that anyone will thrust it in at this point.

IV. 'SAD (D.S.)'

The evidence of its existence comes in Chaucer himself. In his version of the *Romance of the Rose* (l. 211) he says of Avarice, 'full sad...was she', where Guillaume de Lorris had *maigre* (199. Var. *laide*). We may not think *sad* (*d.s.*) a very good translation of either, but all the other senses of *sad* are impossible. He cannot be calling Avarice full-fed, or heavy, or reliable, or composed. He must mean 'gloomy', 'miserable'. But it is not easy, in the fourteenth century, to find any other unambiguous example. The *N.E.D.* finds one in another Chaucerian passage, where Theseus 'with a sad visage...syked stille' (A. 2985). But the *dangerous sense* seems to me here to be at best only possible. In the whole passage Theseus is giving an exhibition of *gravitas*. He has sent for Palamon and Emelye. He waits till they are seated and till the presence

[1] I, Met. iv.

chamber is silent. He then remains silent himself for a while and—admirable touch—'his eyen sette he ther as was his lest' (l. 2983), fixed his eyes on what he chose. He sighed *stille*, quietly, and proceeded to make a high philosophical speech beginning with the First Mover. I cannot feel sure that the *sad visage* was—and I feel quite sure it need not have been—anything more than a grave, a staid, a composed, and an authoritative countenance. He is being *compositus*, *gravis*. More promising is the Lyric 105 in Carleton Brown's *Religious Lyrics of the Fourteenth Century*, where the second line reads 'For sorowe sore I sykkit sadde'. Here the *dangerous sense* seems to me the most probable. But it is not certain. The mourner may have sighed *sadly* as Chaucer's messenger drank *sadly*: continuously, steadily, 'in a big way'.

By the later sixteenth century, *sad (d.s.)*, though not in exclusive possession, is common—'in sad cypress let me be laid', 'tell sad stories of the death of kings', 'sad Celeno' singing a song 'that hart of flint asonder could have rifte'.[1]

As often, we have no difficulty in suggesting ways in which the word could have arrived at this sense. Rather, the possible ways are so numerous that we cannot hope to determine which counted for most.

From the very nature of metaphor a word that means 'heavy' will be very likely to acquire the meaning 'grievous'. A word that means 'fed up' will be very likely to acquire the meaning 'displeased, ill-content'. A word which means 'grave' or even 'steady-going' will

[1] *F.Q.* II, vii, 23.

necessarily mean the opposite of 'light' or 'sportive'. Thus we find *sad* used to mean 'serious', i.e. not joking. 'Speak you this with a sad brow?', are you in earnest?[1] And what is serious will always be thought gloomy by some, and gloom may by litotes be called seriousness. *Pensive*, from meaning 'thoughtful', came to mean 'melancholy' by some such process. Again, what is *sad* in the sense of firm or thoroughgoing or earnest will in some contexts refer to what is also grievous. When Malory wrote 'They drew their swords and gave many sad strokes' (VII, 8), did he mean earnest, all-out strokes (they did not 'pull their punches'), or grim and grievous strokes? Perhaps he could not have told us.

Almost every sense the word ever bore might have had some share in producing *sad* (*d.s.*).

V. OUR POLLY IS A 'SAD' SLUT

So runs the song in *The Beggars' Opera*. We may put beside it, from Farquhar's *Recruiting Officer* (III, ii), 'An ignorant, pretending, impudent coxcomb—Aye, aye, a sad dog' and 'He's a Whig, Sir, a sad dog',[2] and finally Mary Crawford's address to Fanny, 'Sad, sad girl: I do not know when I shall have done scolding you'.[3] I am in great doubt how these arose.

They might owe something to the same sort of transference which has given two meanings to the words *sorry* and *wretch*. In logic one who is *sorry* (Anglo-Saxon *sarig*) ought to be one who is sore, in pain, miserable. But it can

---

[1] *Much Ado* I, i, 183.   [2] Boswell, 12 April 1778.
[3] *Mansfield Park*, ch. XXXVI.

also be one who is vile and unsatisfactory—'a sorry knave'; whence also a sorry inn, a sorry nag, or 'sorry cheer' (a bad meal). A *wretch* (Anglo-Saxon *wrecca*) ought to be an exile, hence (significantly—there is much *Volkwanderung* in the background) in Anglo-Saxon poetry a hero, but soon a 'down and out', a miserable outcast. But a *wretch* can also be a vile person, a villain. 'Princes have been sold by wretches to whose care they were entrusted', says Johnson.[1] Thus the *sorry* man may be not the one who is himself dissatisfied but the one who causes our dissatisfaction; the *wretch* far from feeling wretchedness, may inflict it on others. Possibly in the same way *sad* may be transferred to the person who makes us *sad*, in whichever sense; either makes us 'fed up' (we have soon had quite enough of him), or makes us serious, or makes us melancholy.

But I fancy there is another possibility. Chaucer's messenger drank *sadly*; that is thoroughly, or seriously— meant business'. The spears went *sadly* in the rest because they also meant business. A *sad* instance of anything undesirable could be a serious instance of it. Do Polly's parents, when they call her 'a sad slut' mean that she is a serious, weighty, important instance of sluttery—is among sluts what 'a grave disaster' is among disasters? Are the 'sad dogs' advanced or grave cases of doggery? If so, Mary Crawford's 'sad girl' would be in a separate category. The previous examples have in view a species which is undesirable as a whole (sluts, dogs) and mark out one person as a prime specimen of it. But Mary Crawford of course did not think girls an undesirable species. Her

[1] Boswell, 23 September 1777.

84

usage would show *sad* in this sense going on after the original shade of meaning has been forgotten.

While both are conjectural I cannot help thinking the second process the more likely. The passages where *sad* is used in this way usually have, to my ear, some hint of the humorous about them; never the downright, whole-hearted condemnation of the word *wretch*. This seems to me to fit better with the idea of the 'prime specimen'.

4

WIT

[WITH *INGENIUM*]

IF a man had time to study the history of one word only, *wit* would perhaps be the best word he could choose. Its fortunes provide almost perfect examples of the main principles at work in semantic development. Its early life was happy and free from complications. It then acquired a sense which brought into full play the distinction between the word's and the speaker's meanings. It also suffered the worst fate any word has to fear; it became the fashionable term of approval among critics. This made it a prey to tactical definitions of a more than usually unscrupulous type, and in the heat of controversy there was some danger of its becoming a mere rallying-cry, semantically null. Meanwhile, however, popular usage was irresistibly at work in a different direction; in the end those 'who speak only to be understood' rescued it from the critics and fixed upon it the useful meaning it bears to-day. The chequered story has—what is rare in such matters—a happy ending.

I. EARLY HISTORY

Anglo-Saxon *wit* or *gewit* is mind, reason, intelligence. Rational creatures are those to whom God has given *wit*.[1] A mortally wounded man, until delirium or unconscious-

---

[1] *Genesis B,* 250.

ness overtakes him, still is master of his *gewitt*.[1] And of
course these, or closely similar, senses survived for
centuries. When a man is mad his 'wit's diseased'.[2] As he
grows older his *wit* 'ought to be more', he ought to have
more sense.[3] Davies (anticipating *Paradise Lost* VIII, 76f.)
says that God left some problems dark 'to punish pride of
wit', the pride of man's intellect,[4] and Pope follows him
with the saw that Nature 'wisely curbed proved man's
pretending wit'.[5] In Ireland, and perhaps elsewhere, we
still say 'God give you wit' or 'If you'd only had the wit
to get his address', meaning by *wit* sense or gumption.
In all such usages the ancient meaning is insulated from
the contamination of later meanings by the context. And
the context can have this insulating power even if it is
only a single clause:

> for a calm unfit,
> Would steer too nigh the sands to boast his wit.
> Great wits are sure to madness near allied.[6]

The first *wit* means 'sense', common sense, prudence.
But *wits* in the next line means a good deal more. The
full stop, the adjective *great*, and the fact that the whole
line is a traditional maxim, lead the reader, and perhaps
led Dryden, to make the adjustment unconsciously.

II. WITS

Two quite different causes lead to the frequent use of *wits*
in the plural. One is the old psychology with its five

---

[1] *Beowulf*, 2703.   [2] *Hamlet* III, ii, 336.
[3] *Poema Morale* 2; before 1200.
[4] *Nosce Teipsum. Of the Soule*, etc., stanza 15.
[5] *Essay on Criticism* I, 53.   [6] *Absalom* I, 161.

inward and five outward *wits* or senses.[1] In Benedick's encounter with Beatrice 'four of his five wits went halting off'.[2] This usage, so far as I can see, had almost no effect on other senses of the word.

The second cause is far more interesting. Men differ from one another not only in the amount of *wit* or intelligence they have but in the kind. Each man's *wit* has its own cast, bent, or temper; one quick and another plodding, one solid and another showy, one ingenious to invent and another accurate to retain. Thus as we speak of sceptical or credulous, creative or analytic, 'minds', you could once speak of *wits* to mean types of mind, or 'mentalities', or the people who have them. Thus in Chaucer

> For tendre wittes wenen al be wyle
> Theras they can nat pleynly understande[3]

people of 'tender' mind. The classic place for this usage is the account of 'quick' and 'hard' *wits* in Ascham's *Scholemaster*.

This sense of *wit*, unimportant though it may seem at the first glance, actually opened the way to nearly all the later developments. Without this sense *wit* is something common to all rational creatures or at least to all men of good sense. But a man's *wit* in this sense is something which can distinguish him, which is characteristic of him; his mental make-up.

One obvious result of this is to make *wit* the recognised translation of *ingenium*. Whether its constant use for that purpose actually helped to mould its meaning, or merely

[1] See pp. 147 *sq.* [2] *Much Ado* I, i, 63. [3] *Troilus* II, 271.

allows us to see more clearly just what that meaning was, I do not know. But a study of *wit* which does not take full account of its relation to *ingenium* would be out of court; and a full study, which I do not attempt, would have to spend some time on the Italian *ingegno* as well.

III. 'INGENIUM'

This word, like *natura* in its earlier use, originally meant the character or 'what-sortedness' of a thing, so that Tacitus can talk about the *ingenium* of a hill.[1] It concerns us, however, only when it is applied, as it far more often is, to human beings. 'Precepts', says Seneca, 'lead to right actions only if they meet a pliant *ingenium*.'[2] Here 'nature' or 'character' would do. Elsewhere the word refers specifically to a man's intellectual quality. Epicurus, says Lucretius, surpassed the whole human race in *ingenium* (III, 1043). Helvidius, in Tacitus, had at an early age turned his brilliant *ingenium* to the study of philosophy.[3] The same tendency which has made 'family' mean good family, and 'quality' good quality, brought it about that *ingenium* should usually mean not merely 'cast of mind' but a 'cast of mind above the ordinary'. Quintilian quotes from Cicero 'Whatever my share of *ingenium*, which I know to be small, may be' and 'What I lack in *ingenium* I make up for by hard work' (XI, i). The word obviously means something like cleverness, ability, high intellectual capacity. 'Quickness to learn and memory...are summed up in the single word *ingenium*', says Cicero,[4]

[1] *Histories* II, 4.
[2] *Epistle* 95.
[3] *Histories* IV, 5.
[4] *De Finibus* V, 13.

and adds that those who have them are called *ingeniosi*. But he includes too little, and it is indeed possible on other grounds that some words have dropped out of the text. *Ingenium* really means something more like 'talent' or even 'genius'. This is clear when it is used in the plural to mean 'men who have *ingenium*' (we also speak about 'men of talent' as 'talents'). When Tacitus says that the reign of Augustus has not lacked for its historians *decora ingenia*,[1] we can hardly translate this by anything weaker than 'distinguished talents'. So, when Suetonius records that Vespasian 'patronised *ingenia* and the arts',[2] we must say 'patronised genius' or 'talent' (i.e. men of talent).

IV. 'INGENIUM' AND WIT

The liaison, so to call it, between these two words is much closer than I realised before I looked into the matter.

The one is the almost invariable translation of the other. *Ingenii gloriam* in Boethius[3] becomes 'glory of wit' in J.T.'s version (1609). The Lucretian vaunt that Epicurus surpassed all mankind in *ingenium*, which I quoted a minute ago, is rendered by Burton 'Whose wit excelled the wits of men so far'.[4] Horace writes

> Ingeniis non ille favet plauditque sepultis
> Nostra sed impugnat,[5]

literally 'He does not favour and applaud buried *ingenia* but attacks our own'. Dryden translates it 'He favours not dead wits but hates the living'.[6] Shakespeare, when

---

[1] *Annals* I, i. [2] *Vesp.* xviii. [3] II, Pr. iii.
[4] *Democritus to the Reader.* [5] *Epist.* II, i, 88.
[6] *Defence of the Epilogue. Essays*, ed. Ker, vol. I, p. 163.

he speaks about 'the wits of former days' (Sonnet LIX) means exactly the same; the writers of talent or genius who flourished before his own time.

But *wit* does not appear only as the translation of *ingenium*; both words enter into exactly the same traditional antitheses.

Nullum magnum ingenium sine mixtura dementiae, no great *ingenium* without a dash of insanity, from Seneca's *De Tranquillitate* (XVII, 4), becomes Dryden's 'Great wits are sure to madness near allied'.

'You get what is called affectation (*kakozelon*) when *ingenium* lacks *judicium*.'[1] 'It is a bad sign when a boy's *judicium* gets ahead of his *ingenium*.'[2] This contrasted pair will be familiar to all readers of neo-classical criticism. Harvey, in Cowley's Ode (stanza 13), has 'so strong a wit as all things but his Judgment overcame'. 'Wit and Judgment often are at strife,' says Pope.[3]

'The poem of Lucretius has many flashes of *ingenium*, but also much art.'[4] Pope makes the same dichotomy when he speaks of a work where 'Wit and Art conspire to move your mind'.[5]

An author may be too fond of his own *ingenium*, *nimium amator ingenii sui*.[6] Pope reproduces both this idea and also the antithesis of *ingenium* and *judicium* in one couplet:

> Authors are partial to their wit, 'tis true.
> But are not critics to their judgment too.[7]

---

[1] Quintilian VIII, iii. [2] *Ibid.* II, iv. [3] *Essay on Criticism* I, 82.
[4] Cicero, *Ad Quintum* II, ii. Some emend to 'but not much art'. The choice of reading makes no difference for our purpose.
[5] *E.C.* II, 532. [6] Quintilian, X, i. [7] *E.C.* I, 17.

The difficulty here is to find, for our own purpose, a word to express what *ingenium* and *wit* both clearly mean. One cannot call it either 'talent' or 'genius' without foisting upon the Roman and English writers a far later, and Romantic, distinction; and 'genius' labours further under the disadvantage of having no tolerable plural. But what is hard to express is easy to understand. What is being talked about is the thing which, in its highest exaltation may border on madness; the productive, seminal (modern cant would say 'creative') thing, as distinct from the critical faculty of *judicium*; the thing supplied by nature, not acquired by skill (*ars*); the thing which he who has it may love too well and follow intemperately. It is what distinguishes the great writer and especially the great poet. It is therefore very close to 'imagination'. Indeed, there is one Latin passage where *ingenium* can hardly be translated except by that very word. It comes at the beginning of Cicero's *De Legibus*. Atticus looks round to see the oak which had been mentioned in Cicero's poem *Marius* and asks if it is still alive. 'Yes,' comes the answer, 'it is, and always will be, for it was planted by *ingenium*.' It was an imaginary tree (i, i).

Since English words fail us, and since we may now bid goodbye to Latin itself, for the rest of this chapter I am going to call the sense of the word *wit* which we have been observing 'the *ingenium* sense' or '*wit-ingenium*'. And it seems to me absolutely essential to face this sense squarely and get it firmly fixed in our minds. If we once allow more familiar, though not necessarily later, meanings to colour our reading of the word *wit* wherever the neo-classical writers use it, we shall get into hopeless confusion.

This error has, I believe, been committed by a critic to whose *ingenium* we all owe a willing debt. In his *Structure of Complex Words* (p. 87) Professor Empson, speaking of the word *wit* in Pope's *Essay on Criticism*, says that 'there is not a single use of the word in the whole poem in which the idea of a joke is quite out of sight. Indeed I think that the whole structure of thought in the poem depends on this.' Now I think there are plenty of passages where it is simply *wit-ingenium* with no idea of a joke, however far in the background. 'Great Wits may sometimes gloriously offend' (1, 152). Surely it is the great *ingenia* who are thus entitled to dispense with rule (l. 144) and transcend art (l. 154)? It is an affair of 'nameless graces' (l. 144) attainable only by a 'master-hand' (l. 145); a privilege best reserved for the ancients (l. 161) who have something like a royal prerogative (l. 162). The result pleases, but pleases like 'the shapeless rock, or hanging precipice' (l. 160) which Pope certainly did not find jocular. The truth seems to me to be that he is here handling what is almost a *locus communis*. Democritus, quoted by Horace, had said that *ingenium* was happier than 'painful' or 'beggarly' (*misera*) art.[1] Milton, probably with that very word *misera* in mind, confesses that Shakespeare's 'easy numbers' flow 'to the shame of slow endeavouring art'. Closest to Pope is Boileau's

> par quel transport heureux
> Quelquefois dans sa course un esprit vigoureux,

[1] *De Arte*, 295.

Trop resserré par l'art, sort des règles prescrites,
Et de l'art mesme apprend à franchir leurs limites.[1]

None of these provides a background which makes Professor Empson's view probable. And what of the 'patriarch wits' who survived a thousand years (II, 479)? Does this mean only Aristophanes and Lucian? I think rather, Homer, Sophocles, and Virgil.

But the crucial experiment is still to try. No interpretation of the word *wit* is acceptable unless it can stand up to the couplet

Some have at first for wits, then poets passed,
Turn'd critics next, and proved plain fools at last.[2]

Clearly the whole rhetorical structure is in ruins unless we can find senses for the key-words which provide a continuous descent; a poet must be something inferior to a *wit*, a critic to a poet, and a 'plain fool' to a critic.

Unfortunately the word *poet*, as well as *wit*, now needs explanation. *Poet* has in our time become a term of laudation rather than of description, so that to speak of a 'bad poet' is for some almost an oxymoron. Dr Leavis, if I remember rightly, wrote to a paper to say that Mr Auden was not a poet. But of course there is another sense in which everyone, including Dr Leavis, would have to classify Mr Auden as a poet; the sense any teacher would be using if he said 'No, no. You're confusing Lucan and Lucian. The one was a Latin poet; the other a Greek prose-writer.' The seventeenth- and eighteenth-century usage, if not identical with the teacher's, was far nearer to

---

[1] *L'Art Poétique* IV, 78.   [2] I, 36.

his than to Dr Leavis's. Johnson, who defines *poetry* as 'metrical composition', defines *poet* as 'An inventor; an author of fiction; a writer of poems; one who writes in measure'. We can gauge how far we have travelled[1] by comparing this with the Shorter Oxford Dictionary which, after a definition very like Johnson's, feels obliged to add 'A writer in verse (or sometimes in elevated prose) distinguished by imaginative power, insight, sensibility, and faculty of expression'. Johnson is probably pretty true to the age immediately before his own. Fiction and metre were the chief *differentiae* of the 'poet'. Thus Shadwell is a *poet* in the Epilogue to *The Silent Lovers* (l. 9) and 'our poet' in that to *The Squire of Alsatia*. Even when he wrote verse, to call a man a poet implied neither that he had, nor that he had not, what we now call 'poetic genius'. It was parallel to calling him an architect or an actor. It told you what craft or profession he followed; like calling him 'an author'.

With this proviso, does not Pope's couplet become plain when—but only when—we take *wit* as *wit-ingenium*? 'Some have at first passed for men of genius; then for authors (or literary craftsmen); then for critics; and finally have proved fools.'

In the light of this two Drydenian passages are 'patient' (as the old divines said) of a far more important interpretation than they have usually received. In the *Essay of Dramatic Poesy* we are told that Jonson was 'the more

[1] How far we have travelled from the neo-classic age and also how far it had travelled from the sixteenth century; for *S.O.D.* gives the date 1530 for its loftier sense.

correct poet, but Shakespeare the greater wit'.[1] In the *Original and Progress of Satire* it is said 'if we are not so great wits as Donne, yet certainly we are better poets'.[2] I believe the meaning of both to be almost the opposite of that which naturally occurs first to a modern reader. *Wit* and *wits* are used in the *ingenium*-sense. Dryden is saying that while Jonson was the more disciplined craftsman, Shakespeare was the greater genius; that while we have less genius than Donne we have more literary skill. This is borne out by the fact that he has just censured Donne for insufficient care for 'words' and 'numbers'. In a word, Dryden is almost (not quite) saying that Shakespeare is, in one sense, a greater poet than Jonson; and Donne, in one sense, a greater poet than himself and his contemporaries.

It must be understood that the error of which I venture to suspect Professor Empson is not one in chronology. That sense of the word *wit* which he feels delicately present throughout the *Essay on Criticism* certainly existed in Pope's time, and long before. It was destined to destroy the *ingenium*-sense in the end. The question between Professor Empson and me is whether that slowly rising tide had yet reached all Pope's uses of the word. I believe it had not; the insulating power of the context still protected them. We will now leave *wit-ingenium* in its lofty, yet already precarious, position, and say something of this other sense.

[1] Ker, vol. I, p. 82.   [2] *Ibid.* vol. II, p. 102.

V. EARLY HISTORY OF THE DANGEROUS SENSE'

I take it that *wit* in the sense now current means that sort of mental agility or gymnastic which uses language as the principal equipment of its gymnasium. 'Language' must here be taken in a large sense, to include those proverbs, and quotations almost equivalent to proverbs, which are among the ordinary small change of conversation. Thus the Frenchman's comment on the Munich agreement (*ce n'est pas magnifique, mais ce n'est pas la guerre*) or Lady Dorothy Neville's protest to the cook ('you cannot serve cod and salmon') are *wit* because the familiar *gnomae* which they appositely pervert make part of the whole linguistic situation in which they were said. Pun, half pun, assonance, epigram (in the modern sense) and distorted proverb or quotation are all *witty*. Hence of all the excellences prose can have it is the least translatable. This is the *dangerous sense* of *wit* and I shall refer to it henceforward as *wit* (*d.s.*). But besides *wit* (*d.s.*) and *wit-ingenium* we also need a name for the word's earliest sense, for *wit* meaning mind, rationality, good sense. I call this *wit* (*old sense*).

There is no doubt that *wit* (*d.s.*) was current in the seventeenth century, but it is impossible to determine exactly when it arose. The reason for this impossibility is clear enough. A man's intelligence (*wit* (*old sense*)) impresses other people most and is most talked about if he displays it in conversation. But no way of displaying it in conversation will be so obvious or so attractive to most hearers as repartee, epigram, and general dexterity—*wit* (*d.s.*). The evidence on which men attribute *wit* (*old sense*) to anyone will therefore very often be the *wit* (*d.s.*) of his talk. When *wit* (*d.s.*) has fully established itself in the language a very careful speaker might make a distinction between the quality shown in conversation and the general calibre of mind inferred from it. But not one speaker in a thousand has any care for such things, and until the quality in question has a name the distinction cannot easily be put into words. Hence there will be a period during which such a remark as 'My lord showed prodigious wit in his discourse to-day' is ambiguous. Does it mean 'The *wit* (*d.s.*) of what he said was prodigious', or 'What he said showed (proved) that he has a prodigious *wit* (*old sense*)'? The speaker will not know and will not have raised the question.

We are told that Benedick and Beatrice 'never meet but there's a skirmish of wit between them'.[1] No one doubts that what they displayed *in fact* was *wit* (*d.s.*). But is the speaker using the word in the *dangerous sense*, or does he only mean they set their brains at one another, skirmish with their *wit* (*old sense*)?

So with Falstaff's 'I am not only witty myself but the cause that wit is in other men'.[2] So long as *wit* had its Old Sense, *witty* of course meant wise; as it does, though mockingly, in *Tamburlaine* (I, iv, 686), 'Are you the witty king of Persia?' Is Falstaff calling himself wise? or *spirituel*? The *wit* displayed by the other men was, as the context shows, the 'invention' of things that 'tend to laughter'. This too could be *wit* in more than one sense.

[1] *Much Ado* I, i, 57.   [2] *Hen. IV*, Pt. 2, I, ii, 8.

There is, once more, no doubt about the fact of Falstaff's *wit* (*d.s.*), and little doubt that his *wit* (*d.s.*) is, in part anyway, the thing he is referring to, the ground on which he bases his claim to be *witty*. But this does not prove that *wit* in his language already has the *dangerous sense*.

We may clarify the situation from a parallel case where the two senses of a word admit different spellings. A lady may show her courtesy by making a curtsy; more briefly, may show her courtesy by her curtsy. The fact that someone then speaks of her courtesy on a particular occasion, when her courtesy was wholly contained in her curtsy (she said nothing, and did nothing except making a curtsy), would not prove that *courtesy* had for him the sense *curtsy*. It is our distinction between word's meaning and speaker's meaning. From one point of view the speaker means by 'her courtesy' nothing more or less or other than her curtsy. But that need not be the sense, nor even a sense, of *courtesy* in his language. So here. What the Shakespearian characters are referring to may be in fact *wit* (*d.s.*) so that this becomes the speaker's meaning of the word at that moment. It need not yet be the word's meaning.

But clearly it soon will be one of the word's meanings. If that particular gesture we now call a curtsy becomes the obligatory method by which every lady shows her courtesy on entering a room—so that girls who forget it will be reprimanded by a mother's or duenna's sharp 'Remember your courtesy' (i.e. your good manners)—then, with or without change of spelling, a new sense of *courtesy* in which it means simply this gesture, is almost bound to arise, and its very connection with *cortesia* in general may be forgotten. Similarly, if most of those who praise a man's *wit* are in fact, inside that context, referring to his *wit* (*d.s.*), this is almost bound to become a new and distinguishable meaning of the word. The ambiguity of the Shakespearian passages is just what one might expect; the sort of thing that happens if we catch a new sense at the very moment when it is first branching off the parent stem.

Two less ambiguous passages illustrate a faint movement of the word away from its old sense in a direction which might finally lead to its meaning *wit* (*d.s.*). 'Sharp and subtle discourses of wit', says Hooker, 'procure great applause, but being laid in the balance with that which the habit of sound experience plainly delivereth, they are over weighed' (v, vii, 1). Burton defines *wit* as 'acumen or subtilty, sharpness of invention' (1, 1, 2, 10). Neither amounts to much. But the idea of levity (of the *peu solide*) which is there in Hooker, and that of sharpness in Burton, have perhaps some small significance. *Wit* is becoming something less staid and tranquil than intelligence.

It is in the second half of the seventeenth century that we find the most abundant and amusing evidences of the word's drift towards its *dangerous sense*; amusing because they consist almost entirely of disclaimers. Everyone starts telling us what the word does *not* mean; a sure proof that it is beginning to mean just that.

1650: Davenant, describing something 'which is not, yet is accompted, Wit', includes in it 'what are commonly called *Conceits*, things that sound like the knacks or toyes of ordinary *Epigrammatists*'.[1]

1664: Flecknoe warns us that *wit* must *not* include 'clenches (puns), quibbles, gingles, and such like trifles'.[2]

1667: Dryden tells us that *wit* does *not* consist of 'the jerk or sting of an epigram nor the seeming contradiction of a poor antithesis…nor the jingle of a more poor paranomasia'.[3]

1668: Shadwell corrects those ignorant people who believed 'that all the Wit in Playes consisted in bringing two persons upon the Stage to break Jests, and to bob one another, which they call Repartie'.[4]

1672: Dryden classifies 'clenches' as 'The lowest and most grovelling kind of wit'.[5]

1700: Dryden says that 'the vulgar judges…call conceits and jingles wit'.[6]

Clearly the thing which they deny to be *wit*, or admit only to be 'the lowest and most grovelling' species of it, is *wit* (*d.s.*). And this, as I have said, proves that *wit* (*d.s.*) was increasingly the current meaning of the word *wit*. To be sure, Dryden's reference to 'vulgar judges', and perhaps the language of all these critics, might lead us to believe that a group of cultivated speakers were defending their own usage against a vulgarism perpetrated only by 'lesser breeds without the law'. But it is no such thing. They themselves used *wit* in the sense they reprobate.

[1] Preface to *Gondibert*.   [2] *Discourse of the English Stage*.
[3] Preface to *Annus Mirabilis*, Ker, vol. I, p. 14.
[4] Preface to *The Sullen Lovers*.
[5] *Defence of the Epilogue*, Ker, vol. I, p. 173.
[6] *Preface to the Fables*, Ker, vol. II, p. 256.

Watch Dryden off his guard when he is just using, not thinking about, the word.

'As for comedy,' he says, 'repartee is one of its chief graces; the greatest pleasure of the audience is a chace of wit, kept up on both sides and swiftly managed.'[1] Or again, 'They say the quickness of repartees in argumentative scenes receives an ornament from verse. Now what is more unreasonable than to imagine that a man should not only light upon the wit, but the rhyme too, upon the sudden.'[2] The 'copiousness' of Ovid's 'wit' was such that he 'often writ too pointedly for his subject'.[3] Only intolerable straining could give *wit* anything but its *dangerous sense* in such passages. What Dryden probably believed, and would certainly have wished others to believe, about his use of the word is not true. 'Out of school' he often talked like the 'vulgar judges'.

Often, not always, *wit-ingenium* and *wit* (*d.s.*) were both equally parts of his vocabulary; and so, I suspect, was *wit* (*old sense*) too. The situation is common enough. You and I at nine o'clock any morning, poring over the pencilled washing bill presented by our bedmakers, complain 'I can't read the last figure'. At ten, during a supervision, we mention a figure (of rhetoric). At our elevenses we say to a friend that the young woman who has just left the tap-room has a fine figure. So then. Dryden, joined on his way to the coffee-house by an elderly friend, and asked whether it were not true that my Lord Clarendon was a man of great *wit*, would at once understand *wit*

[1] *Dramatic Poesy*, Ker, vol. 1, p. 72.   [2] *Ibid.* p. 92.
[3] *Preface to Ovid's Epistles*, Ker, vol. 1, pp. 233-4.

(*old sense*). Seated an hour later among Templars and poets and discussing the nature of poetry he would use *wit-ingenium*. Yet, before the talk was out, if some bright youngster delighted them with brilliant repartee, he might praise that youngster's *wit* (*d.s.*). He would slip in and out of the different meanings without noticing it. It is all ordinary and comfortable until one of the meanings happens to become strategically important in some controversy. A bad linguistic situation then results.

VI. THE AFFLICTIONS OF 'WIT-INGENIUM'

The growing currency of *wit* (*d.s.*) would in any circumstances have endangered *wit-ingenium*. But the latter sense suffered from an internal weakness as well. It was a term of laudation; by attributing *wit-ingenium* to a man or calling him (in that sense) 'a *wit*', you praise him. This brings the distinction between word's meaning and speaker's meaning into play in a very acute form.

A Hottentot and a Dane might hammer out an agreed definition of *beauty*, and in that sense, lexically, 'mean' the same by it. Yet the one might continue, in a different sense, to 'mean' blubber lips, woolly hair, and a fat paunch while the other 'meant' a small mouth, silky hair, 'white and red', and a slender waist. And two men who agree about the (lexical) 'meaning' of *comic* would not necessarily find the same things funny.

This is even more obviously true of a word like genius. It may lexically 'mean' to all of us the mental quality, character, or state which produces, say, great literature. But we do not all think the same sorts of literature great.

We shall therefore attribute *genius* to quite different authors, and we shall include in our conception of *genius* different mental powers. Lexical agreement can co-exist with fierce disagreements about denotation.

In just this way there was, during the seventeenth and early eighteenth centuries, a wide agreement among critics—'in school', when they were on their guard—on the meaning of *wit*. They agreed that the *ingenium* sense was its true or proper meaning. Never, never (till, next moment, they forgot) would they consent to the meaning *wit* (*d.s.*). No; this noble word meant the essential faculty of the poet, the inner cause of excellence in writing. But while this lexical agreement still lasted taste began to change. *Wit* was the cause of excellence, but people began to think different things excellent. And no one was ready to give up the magic word *wit*. However little the new poetry resembled the old, those who claimed excellence for it claimed that it showed *wit*. As new shopkeepers who have 'bought the goodwill' of their predecessor's business keep his name for a while over their door, so the literary innovators want to retain the prestige, almost the 'selling-power', of the consecrated word. It occurred to no one to say 'The school of *wit* is over; we offer excellence of a different kind.' They preferred to say 'What we offer is "the real" or "true" *wit*'. Hence the constant, and linguistically barren, definings and re-definings of the word. They are merely tactical. The word has to be stretched and contracted so as to cover whatever you and your friends write or enjoy and to exclude what the enemy writes or enjoys.

Cowley 'meant' by *wit* the essential gift of the poet.
But then, for him, the essential gift was the power to
produce that *concordia discors* which has been called 'Metaphysical Wit' ever since Johnson's day:

> In a true piece of *Wit* all things must be,
>   Yet all things there agree,
> As in the Ark, join'd without force or strife,
> All *Creatures* dwelt; all creatures that had *Life*.[1]

Dryden also 'meant' by *wit* the essential gift of the poet.
And in 1667 he defined this gift as 'the faculty of imagination...which, like a nimble spaniel, beats over and
ranges through the field of memory'.[2] His ideal is already
a little different from Cowley's; there is less emphasis on
the *discors*, the heterogeneity of the things the poet unites.
But ten years later he and Cowley are leagues apart, each
'hull down' to the other.[3] *Wit* is now 'propriety of
thoughts and words'. He produces this with some self-congratulation. He liked it so well that he repeated it in 1685.[4]

This definition, as Addison observes,[5] would commit
us to the consequence, 'Euclid was the greatest wit that
ever set pen to paper'. It may also be asserted almost
safely that no human being, when using the word *wit* to
talk with and not talking *about* the word *wit*, has ever
meant by it anything of the sort. Nor does Dryden himself anywhere make the slightest use of this definition;
there is perhaps none to be made, since it leaves no room
for any distinction in *wit* between the greatest literature

[1] *Ode to Wit*, stanza 8.
[2] *Preface to Annus Mirabilis*, Ker, vol. I, p. 14.
[3] *The Author's Apology etc.*, Ker, vol. I, p. 190.
[4] Ker, vol. I, p. 270.   [5] *Spectator*, 62.

in the world and any competent piece of draughting.
We might tax our brains for a long time to explain how
a man of Dryden's stature could have said anything so
false to all actual usage, so useless, and so unsupported, if
we did not realise its tactical function. He is thinking
neither about what the word actually meant nor about
what it could, in the interests of clarity and precision and
general utility, be made to mean. It is a valuable vogue-
word. Therefore a strong point in the critical battle. He
wants to deny the enemy the use of it. What use, if any,
his own side can make of it hereafter may be left for
consideration. 'Propriety' is a garrison word; thrown in
to exclude Ovid and Cowley and Cleveland from the
highest poetical honours.

Pope also meant by *wit* the essential gift of the poet.
But with him the wheel has come almost full circle. *Wit*,
for Cowley, depends on the unexpected thought which
yokes together 'things by nature most unneighbourly'.
For Pope it is the perfect expression of well-worn
thoughts, the pellucidity and finality which rescue the
obvious from neglect—

> True Wit is Nature to advantage dress'd,
> What oft was thought but ne'er so well express'd.[1]

But the tell-tale word is 'true'. No one describes as '*true*
happiness' the life we all enjoy; it is just 'happiness'. No
one who is being agreeable calls himself our '*true* friend';
freedom and what Hegelians call '*true* freedom' are
almost mutually exclusive. If *wit* were the current name

---

[1] *Essay on Criticism*, II, 297.

for the thing Pope describes, then he would have called it simply *wit*, not *true wit*. The adjective shows that he is twisting the noun into a sense it never naturally bore.

In the story I have to tell Dryden and Pope cut a sufficiently poor figure; it is therefore only fair to add at once that this did not come about through any lack of intelligence. Both show elsewhere that they knew, and could have done, much better. 'Ben Jonson...always writ properly and in the character required; and I will not contest further with my friends who call that wit; it being very certain that even folly itself, well represented is wit *in a larger signification*'.[1] Here we exchange dogmatism about what the word ought to mean for distinction between two of the things it actually meant. And Pope can write

> Thus Wit, like faith, by each man is applied
> To one small sect, and all are damn'd beside.[2]

In his own definition of 'true wit' he wrote from within one of the sects and on its behalf. Here he stands above the conflict; for a moment.

VII. HAPPY ENDING

These tactical definitions, having served their momentary purpose, were dropped by their inventors and rejected by other speakers. If they had any influence on the history of the language, they probably helped to hasten the death of the *ingenium* sense by diminishing its utility. But even this is very doubtful.

[1] Italics mine. *Defence of the Epilogue*. Ker, vol. I, p. 172.
[2] *E.C.* II, 396.

The *ingenium* sense had an external enemy in the increasing popularity of the *dangerous sense*. But it also had what we may call an internal enemy. Lexically, as I have said, *wit-ingenium* had long meant the essential gift of the poet. That was the word's meaning. And the speaker's meaning, of course, was the gift required for producing the sort of poetry the speaker approved. And ever since the last quarter of the sixteenth century most people had approved a pointed, figured, conceited sort of poetry. Gascoigne and the young Shakespeare and Du Bartas had not, any more than Cowley and Cleveland and Butler, been offering 'what oft was thought'. Nor had Ovid, nor the young Dryden, nor always the young Milton. Modern critics rightly distinguish the Elizabethan from the 'Metaphysical' conceit; but all these poets, set against either medieval or eighteenth- and nineteenth-century poets, are a continuous dynasty. And by the time the mature Dryden and the young Pope are fighting for the recognition of a new kind of excellence, the long reign of that dynasty has associated *wit-ingenium* indissolubly with one kind of poetic *ingenium*. The speaker's meaning has become the word's meaning. The effort to appropriate the word *wit* to the new excellence is hopeless, just as now it would be hopeless to try to extend the word *tragedy* to cover plays (like the *Helena*, the *Iphigenia in Tauris*, or the *Cid*) that have a happy ending. It has been too long associated with deaths in Act v. So *wit*, as a term of praise for poetry, had been too long associated with a particular kind of poetry.' And it was useful because it described the virtues of that kind, not of poetry in general. In this sense the meaning that survived the critical controversies may be called *wit-ingenium demoted*, the thing described by Addison, when, correcting Locke, he says that *wit* is not merely 'the assemblage of ideas... wherein can be found any resemblance or congruity', because 'every resemblance of ideas is not that which we call wit, unless it be such an one that gives delight and surprise'.[1] After that comes the perfection of Johnson, 'a kind of *discordia concors*, a combination of dissimilar images, a discovery of occult resemblances in things apparently unlike'.[2] This belongs to a different world from the Popian and Drydenian definitions. Here is a man with no axe to grind, a man defining what he believes (no doubt rightly) to be the actual use of the word in one of its senses.

In one of its senses. For *wit-ingenium* even when thus demoted is still not quite synonymous with *wit (d.s.)*. But they certainly have more in common with each other than either has with *wit (old sense)* or with any of the pseudo-senses the controversial critics gave the word. Both display the unexpected, the lively, the dexterous. Both, if disliked, are liable to be called 'cleverness', or 'fireworks'. Thus, unforeseen, a very happy linguistic situation has come about. Outside literary circles *wit* means *wit (d.s.)*. But those within the literary circles, while fully accepting *wit (d.s.)*, have no difficulty in accepting the word *wit* (guarded with some such addition as *metaphysical* or *baroque*) as a name for the characteristic quality of Donne and Herbert. And most of us do not

[1] *Spectator*, 62.   [2] *Life of Cowley*.

feel that the one *wit* and the other are what Aristotle calls 'things accidentally homonymous'. We have rather the conception of *wit* as something with a very wide range (from the *Nocturnall upon S. Lucies Day* to *The Importance of Being Earnest*) but also with a continuity throughout that range. Thus, after terrible danger, *wit* becomes once more a really useful word, as useful as it was in Anglo-Saxon. It enables us to distinguish; to point at this, and therefore not at that. In reaching this happy condition the word has, no doubt, had to abandon its large and lofty sense of *ingenium*. What has been (usefully) appropriated to one kind of literary excellence or even to one area of related excellences, cannot go on meaning literary excellence in general. As for its still more general meaning, its *old sense*, that survives in expressions like 'God give you *wit*'. It is enabled to do so because it occurs in wholly un-literary contexts and therefore never clashes with *wit* as a critical term. *Fallentis semita vitae*; it lives by keeping out of its rival's way.

5

FREE

THE materials of this chapter will illustrate two principles
mentioned in the Introduction. They are all moralised
status-words. And they all show parallelism of semantic
movement in different languages.

I. 'ELEUTHEROS'

Eleutheros means 'free', not a slave. One can also be
eleutheros apo, free from, pain, fear or the like. A community is *eleutheros* when it is autonomous; Xenophon
can speak of two communities being *eleutherous apo*, free
from, one another; mutually independent.[1] All this
would be unimportant if the word had not taken on a
secondary, a social-ethical, sense. To call a man *eleutheros*
in the first sense merely identified his legal status; to call
his behaviour *eleutheros* in the second was to say that it
displayed the qualities which, on the Greek view, a freeman ought to have. There is also another adjective,
eleutherios, which is used with this second meaning only.
Eleutheros is used with both.

The character of the *eleutheros* (or *eleutherios*) is, of
course, contrasted with that of the slave. It would be
dangerous in modern English to say 'with the servile

[1] *Cyropaedia* III, ii, 23.

character', for that would probably conjure up a false image. By a 'servile' man we mean, I take it, an abject, submissive man who cringes and flatters. That this was not the ancient idea of the typical slave is plain from the slaves in Greek and Roman comedy and also from the contrasts implied in the words we are now studying. It was a slave-girl who taunted Monica with her tippling, while quarrelling with her young mistress *ut fit*, 'the way they do'.[1] The true servile character is cheeky, shrewd, cunning, up to every trick, always with an eye to the main chance, determined 'to look after number one'. Figaro or Mrs Slipslop fill the requirements pretty well. Sam Weller has the right knowingness, the diamond-cut-diamond realism, but he is disinterested. Absence of disinterestedness, lack of generosity, is the hall-mark of the servile. The typical slave always has an axe to grind. Hence the miserably betrayed Philoctetes in Sophocles' play (l. 1006) says to the cunning Odysseus 'Oh you— you who never had a sound or *eleutheron* thought in your mind!' Odysseus has done nothing without 'an ulterior motive'.

It was of course recognised, as by Aristotle so by others, that servile status and servile character did not always coincide. Hence a fragment of Menander runs 'Live in slavery with the spirit of a freeman (*eleutherôs*) and you will be no slave'.

Generosity being part of the freeman's character, the abstract noun *eleutheriotes* can mean generosity about money, bountifulness, readiness to give; the word

[1] St Augustine, *Confessions* IX, 8.

generosity itself, as we noticed before, shows a very similar development. *Aneleutheria*, the opposite of *eleutheriotes*, of course means stinginess.[1]

II. 'LIBER'

Latin *liber* and *liberalis* are related almost exactly as *eleutheros* and *eleutherios*. *Liber* is 'free', not a slave; or free, used of an inanimate object, in the sense of unconfined, unopposed. The sea, in Ovid, as opposed to the rivers, is the plain of freer (*liberioris*) water.[2] One's mind or judgement can be *liber* when one is not 'committed' or bound by previous engagement or prejudice. Honest jurymen who come to the case with an 'open' mind are *liberi solutique* in Cicero's *Verrines*, 'free and without ties'. Conduct is *liberalis* when it is such as becomes a freeman. Justice, according to Cicero,[3] is the most magnificent virtue and most suitable-to-a-freeman (*liberalis*). This ethical sense is often specialised and narrowed to denote the quality which we still call *liberality*. '*Liberales* are the sort of people who ransom prisoners of war'.[4]

Since the word *liberalis* is metrically two trochees it can never occur in dactylic verse. In poetry, therefore, *ingenuus* (free-born) is used instead, with, I think, precisely the same range of meaning. That is, it may refer merely to status, but much more often has the ethical-social meaning; as when Juvenal says 'a boy of *ingenuus* countenance, with an *ingenuus* modesty (*pudor*)', in XI, 154. The passage is interesting in two ways: first, because this

---

[1] Aristotle, *Ethics*, 1119 b.   [2] *Metamorphoses* I, 41.
[3] *Republic* III, viii.   [4] Cicero, *Offices* II, xvi.

boy was in fact a slave, and secondly because the *pudor* brings out by contrast the ancient idea of the typical slave. The slick waiters, alternately fawning and insolent, in the worst type of 'posh' hotel would have seemed to the ancients typically 'servile'; the kind, unpretentious old servants whom men of my age can still remember (especially in the country) would not. The later history of the derivative *ingenuous* is also instructive; like a free-man, thence open, unsuspicious, ready to trust because trustworthy, thence (in the good sense) *simple*, thence too simple, credulous, finally fatuous, a dupe, a gull. Greek *euethes*, originally 'good-natured' but finally 'silly', shows the same development. So does *silly* itself, and *innocent*. These developments in fact embody the comment of the typical slave on the *ingenuus*, whose lack of suspicion he regards as folly. If Sam Weller had been a typical *servus* he would merely have despised (instead of both honouring and smiling at) the innocence of Mr Pickwick.

III. 'FREE'

Like the Greek and Latin words this originally refers to legal status. The opposite is slave—*theow* in classical Anglo-Saxon, or, later, Old Norse *thrael*. All sons of free men, *freora manna*, are to be taught to read, says King Alfred in the preface to his version of the *Cura Pastoralis*. It also means 'free' in the physical sense, free to move. After her miraculous healing the blind woman in the old version of Bede, who had been led to the shrine by her maids, went home '*freo* on her own feet' (IV, 10). These, the oldest senses of the word, are now, oddly enough, its *dangerous senses*; for the others, those that correspond roughly to *eleutherios* and *liberalis*, are mainly obsolete.

I say 'correspond roughly' because there is a perceptible difference between the ancient and the English developments. Both may be described as 'social-ethical', but in the Greek and Roman words the ethical predominates and the social almost vanishes in the end. This is not so of English *free*. Its background is feudal, not republican; it belongs to a world in which manners were more elaborate than in antiquity and far more valued.

In *Piers Plowman* we read that Mede is married more for her money than for any virtue or beauty or any *high kinde*—any noble blood.[1] The B text at the corresponding point reads *free kinde*.[2] The adjectives are probably almost synonymous in this context. There need be no ethical implication in either; and the social pretension is higher than that of *eleutheros* or *liberalis*. Often the word refers neither to blood nor to morality but to manners, as when the thirteenth-century *Floris and Blancheflor* (l. 498) describes a burgher as 'fre and curteys', polite and courteous. Like the adjective *kinde* it tails off into the vaguest, most unspecified, laudation, so that Christ in the York *Harrowing of Hell* (l. 5) can say 'mi Fader *free*'. It shows its fullest charge of meaning in Chaucer's line 'Trouthe and honour, fredom and courtesye';[3] knightly behaviour, in which morality up to the highest self-sacrifice and manners down to the smallest gracefulness in etiquette were inextricably blended by the medieval ideal.

[1] C. III, 82.   [2] B. II, 75.   [3] *C.T.* A. 46

Inevitably, since 'largesse' is a most important aspect of *fredom*, this sense throws out the branch 'munificent, open-handed'; 'fre of hir goodes', generous with their property,[1] or 'to fre of dede', over-liberal in its action.[2] This could also, however, be reached without going through the sense 'noble, courteous', simply from the sense 'unrestrained' (as in the translation of Bede); uninhibited, unchecked, in one's dealings with one's own property.

The larger sense is perhaps well brought out in Chaucer's line 'Free was daun John and namely of dispence':[3] he had in general the manners of a gentleman, and especially in the way he spent his money. The *Franklin's Tale* gives us a sort of competition in *fredom* (magnanimity, generosity) and hands over to the reader the problem 'which was the moste free'.[4] Boccaccio in the corresponding passage asks who had shown the greatest *liberalità*.

From the sense 'unrestrained' another branch goes off. Behaviour which is informal, familiar, facile, the reverse of 'stand-offish', can be *free*. Thus Quarles says 'The world's a crafty strumpet...if thou be free she's strange; if strange, she's free'.[5] Hence a pejorative usage. One may be more familiar, less formal, than the social situation justifies, and may receive, as in Sheridan, the rebuff 'Not so free, fellow'.[6] Finally *free* can almost mean 'abusive'. 'The mistress and the maid shall quarrel and give each

---

[1] *Piers Plowman*, B. x, 74.   [2] *Pearl*, 481.
[3] *C.T.* B. 1233.   [4] F. 1622.
[5] *Emblems* I, iv.   [6] *St Patrick's Day* II, ii.

other very free language.'[1] 'A *freedom*' can likewise be an
unwarranted breach of social restraint, a 'liberty' unduly
'taken', and even an indecency: 'I do not know a more
disagreeable character than a valetudinarian, who thinks
he may do anything that is for his ease and indulges himself in the grossest freedoms'.[2]

It is probably by an influence from this sense that we
should explain Shakespeare's use of *liberal* to mean, in
various senses, (too) 'free-spoken'; as where the young
wag in *The Merchant* is warned that his chatter among
strangers may 'show something too liberal' (II, ii, 187).

Very distinct from all these, though doubtless springing
from the idea of 'unrestrained, not tied, not confined', is
free in the sense 'costing nothing' (Latin *gratis* and Greek
dorean). Thus *dorean* is rendered as *freely* in the Authorised
Version; 'freely ye have received', and, earlier, in the
Wycliffite translation, *freli*.

IV. 'FRANK' AND 'VILLAIN'

There is a sharp contrast between the histories of *frank* and
free. The social-ethical meanings of *free* have vanished;
but, for *frank*, only the ethical meaning, and that in a very
narrowed sense, survives.

Originally *frank* is of course a national name—'a
Frank'. Its legal, social, and ethical meanings are ultimately derived from the state of affairs in Gaul after the
Frankish conquest. Any man you met would probably
be either a Frank, hence a conqueror, a warrior, and a
landowner, or else a mere 'native', one of a subject race.

[1] Steele, *Spectator*, 493.   [2] Boswell, 16 September 1777.

If the latter, he was (typically) a serf, an un-free peasant attached to an estate which had once been a Roman *villa*; he was in fact a *villanus* or *vilains*. *Frank* and *villain* (or *frans* and *vilains*) is the essential contrast.

English *villain* could still be used in its literal sense by Lancelot Andrewes: 'they be men, and not beasts; free-men, and not villains'.[1] But long before his time it had dwindled into a term of abuse, and finally into a term of mere (i.e. unspecified) abuse: *villain* (*d.s.*), a synonym for 'bad man', useless except as a technical term in dramatic criticism (for 'Shakespeare's villains' is a convenient enough expression). The process was of course gradual, and it is not easy to be sure what stage of it is represented by each occurrence of the word in the old texts.

At first its pejorative meaning was closely connected with its literal; the image of the actual *vilains* or peasant was still operative. Peasants, since we abolished them, have in this country been so idealised that we may go as far astray about the old overtones of 'peasant' as about the ancient idea of the servile character. We get an inkling of them when Love, in the *Romance of the Rose*, says 'no villain or butcher' has ever been allowed to kiss his lips (l. 1938). He goes on to say that the *villain* is brutal (*fel*), pitiless, disobliging, and unfriendly (ll. 2086–7). If you would avoid *vilanie*, the peasant character, you must imitate courteous Gawain, not surly Kay (ll. 2093 f.). Danger is later described as a *vilains*; he leaps suddenly from his hiding place, huge, dark, bristly, with blazing eyes, loud and violent (ll. 2920 f.). But notice that while

[1] Sermon before the Queen, 24 February 1590.

vilains is still thus closely connected with the image of the actual peasant, it quite clearly refers to a psychological type, not to an actual rank. Love takes care to tell us that '*vilanie* makes the *vilains*' (l. 2083). Theoretically, one who was a *vilains* by status might not have the vice of *vilanie*; certainly many a man who is not a *vilains* by status will be guilty of it. *Churl*, itself originally a status word, would be the nearest English equivalent to Old French *vilains* in this sense, if it had not come to lay more emphasis on niggardliness in particular than on the generally sullen and uncooperative character of the peasant.[1] *Boor* is perhaps now our best translation.

The noun *vilein* is of doubtful occurrence in Chaucer, but *vileinye* is common. The central area of its meaning is rudeness, bad manners. The Knight never 'said *vileinye*', spoke rudely, to anyone (A. 70). Chaucer hopes that his setting down the bawdy tales will not be counted against him as *vileinye* (l. 726). The young roisterers in the *Pardoner's Tale* are reproved for speaking *vileinye* to an old man (C. 740). By an easy transition, to dispraise or vilify anything is to speak *vileinye* of it; the Wife of Bath asks why one should speak *vileinye* 'of bigamye or of octogamye' (D. 34) or of Lameth (D. 53). Hence a shame or indignity done to anything, like Creon's refusal to permit the burial of the enemy dead (A. 941), can be a *vileinye*.

We get nearer to a purely ethical sense when the Wife of Bath argues that if nobility were really transmissible by heredity, then those of a good stock would never cease to practise *gentillesse* nor begin practising 'villeinye or vyce'

[1] Probably under the influence of A.V. I Samuel xxv. 3–11.

(D. 1133–8). But the context still attaches the word very closely not to moral defects in general but to those moral defects which were felt to be especially inappropriate in the highest ranks—the opposites of *gentillesse*. Twice we find rape described as *villeinye*. The wife of Hasdrubal committed suicide to make sure that no Roman 'dide hir vileinye' (F. 1404), and Tarquin is asked in an apostrophe how he could have done Lucretia 'this vilanye'.[1] But note the preceding lines. He ought to have acted as a lord and a 'verray knight', instead of which he has 'doon dispyt to chivalrye'. Rape will naturally be the first of all moral offences to be called *vileinye* because, besides being a sin against the Christian law, it is the direct antithesis of *gentillesse*, of courtesy and of deference to ladies. Tarquin's sin is a *vilein's* act because it is, as our fathers, if not we, would say, 'the act of a cad'. Indeed the word *cad*, with its contemporary semantic wobble between social and moral condemnation, is a good enough parallel to *vileinye* in this sense. And once *vileinye* means something like 'caddishness' it is already on the downward path which will finally lead it to become a word of mere, unspecified opprobrium. Once or twice in Chaucer it has almost reached this stage. When the act of those enemies who had beaten the wife of Melibeus and mortally wounded his daughter is described as a *vileinye* (B. 2547), or John warns Aleyn that the miller is a dangerous man who might do them a *vileinye* (A. 4191), the content of the word is perhaps hardly more precise than 'a rotten trick' or 'a bad turn'. In the *Second Nun's Tale*, when we

[1] *Leg.* 1823.

hear that no one can see the rose and lily garlands brought by the angel unless he 'be chaast and hate vileinye' (G. 231), perhaps we have reached a purely ethical meaning.

In the Elizabethan drama *villain*, and the associated words, are, so to speak, treacherous. At first the modern reader in most contexts will give them the *dangerous sense* without hesitation. Because they are opprobrious, that sense will always seem to fit the context; that is why it is so dangerous. 'Remorseless, treacherous, lecherous, kind-less villain!';[1] 'I never loved my brother in my life'— 'More villain thou';[2] 'Some villain hath done me wrong'[3]—what should all these be but *villain (d.s.)*? Perhaps they all are. But it is not absolutely certain.

Antipholus of Syracuse describes his man Dromio as 'a trusty villain' whose 'merry jests' often cheer him up.[4] We have here of course the affectionate use of an oppro-brious term in reverse—like 'a trusty rogue'. But it is hard to believe that the opprobrium stored in the term before it is reversed can be as strong as that of *villain (d.s.)*. Something more like 'rogue' or (in older usage) 'wretch', or 'rascal'. And 'rascal'—certainly not *villain (d.s.)*—is surely the sense required when Petruchio repeatedly calls his man Grunio a *villain*, and once a *knave*.[5] Again, in *Measure for Measure* (v, i, 264) the luckless Lucio says that Friar Lodowick 'spoke most villanous speeches of the Duke'. The point of the joke is that it was Lucio himself who had spoken those speeches, as no one knows better than the Duke. And they were not those of a *villain (d.s.)*.

[1] *Hamlet* II, ii, 619.   [2] *As You Like It* III, i, 14.
[3] *Lear* I, ii, 183.   [4] *Errors* I, ii, 19.   [5] *Taming* I, ii, 8–19.

He was not plotting the Duke's murder or deposition, only telling 'pretty tales', talking bawdy about his betters. His speeches were, in fact, *vileinye* in Chaucer's rather than in the modern sense; rude, scandalous.

Since words mean many things in the same period, these usages do not of course disprove the interpretation *villain* (*d.s.*) in the previous passages from *Hamlet*, *As You Like It* and *Lear*. But they provide the background against which its probability can be judged. I am inclined, myself, to think that *villain* (*d.s.*) need not be fully present in any of them. It may be present in all as the speaker's meaning. The speaker certainly regards the other party as what *we* would call a *villain*; but I am not certain that he selects this particular term of abuse because it already (lexically) has the meaning 'very wicked man'. The purpose of all opprobrious language is, not to describe, but to hurt—even when, like Hamlet, we make only the shadow-passes of a soliloquised combat. We call the enemy not what we think he is but what we think he would least like to be called. Hence extreme hatred may select the word *villain* precisely because it is not yet merely moral but still carries some implication of ignoble birth, coarse manners, and ignorance. For all except the best men would rather be called wicked than vulgar. Compare the scene where Somerset calls Suffolk away from the *de jure* Duke of York with the words 'Away!... We grace the *yeoman* by conversing with him'.[1]

All this I admit to be uncertain. But there is one place where I very greatly hope that *villain* has hardly any of

[1] *Hen. VI*, Pt I, II, iv 81.

the *dangerous sense* in it. The opening soliloquy of *Richard III* does not, on any view, show Shakespeare at his subtlest. But the crudity of 'I am determined to prove a villain' (I, i, 30) is, even on that level, almost comic if Richard means *villain* (*d.s.*). But if we dare suppose that the word has predominantly—or, better still, exclusively —its older sense, the line is immeasurably improved. For then, Richard, having produced as good, and contemptuous, a parody as his distorted body can of those who 'court an amorous looking glass', suddenly relapses into himself, looks as clumsy, as coarse, as uncouth as he knows how—becomes the very image of the *vilains*, fixes the audience with a glance of ogre-ish glee, and says in effect 'Well; since I can't be a lounge-lizard, I'll be— gad, I'll be—a Tough'.

Some other usages, which obviously come by hyperbole, are consistent with almost any meaning of the word. Such are 'a villainous house for fleas', 'villainous smell', 'villainous melancholy', or 'villainously cross-gartered'. These will surprise no one who remembers how, at various periods, every inconvenience or discomfort, has been called *scurvy*, *abominable*, *shocking*, *incredible* or *shattering*.

In Old French, *frans*, the form which *frank* assumed, can mean *free*, unencumbered. There is a line quoted by Chalcidius 'When you have laid aside your body and soar *free* (*liber*) to the sky';[1] the *Romance of the Rose* (l. 5030) translates 'You will go *frans* into the holy air'. This usage is found also in English; Lord Berners in his

[1] *In Timaeum* CXXXVI.

version of *Huon* writes 'he and all his companye shal depart frank and free at their pleasure' (XLIII).

Its social-ethical sense once had pretty much the same range as that of *free*. The god of love, in the *Romance of the Rose*, says that the servant when he accepts must be courteous and *frans* (l. 1939). The quality which the *frans* has is of course *franchise* (courtesy, gentle manners, the gentle heart) both in French and English; among Gawain's virtues are '*franchise* and fellowshipe'.[1] But later usage restricted the word to a sense which may owe something both to the idea of 'unrestrained' and to that of the noble or chivalrous. This double implication, or double semantic root, may have helped the sense in question to triumph. The *frank* person is unencumbered by fears, calculations, and an eye to the main chance; he also shows the straightforwardness and boldness of a noble nature. Hence 'with frank and with uncurbed plainness'[2] or 'bearing with frank appearance their purposes towards Cyprus'.[3]

Like *free*, it too can mean *gratis*, not to be paid for; in *Mother Hubbards Tale*, we find 'Thou hast it wonne for it is of frank gift' (l. 531). This sense long survived in 'the frank' which members of Parliament were once entitled to put on their letters.

V. AN OBSOLETE BRANCH-LINE

Like *eleutheria* and *libertas*, *freedom* and *franchise* can of course mean the legal freedom of a community. But the ancient words are used chiefly, if not entirely, in reference

---

[1] *Gawain*, 652.   [2] *Hen. V*, I, ii, 244.   [3] *Othello* I, iii, 37.

to the freedom of a state. The contrast implied is sometimes between autonomy and subjection to a foreign
power; sometimes between the freedom of a republic and
the rule of a despot. The medieval words nearly always
refer to something different; to the guaranteed freedoms
or immunities (from royal or baronial interference) of a
corporate entity which cuts across states, like the Church,
or which exists within the state, like a city or guild. Thus
Gower says a knight should defend 'The common right
and the franchise of Holy Churche';[1] or Shakespeare,
'If you deny it let the danger light upon your city's
freedom'.[2]

This led to a development unparalleled, I believe, in the
ancient languages. By becoming a member of any cor-
poration which enjoys such *freedom* or *franchise* you of
course come to share that *freedom* or *franchise*. You become
a *freeman* of, or receive the *freedom* of, that city; or you
become 'free of the Grocers'.[3] These are familiar. But a
further development along this line is more startling.
Freedom can mean simply 'citizenship', and when the
centurion tells Saint Paul that he had paid a lot of money
to acquire Roman citizenship (*politeia*), the Authorised
Version says 'At a great price obtained I this freedom'.[4]
Philemon Holland translating Suetonius writes 'Unlesse
they might be *donati civitate*...enioye the fraunchises and
freedom of Rome'. This meaning is fossilised in the
surviving English use of *franchise* to mean the power of
voting, conceived as the essential mark of full citizenship.

[1] *Confessio* VIII, 3023.   [2] *Merchant* IV, i, 39.
[3] Jonson, *Alchemist* I, i.   [4] Acts xxii. 29.

VI. 'LIBERAL' AS A CULTURAL TERM

We had brought the ancient words to a social and ethical sense; it remains to consider the all-important cultural meaning which grew from it.

The freeman, and still more the *eleutherios* or *liberalis* who not only is but ought to be a freeman, has not only his characteristic virtues but his characteristic occupations. Some of these are necessary; statesmanship, says Pseudo-Plato, is the most *liberal* (*eleutheriotaten*) of studies.[1] But the idea that leisure occupations, things done for their own sake and not for utility, are especially *eleuthera*, soon comes into play. It is perhaps present when Xenophon says 'They have a square (*agora*) called the Free (*eleuthera*) Square from which tradespeople and their noises and vulgarities (*apeirokaliai*) are excluded'.[2] The tradespeople need not be, and probably are not, slaves. But they are engaged in activities which have no value except in so far as they contribute to some end outside themselves. The contrast becomes explicit when Aristotle says in the *Rhetoric* 'of one's possessions those which yield some profit are the most useful, but those which exist only to be enjoyed are *eleutheria*'. This is the first step. Only he who is neither legally enslaved to a master nor economically enslaved by the struggle for subsistence, is likely to have, or to have the leisure for using, a piano or a library. That is how one's piano or library is more *liberal*, more characteristic of one's position as a freeman, than one's coal-shovel or one's tools.

[1] *Axiochus*, 369.   [2] *Cyropaedia* I, ii, 3.

But there is a further development, which we owe (I believe) entirely to Aristotle; a brilliant conceit. (There is no reason why we should not attribute a conceit to him; he was a wit, and a dressy man, as well as a philosopher.) It comes in the *Metaphysics*.[1] 'We call a man free whose life is lived for his own sake not for that of others. In the same way philosophy is of all studies the only free one; for it alone exists for its own sake.'

Here is an astonishing change. Up till now a study could be *free* because it was the characteristic occupation of a freeman. Aristotle now makes it 'free' in a quite new sense; namely, by analogy. It is a free study because it holds among other studies the same privileged position which the freeman holds among other men. The conceit is all the better for taking up into itself the much simpler idea that disinterestedness is an essential part of the 'free' character. The free study seeks nothing beyond itself and desires the activity of knowing for that activity's own sake. That is what the man of radically servile character— give him what leisure and what fortune you please—will never understand. He will ask, 'But what *use* is it?' And finding that it cannot be eaten or drunk, nor used as an aphrodisiac, nor made an instrument for increasing his income or his power, he will pronounce it—he has pronounced it—to be 'bunk'.

How far Aristotle's ideal is from a mere dilettantism can best be seen by giving it the background which two other passages supply. In *Metaphysics* we learn that the organisation of the universe resembles that of a household,

[1] 982 b, Everyman ed., p. 55.

in which 'no one has so little chance to act at random as the free members. For them everything or almost everything proceeds according to a fixed plan (*tetaktai*), whereas the slaves and domestic animals contribute little to the common end and act mostly at random.'[1] The attitude of any slave-owning society is and ought to be repellent to us, but it is worth while suppressing that repulsion in order to get the picture as Aristotle saw it. Looking from his study window he sees the hens scratching in the dust, the pigs asleep, the dogs hunting for fleas; the slaves, any of them who are not at that very moment on some appointed task, flirting, quarrelling, cracking nuts, playing dice, or dozing. He, the master, may use them all for the common end, the well-being of the family. They themselves have no such end, nor any consistent end, in mind. Whatever in their lives is not compelled from above is random—dependent on the mood of the moment. His own life is quite different; a systematised round of religious, political, scientific, literary and social activities; its very hours of recreation (there's an anecdote about them) deliberate, approved and allowed for; consistent with itself. But what is it in the structure of the universe that corresponds to this distinction between Aristotle, self-bound with the discipline of a freeman, and Aristotle's slaves, negatively free with a servile freedom between each job and the next? I think there is no doubt of the answer. It is the things in the higher world of aether which are regular, immutable, consistent; those down here in the air that are subject to change, and chance and

[1] 1075 b.

contingence.[1] In the world, as in the household, the
higher acts to a fixed plan; the lower admits the 'random'
element. The free life is to the servile as the life of the
gods (the living stars) is to that of terrestrial creatures.
This is so not because the truly free man 'does what he
likes', but because he imitates, so far as a mortal can, the
flawless and patterned regularity of the heavenly beings,
like them not doing what he likes but being what he
is, being fully human as they are divine, and fully
human by his likeness to them. For the crown of life—
here we break right out of the cautious modesty of most
Greek sentiment—is not 'being mortal, to think mortal
thoughts' but rather 'to immortalise as much as possible'
and by all means to live according to the highest element
in oneself.[2]

Of course humanity is not often on the Aristotelian
height. The *eleutheria mathemata* of the Greeks, the
liberalia studia or *liberales artes* of the Latins are soon taken
over by the curricula and every teacher or student knows
which they are; one no longer needs to think why they
are called *liberal*. You need merely enumerate: 'Arts',
says Cicero, 'which include *liberales et ingenuae* know-
ledges, such as Geometry, Music, the knowledge of letters
and poets and whatever is said about natural objects,
human manners and politics'.[3] One even meets the idea
(strange to those who have studied the lives of the
Humanists) that the pursuit of such studies tends to
improve one's behaviour: 'to have learned well the

[1] *De Mundo*, 392 a.   [2] *Ethics*, 1177 b.
[3] *De Oratore* III, xxxii.

liberal arts' (*ingenuas*, because it comes in a hexameter) 'softens the manners and banishes ferocity'.[1] Finally, in the Middle Ages, the *Liberal Arts* settle down into the well known list of seven—grammar, dialectic, rhetoric, music, arithmetic, geometry, and astronomy. Arithmetic might hardly have won its place if Aristotle's idea of the *liberal* had been kept steadily in view.

That idea is, however, still operative in the eighteenth and nineteenth centuries in the conception of an inquisitiveness which is 'generous' or 'noble' or 'liberal' because it seeks knowledge for its own sake. Johnson speaks of 'such knowledge as may justly be admired in those who have no motive to study but generous curiosity',[2] and praises Boswell, back from Corsica, as one 'whom a wise and noble curiosity has led where perhaps no native of his country ever was before'.[3] Macaulay says that the Jesuits, as missionaries, 'wandered to countries which neither mercantile avidity nor liberal curiosity had impelled any stranger to explore'.[4]

The *liberal* motive is here contrasted equally with the religious and the mercantile. This suggests a problem for those who wish to embrace both the Christian and the Aristotelian scheme. What excellence can either ideal concede to the other? The only nineteenth-century author, so far as I know, who fully faced the question was Newman, in a very firm piece of thinking which makes clear how, in his view, that which is necessarily subordi-

[1] Ovid, *Ex Ponto* II, ix, 47.
[2] *Journey to the Western Islands, Ostig.*
[3] Boswell, 14 January 1766.   [4] *History* VI.

nate has nevertheless its own relative autonomy and its own proper excellence—

That alone is *liberal* knowledge which stands on its own pretensions, which is independent of sequel...refuses to be informed (as it is called) by any end. The most ordinary pursuits have this specific character if they are self-sufficient and complete; the highest lose it when they minister to something beyond them....If, for instance, Theology, instead of being cultivated as a contemplation, be limited to the purposes of the pulpit or be represented by the catechism, it loses—not its usefulness, not its divine character, not its meritoriousness (rather it increases those qualities by such charitable condescension) but it does lose the particular attribute which I am illustrating; just as a face worn by tears and fasting loses its beauty....And thus it appears that even what is supernatural need not be *liberal*, nor need a hero be a gentleman, for the plain reason that one idea is not another idea.[1]

Unless followed by the word 'education', *liberal* has now lost this meaning. For that loss, so damaging to the whole of our cultural outlook, we must thank those who made it the name, first of a political, and then of a theological, party. The same irresponsible rapacity, the desire to appropriate a word for its 'selling-power', has often done linguistic mischief. It is not easy now to say at all in English what the word *conservative* would have said if it had not been 'cornered'. by politicians. *Evangelical, intellectual, rationalist,* and *temperance* have been destroyed in the same way. Sometimes the arrogation is so outrageous that it fails; the Quakers have not killed the word *friends*. And sometimes so many different people

[1] *Scope and Nature of University Education,* IV.

grab at the coveted word for so many different groups or factions that, while it is spoiled for its original purpose, none of the grabbers achieve secure possession. *Humanist* is an example; it will probably end by being a term of eulogy as vague as *gentleman*.

We cannot stop the verbicides. The most we can do is not to imitate them.

6

SENSE

[WITH *SENTENCE, SENSIBILITY, AND SENSIBLE*]

I. INTRODUCTORY

EVERYONE who speaks English is familiar with two meanings for the word *sense*: (*a*) ordinary intelligence or 'gumption', and (*b*) perception by sight, hearing, taste, smell or touch, which I shall call *aesthesis*. In our individual linguistic histories gumption is undoubtedly the earlier meaning. We had all been told to 'have sense', or asked why we 'had not more sense', years before we ever heard *sense* used to mean aesthesis. The aesthesis meaning belongs to a comparatively late, bookish, and abstract stratum of our vocabulary.

On the other hand there is no evidence that we reach the meaning aesthesis by a metonymy or any other kind of extension from the meaning gumption. In modern English the two meanings are not at all related as parent and child. They can be explained only by the pre-English history of the word; not of course that most English speakers have known or cared anything about that history, but that in their daily usages they have unconsciously availed themselves of the situation it had created.

Of the thousands who use the word *sense*, sometimes to mean gumption, and sometimes to mean aesthesis, only the tiny minority who are interested in language ever notice that they are doing so. A sudden transition from the one meaning to the other would affect most speakers like a pun.

II. 'SENTIRE'

Sense is from *sensus*, the noun that goes with the verb *sentire*, and at the verb our story must begin. Its central area of meaning seems to me to have been something like 'to experience, learn by experience, undergo, know at first hand'. 'Catiline', says Cicero, 'is going to learn, going to find out (*sentiet*), that the consuls in this town are wide awake.'[1] That is, he is going to learn by (bitter) experience. The braggart in Phaedrus (v, ii) assures his fellow traveller that he will pursue the man who has robbed them both and 'see that he learns' (*curabo sentiat*) what sort of people he has meddled with. The English would be 'I'll show him'. As prices went up, says Tacitus, the mass of the people gradually came to know (*sentire*) the ills of war;[2] as we might say 'began to find out what war really means'. It can also be used of another sort of first-hand experience; that is, like *know* in the Authorised Version, it can mean 'to have carnal knowledge of, sexual intercourse with'. Thus Ovid, addressing Neptune, can say 'Ceres knew (*sensit*) you in the form of a horse, Medusa knew (*sensit*) you as a bird, Melantho knew (*sensit*) you as a dolphin'.[3] In some contexts English *see* would be a good translation, but with no precise restriction to visual experience (cf. 'He has seen

[1] *Catiline* II, xii, 27.   [2] *History* I, 89.
[3] *Metamorphoses* VI, 118–20.

active service'), so that we could render Horace's lines 'With you I saw (*sensi*) the fight at Philippi and the *sauve-qui-peut* rout'.[1] The same author can use *sentire*—perhaps with less of conscious personification than we suppose—of a vine which 'will not feel (*sentiet*) the withering south-wind'.[2] For *feel* we could equally well put *get*, *catch*, *suffer*, or perhaps, in older English, *taste*. But we should have to use *see* again for the line where Virgil's Venus saw (*sensit*) that Juno had been talking disingenuously.[3] Strictly speaking, no doubt, such a 'seeing' would involve rapid half-unconscious inferences, but it would be felt as immediate; and certainly as first-hand compared with any knowledge of your opponent's motives which you could get from a report by a third party.

Now the two most obvious instances of knowledge at first hand or by experience are (*a*) that of our own conscious psychological state at the moment, and (*b*) that which we receive by sight, hearing, touch, smell and taste. We shall not therefore be surprised if *sentire* is used of both. I know or perceive or (as the French would say) experiment, my present thought and emotions; *sentio* will do for that. I also know or perceive or experiment the hardness of this pen, the white of this paper, and the temperature of the room; *sentio* will do for that too. Thus from the beginning the verb has a tendency to bifurcation of meaning. How soon, or whether at any time, the Romans felt it to have what we should call 'two meanings'

[1] *Odes* II, vii, 10.   [2] *Odes* III, xxiii, 5.
[3] *Aeneid* IV, 105.

is a question for classical scholars. We, who are concerned with the later developments, may certainly (in view of those later developments) say that the word is already bifurcated in classical Latin. We shall therefore distinguish *sentire* (*A*) from *sentire* (*B*). *Sentire* (*A*) has what may loosely (with no pretence at philosophy) be called the introspective meaning; *Sentire* (*B*), the aesthesis meaning.

III. 'SENTIRE (A)'

Although *sentire* (*A*) is itself a product of bifurcation, within it another bifurcation immediately threatens us. Of this subordinate bifurcation I do not think the Romans were aware. Our more analytic minds impose it. As translators we have to decide in each case whether we are going to render *sentio* (*A*) by 'I feel' or 'I think'. Very often we cannot decide, and possibly a Roman would not have understood what we are asking. At the end of the first chapter of his *Histories* (Book I) Tacitus congratulates himself on the felicity of a period in which you can *sentire* (feel? or think?) what you please and say *quid sentias* (what you think? or feel?). Seneca says to Lucilius, 'I want my letters to run just as my talk would run if we were sitting or walking together...if possible I would rather show than say *quid sentiam* (what I feel? or think?)...This at least I'd like to assure you of: my *sentire* (my really thinking? my feeling? my really meaning?) all I said'.[1] Cicero says of some philosopher 'If he *sensit* as he speaks, he is depraved'.[2] If he meant what he says? If he felt as he talks? If he thought as he talks?

[1] *Epistles* LXXV.   [2] *Republic* III, xxi.

There is an apparent (but, I think, only apparent) parallel to this in modern colloquial English, 'I feel that last step in your argument is a bit doubtful'. But *feel* here is almost certainly used as a polite litotes, a deliberate understatement. To avoid the rudeness of saying 'I have detected a *non sequitur* which I will now demonstrate', we feign that what is really, or what we take to be, a rational perception, is merely a fugitive emotion. The mixture of *think* and *feel* in *sentire* has almost certainly nothing to do with understatement.

There is, then, a central semantic area of *sentire* (*A*) which resists our efforts to dichotomise. But there are also usages which fall neatly on one side or other of the line we want to draw, giving us *sentire* (*A*1) (to feel) and *sentire* (*A*2) (to think).

Sentire (*A*1) can be illustrated from the famous couplet in Catullus: 'I love and hate. You ask me how? I don't know; but I feel it (*sentio*) happening and it is torture' (LXXXV). So also in Seneca, 'to feel (*sentire*) grief at the loss of a friend'.[1] The usage is not, however, very common.

Sentire (*A*2), on the other hand, is common and unambiguous. The verb here means not only to think or opine, but to 'take a view', to arrive at an opinion and give formal expression to it. Thus in Cicero, 'I joined in opinion (*assensi*) with those who seemed to take the mildest opinion' (*lenissime sentire*);[2] or in Aulus Gellius, 'if the judges take a view, come to a decision (*senserint*), in my favour'. This meaning was of great importance for later linguistic history.

---

[1] *Epistles* XCIX.   [2] *Ad Familiares* v, ii.

IV. 'SENTIRE (B)'

This is the aesthesis meaning: to perceive by one of the 'senses'. It is quite simple and need not detain us. 'We perceive (*sentimus*) the various smells of things', says Lucretius (I, 298), or 'You can perceive (*sentire*) the sound' (IV, 560). It is often assumed, I fancy, that this is the oldest meaning of *sentire*, but that assumption would not make the general history of the word easier to understand.

V. THE NOUNS

The verb *sentire* is privileged to have two nouns. One is *sentientia* (like *conscientia* with *conscire*) which in classical Latin has become *sententia*. The other is *sensus*. There is a difference between them. *Sententia* is the noun of *sentire* only in its *A*-meaning; but *sensus* is the noun of *sentire* in all its meanings.

VI. 'SENTENTIA' AND 'SENTENCE'

1. Since *sentire* (*A*2) means to think or opine, a man's opinion, what he thinks, is his *sententia*. This usage is familiar to everyone from the often-quoted Terentian *quot homines, tot sententiae*, 'There are as many opinions as there are men'. Middle English *sentence* retains this meaning; 'the commune sentence of the peple false is'.[1] By an important specialisation, *sententia* can mean the considered, final opinion of a judge: 'Cato as judge gave his *sententia*,' says Cicero.[2] Hence English *sentence* comes to mean the judge's decision about the punishment and

[1] Thomas Usk, *Testament of Love* III, ix.   [2] *De Officiis* XVI, 66.

finally the punishment itself—'the sentence was death'.
This is an excellent example of the merely homophonic
status to which the different uses of a word are finally
reduced. If you said 'Jeremy Taylor can boast the longest
sentence of any English writer' and someone replied
'Poor Wilde had a longer one', this would be a pure
pun.

2. A man's opinion or *sententia*, what he thinks, can of
course be distinguished from the words in which he
expresses it. From this point of view *sententia* comes to
signify meaning as opposed to words, content as opposed
to form. 'The Stoic doctrine about living according to
Nature has, I believe, the following meaning (*sententia*)',
says Cicero.[1] Old French and Middle English *sentence*
can both be used in the same way. 'This is the meaning
(*sentence*) of Plato's words in French', says Jean de Meung.[2]
Chaucer boasts of giving us 'playnly every word' of
Troilus' song and not merely the *sentence*, the drift or
meaning.[3]

3. If a man's meaning can be contrasted with his
words, so the meaning of words can of course be contrasted with their sound. Thus we find Lucretius saying
that you may be able to hear the sound of someone talking
in the next room when you cannot make out the *sententia*
or meaning (IV, 561).

4. Because *sententia* is 'meaning', the minimum unit of
speech or writing which has a complete meaning can be
a *sententia*. Thus Quintilian says the whole point of

[1] *De Officiis* III, iii, 13.   [2] *Roman de la Rose*, 19081.
[3] *Troilus* I, 393.

Lysias' style would have been lost if he had had a system (*ratio*) for 'beginning and ending *sententias*, his sentences' (IX, iv).

5. When we say that an utterance is 'full of meaning' we do not merely claim that none of it is meaningless; we claim that it is profound, worth chewing on, 'significant'. Just in the same way *sententia* can signify not bare 'meaning' but 'depth of meaning', meaningfulness, pith, profundity. Speaking of the old maxim 'know thyself', Cicero says it was attributed to a god because it has so much *sententia*—goes so deep, has 'so much in it'.[1] This is an important usage of Middle English *sentence*. The speech of Chaucer's clerk was 'short and quik and full of heigh sentence';[2] economical, full of life, and pregnant. There was no dead wood.

6. Both the preceding usages may have helped *sententia* to the meaning 'maxim, saw, apophthegm, aphorism'. Quintilian rightly regards *sententia*, in this usage, as the equivalent of Greek *gnome* (VIII, v). A style full of *sententiae* is a gnomic style. English *sentence* long retained this as one of its commonest meanings: 'a sentence or an old man's saw', we read in *The Rape of Lucrece* (l. 244). Overbury's 'Meere Scholer' is one who 'speaks sentences'. As late as Johnson's time we find 'A Greek writer of sentences', an aphorist.[3]

From *sententia* meaning a maxim, through *sententiosus*, we get our adjective *sententious*. Originally it had no derogatory implication. In his *Second Sermon on the Lord's*

---

[1] *Laws* I, xxii, 58.   [2] *Prologue*, A. 306.
[3] *Rambler*, 79.

Prayer Latimer observes 'it is better to say it sententiously one time than to run over it an hundred times with humbling and mumbling'. To say it *sententiously* is to say it meaningfully, thinking of what you say. When Milton describes the Greek tragedians as teaching by 'brief sententious precepts' he is referring simply to their gnomic manner.[1] By Fanny Burney's time the word is beginning to have its modern force; in *Caecilia* (IV, 1) the truth of a remark can 'palliate' its 'sententious absurdity'. The development had long been prepared, for ever since the sixteenth century the conversation of those who dealt much in saws and adages had been despised. Overbury's 'mere scholar' we had a moment ago; you may add Donne's clownish mistress, 'natures lay Ideot', whose talk, till he taught her better, had consisted of 'broken proverbs and torne sentences'.[2] The word has also, I suspect, been infected by the phonetic proximity of *pretentious*. A word needs to be very careful about the phonetic company it keeps. The old meaning of *obnoxious* has been almost destroyed by the combined influence of *objectionable* and *noxious*, and that of *deprecate* by *depreciate*, and that of *turgid* by *turbid*.

VII. 'SENSUS' AND 'SENSE'

The least specialised meaning of this noun seems to me to correspond exactly to that given for the verb in paragraph II. *Sensus* is first-hand experience, immediate awareness of one's own mental and emotional content. We have *sensus* of that which is *erlebt*. Ovid in

---

[1] *Paradise Regained* IV, 264. [2] Elegy VII, 19.

exile envies Niobe for being turned into stone because she thus lost the *sensus* of her sorrows.[1] Cicero's own *sensus* tells him how strong love between brothers can be.[2] In English he might have said 'I know from what I feel myself' or 'My own heart tells me'. But it would be better to render it 'I know because I've tried' (or 'because I've been through it'), for we must not fix a too narrowly emotional meaning on *sensus*. We want a meaning which will cover another Ciceronian passage. In the *Republic* (I, xxxviii) one disputant says to another 'Use the evidence of your own *sensus*'. 'My *sensus* of what?' comes the reply. The required *sensus* turns out to be that of controlling anger by reason. In this context it is hardly possible to translate *sensus* by any word but 'experience'; in others 'awareness' or (sometimes) 'consciousness' will do.

Such unspecified awareness is of course a common meaning of *sense*. 'Of the highest vertue', says Bacon, the common people 'have no sense or perceiving at all';[3] compare Wordsworth's 'sense sublime Of something far more deeply interfused'. In much the same way we are said to have or lack a *sense* of honour, decency, danger, inferiority, or almost what you will. This meaning now exists, in an almost fossilised condition, in 'sense of humour'. We hardly remember that this was originally an awareness of humours (idiosyncrasies) in our neighbours.

So much for the central, hardly differentiated, meaning of the word. We have now to follow its *A*- and *B*-bifurcations—its intellectual and sensory meanings.

[1] *Ex Ponto* I, ii, 32.   [2] *Ad Familiares* IV, ii, 10.   [3] *Of Praise.*

VIII. 'SENSUS' AND 'SENSE (A)'

1. Like *sententia*, it can mean opinion. 'His *sensus* about politics pleases me greatly', says Cicero—I like his political views.[1] This may be the meaning of *sense* when Shakespeare says, 'For in my sense 'tis happiness to die'.[2] It is certainly so when Macaulay speaks about 'the unanimous sense of the meeting' or 'the sense of the best jurists'.[3]

2. *Sensus* is also used in the Vulgate to render Greek *nous*. *Nous* is a hard word. When St Paul says 'Every one must be fully confident in his own *nous*'[4] and the Vulgate translates 'Every one must be full to overflowing (*abundet*) in his own *sensus*', one is tempted to equate *nous* with opinion—in which cases *sensus* would have exactly the same force as in the preceding examples. But I think *nous* comes to mean something like opinion only because it means mind (as we also, till lately, could have said 'I told him my mind on the question') and our next example confirms this. St Paul speaks of the *nous* which God cannot accept;[5] Vulgate translates this as *reprobum sensum*. *Nous* and *sensus* here mean something like 'frame' or 'state' of mind. Both passages are important for their effect on the vernaculars. Thanks to the first, it was good French centuries later for Descartes to say *chacun abonde si fort en son sens*;[6] thanks to the second, Burton can say 'They are in a reprobate sense, they cannot

---

[1] *To Atticus* xv, 7.   [2] *Othello* v, ii, 288.
[3] *History*. Both in ch. x.   [4] Romans xiv. 5.
[5] *Ibid*. i. 28.   [6] *Discourse on Method* vi.

think a good thought',[1] and Milton, 'Insensate left or to sense reprobate'.[2] In all three passages this meaning is derived, ultimately from the Vulgate. It entered English through the Rheims version of 1582, which reads at xiv. 5 'let every man abound in his own sense', and at i. 28 'a reprobate sense'. That English and Protestant authors, one of them a good Greek scholar, should depend for a scriptural phrase either on Vulgate or Rheims will seem strange to many. Very ill-grounded ideas about the exclusive importance of the Authorised Version in the English biblical tradition are still widely held.

3. Like *sententia*, *sensus*, and of course *sense*, signify the meaning of a word. 'This was the *sensus* of the word', says Ovid.[3] The whole of this book is about the *senses* of words. Here we have a usage from which, even without the help of developments still to be noticed, the meaning 'gumption' might have been developed. 'Talk *sense*' and 'Have sense' are very similar rebukes. But the first follows easily from *sense* signifying meaning: 'Say things that have some meaning, stop uttering the non-significant.' 'He has no sense' could have arisen (though the actual history is more complicated) as an ellipsis of 'His conversation has no sense'.

4. By exaggeration *sense* (meaning) is often used loosely for important or pertinent meaning, so that, like *sententia*, it is equivalent to 'depth of meaning'. The passage from Overbury, which I gave in a truncated form above, runs in full, 'A meere scholar speaks sentences more familiarly

[1] Pt III, Sect. 4, Mem. 2, Subs. vi.
[2] *Samson Agonistes*, 1685.   [3] *Fasti* v, 484.

than sense'. I do not think this means that his discourse
was often meaningless, in the strict use of the word—only
that it was, as we say, 'gas', there was 'nothing in it'.
Similarly when Herbert says of the sermon

> if all want sense,
> God takes a text, and preacheth patience,[1]

he hardly envisaged a preacher who talked actual
gibberish; the 'want of *sense*' would be vapidity, emptiness, ignorance or the like. This usage also can clearly help
us towards the meaning 'gumption'.

5. Like *sententia*, *sensus* can also mean a grammatical
sentence. 'It is best by far', says Quintilian, 'to end the
sensus with a verb' (ix, iv). So in Dryden, 'Mr Waller
first showed us to conclude the sense most commonly in
distichs'.[2]

6. To lack awareness (*sensus*), to have no opinion
(*sensus*), to utter what has little or no meaning (*sensus*);
all these are the marks of an unintelligent man. And
sensus can also mean 'frame of mind'. Here are four
semantic pressures helping the word *sensus* to some
meaning like 'intelligence' or 'gumption'. In post-
classical Latin it yields to them. We read in the *Digest* that
neither a beast nor a madman has *sensus*. We also find the
adjective *sensatus* used to mean 'sensible, intelligent'
(classical Latin would probably have said *cordatus*). This
development may also have been encouraged by an
expression which we must now investigate.

[1] *Church-Porch*, 431.
[2] Preface to *The Rival Ladies*, *Essays*, ed. W. P. Ker, vol. i, p. 7.

IX. COMMUNIS SENSUS' AND 'COMMON SENSE'

This has in its time borne a good many different meanings.

1. *Koinos* is the Greek for 'common', and we have already seen that *sensus* can be used as a translation of Greek *nous*. *Koinos nous* is defined by Epictetus thus: 'There are some things which undistorted men perceive by the use of their common faculties. This state of affairs is called *Koinos nous*' (III, vi, 8). Here we have, almost exactly, what *common sense* often means; the elementary mental outfit of the normal man. *Communis sensus* would be a very natural way of turning *Koinos nous* into Latin, but clear examples of *communis sensus* to mean intelligence are not very easy to find. This, from Phaedrus, is, I think, certain. The Fox, finding a tragic mask, remarks after sniffing and trundling it 'What a fine physiognomy to have no brain inside it!' The moral applies, says Phaedrus, to those people who have office and fame but no *sensus communis* (I, vii).

2. Distinct from this, so far as I can see, is the use of *communis sensus* as the name of a social virtue. *Communis* (open, unbarred, to be shared) can mean friendly, affable, sympathetic. Hence *communis sensus* is the quality of the 'good mixer', courtesy, clubbableness, even fellow-feeling. Quintilian says it is better to send a boy to school than to have a private tutor for him at home; for if he is kept away from the herd (*congressus*) how will he ever learn that *sensus* which we call *communis*? (I, ii, 20). On the lowest level it means tact. In Horace the man who talks to you when you obviously don't want to talk lacks

communis sensus.[1] To say 'lacks *common sense*' would be a mistranslation. But the fact that the mistake is so tempting and the alteration so comparatively slight shows that these two semantic regions have at least a strip of common frontier. In that way even this usage may have made some small contribution to the later meaning.

3. Quite distinct from these is *communis sensus* or 'common wit' as a technical term in medieval psychology; originally, I presume, a rendering of Greek *Koine aisthesis.*[2] The old psychologists gave man five 'outward', and five 'inward', wits (or *senses*). The five outward wits are what we call the five *senses* to-day. Sometimes they are called simply the *senses*, and the five inward ones are called simply the *wits*; hence in Shakespeare 'my five wits nor my five *senses*'.[3] Which five you lose, or whether you lose all ten, when you are frightened 'out of your wits' or 'out of your senses', I don't know; probably the inward ones.

The five inward wits were originally memory, estimation, fancy, imagination, and common wit (or *common sense*). By Burton's time the list has been reduced to three,[4] but common sense is still one of them, and his account of it will serve our turn; it is 'the judge or moderator of the rest...by whom we discern all differences of objects; for by mine eye I do not know that I see, or by mine ear that I hear, but by common sense, who judgeth of sounds and colours: they [*sc.* the eye and ear] are but the organs to bring the species (appearances,

---

[1] *Satires* I, iii, 66. [2] Aristotle, *De Memoria*, 450 a.
[3] Sonnet CXLI. [4] See Pt I, Sec. I, Mem. 2, Subs. vii.

sense-data) to be censured (judged)'. It is in fact something like apperception; it turns mere sensation into
coherent experience. We see its function in the 1590
Arcadia (III, xviii, 9) when Sidney explains how two
combatants could go on fighting despite their severe
wounds—'Wrath and Courage barring the common sense
from bringing any message of their case to the minde'.

It will be noticed that a man in whom the common
sense or wit is suspended is not entirely in his right mind.
One in whom it was permanently lacking would be an
imbecile. Here we have yet another semantic pressure
which could help *common sense* towards the meaning
'gumption'.

4. *Sensus*, as we have seen, means all the *erlebt*; our
experience, emotions, thoughts, apprehensions, and
opinions. The *communis sensus* of mankind is what all men
have 'been through' (e.g. pain and pleasure), or feel
emotionally (fears and hopes), or think (that half a loaf's
better than no bread) or have some apprehension of (the
comic, the praiseworthy), or agree to be true (that two
and two make four).

Now the word *communis* is here ambivalent.

(*a*) It may contrast the *sensus* of the human race in
general, unfavourably, with what experts think and
know or what choicer spirits apprehend and feel. *Common*, taken that way, is 'common or garden', nothing
above the ordinary; if you like, vulgar.

Thus Cicero says that in all arts except one (oratory)
that is best which is furthest from the *sensus* of the ignorant; but in public speaking you have to stick to the

common mode of speech and the custom of the *communis sensus*.[1] You are not addressing men of learning or fine feeling; you can use only what will 'find an echo in *every* bosom'. In *Love's Labour's Lost* the 'godlike recompense' of study or learning is to know 'things hid and barr'd from common sense' (I, i, 55-7), things beyond the thought and apprehension of ordinary men. When Spenser says that the pains of lovers seem ''gainst common sense, to them most sweete'[2] he does not mean, as we should if we used the same words, that the lovers are fools who like their pains contrary to all reason. He means that the gentle heart finds somehow sweet what the 'swainish and ungentle breast' with its merely 'common' apprehension would find simply disagreeable.

(*b*) But *common* may also contrast the *sensus* of humanity in general, favourably, with what is thought or felt by the irrational, the depraved, the sub-human. *Common*, so taken, has no association with *vulgar*. It is the *quod semper*, *quod ubique*, the normal and indeed the norm.

It is this, though he happens not to use the words *common sense*, that Hooker is thinking of when he says that 'the general and perpetual voice of man is as the sentence of God himself' (I, viii, 3). So is Cicero, when he says that some principle is vouched for 'by truth and the nature of things and the *sensus* of every man'.[3] Seneca is particularly illuminating. He first produces philosophical authority to show that the wise man is self-sufficient. But then he confirms it[4] from a passage out of

---

[1] *De Oratore* I, iii, 12.   [2] *F.Q.* IV, x, 2.   [3] *De Finibus* IV, 19.
[4] Epistle 9.

a comic poet in order to show that these *sensus* (plural) are *communes*, are 'universal convictions'. The 'common sense' or vote or sentence of humanity is august enough to confirm even the teachings of the Stoics. St Augustine speaks of people 'divorced by some madness from the *communis sensus* of man'.[1] Centuries later the Jesuit Mariana writes that *communis sensus* 'is, as it were, the voice of Nature whereby we may discern good from evil'.[2]

Thus the ambivalence of the word *common* brings it about that one's *sense* may be disparaged by that adjective; but equally, one's *sense* may be all the better for its 'commonness'. But it is time to return to the *B*-branch.

X. 'SENSUS' AND 'SENSE (B)'

1. *Sensus* is the sensory awareness of anything. 'If', says Cicero, 'an organism admits the *sensus* of pleasure, it also admits that of pain.'[3] So in English: 'then first with fear surpris'd and *sense* of pain'.[4]

2. A faculty of sensory perception, one of the *five senses* or outward wits. 'Every organism has *sensus* [plural]', says Cicero in the place I have just quoted. What before fruition pleased the lovers in all ways, afterwards 'takes [charms] but one sense', said Donne.[5] In English there is (or perhaps was) a common use of the singular *sense*, collectively, to mean all the *senses*, the whole life of what medieval psychologists called the sensitive (as distinct from the vegetable or rational) soul. This appears in Donne's reference to 'dull sublunary

[1] *The Two Souls*, 10.   [2] *De Rege* I, vi, 1598.
[3] *De Natura Deorum* III, 13.   [4] *P.L.* VI, 394.   [5] *Farewell to Love*, 18.

lovers, love Whose soul is sense',[1] or Tennyson's 'sense at war with soul'—that is, in older and more precise terms, the sensitive soul at war with the rational. There is little doubt that *sense* is being thus used collectively when Hamlet says (III, iv, 71), 'Sense, sure you have, Else you could not have motion'. One might be momentarily tempted to take *sense* here for gumption or judgement; but if it meant that, only a rather strained and remote connection with motion could be made out. If, on the other hand, Hamlet means 'You must have senses, must have a sensitive soul', he is making a clear and simple application of the maxim, originally Aristotelian, that 'the external senses are found in all creatures which have the power of locomotion'.[2]

(Since we have here run across the sensitive soul it may be worth noticing that its name in Middle English is sometimes 'sensualitee'. That is why Chaucer's Parson says that *sensualitee* 'sholde have lordshipe...over the body of man'.[3] When our foot 'goes to sleep', *sensualitee*, the sensitive soul, has suffered a local loss of lordship over the body. Needless to say, the word, thus used, has no ethical content.)

XI. 'SENSE' AND 'SENS' IN LATER TIMES

1. The first thing to notice is the continued, and equal, vigour both of what I have called 'the introspective', and what I have called 'the aesthesis', meanings. Preserved by the insulating power of the context, they

[1] *Valediction Forbidding Mourning*, 14.
[2] *De Sensu*, 436 a.   [3] *C.T.* l. 2262.

flourish happily side by side without the slightest mutual contamination. Here are two lines from Pope:

What thin partitions sense from thought divide.[1]

While pure Description held the place of sense.[2]

In the first it would never have occurred to Pope, and has never occurred to any reader of Pope, to give *sense* any meaning but aesthesis—perception by the five outward wits. Equally, when we read *sense* in the second line, the idea of aesthesis never comes into our heads. This is obviously Herbert's use ('if all want sense'). Description fills up the void left by the lack of profundity, of pertinent comment on life, of intellectual meat. In a word, *sense* in the second line is almost synonymous with 'thought' in the first line, there contrasted with *sense*. The intrusion of either meaning into the wrong line would produce non-sense. No one commits it. No one needs any semantic gymnastics to avoid it. No one notices that there was anything to avoid. Both meanings are 'handed to us on a plate', as separate as if they were accidental homophones.

2. In earlier sections of the chapter we have seen *sense* signifying thought, awareness, meaning, depth of meaning, apprehension, and (in Late Latin) intelligence. We have seen *common sense* signifying apperception, and then the convictions common to all undepraved or normal men. As Epictetus was pretty well known (he is one of Pepys's favourites) his *koinos nous* had probably gone into the pot too. All these, simmering together, finally give the meaning gumption. For there is no need to distinguish

[1] *Essay on Man* I, 226.   [2] *To Arbuthnot*, 147.

sens from *le bon sens* or *le sens commun*, nor *sense* from
'good sense' and 'common sense'. Whatever the idea (or
ideas) of a *common sense* contributed to the final flavour of
the brew, it is now indistinguishable. Thus Descartes opens
his *Discourse on Method* with a definition of *le bon sens ou
la raison*; but by the second paragraph it has changed into
la raison ou le sens. Descartes does not notice the change.
With or without *bon*, *sens* is a synonym for *raison*.

3. An unexpected phenomenon now meets us. The
passages quoted above from Seneca, Mariana, and
Hooker make the *common sense* of mankind something
very august. It is the voice of Nature, or even 'is as the
sentence of God himself'. Lay beside these Descartes'
statement that *le (bon) sens* is pretty equally bestowed on
all men by nature; or Locke's 'He would be thought void
of common sense who asked...why it is impossible for
the same thing to be and not to be'.[1] What has happened?
There is no logical contradiction. But there is a change of
atmosphere; the temperature has dropped. There are
causes behind this which I cannot here properly develop;
a weakening in the Renaissance conception of the dignity
of Man, and a growing tendency to assign moral premisses
to some faculty other than reason, so that reason (or *sense*)
is now concerned only with truth, not also with good.
But the ambivalence of *common* has also been at work.
This permits what may be called either a maximising or
a minimising view of that *sense* (or reason) which is
common to all men. On the one hand, because it is
universal, cutting across all frontiers and surviving in all

[1] *Essay* i, iii, 4.

153

epochs, it may be reverenced. On the other, if it is as *common* as that—like having two legs or a nose in your face—it can't be anything very wonderful. To fall below it may be idiocy; to come up to it can't possibly be a ground for self-congratulation. Locke's words bring this out; a man doesn't plume himself on grasping the principle that two contraries can't both be true.

Now the curious thing is that the age which of all others made *sense* or *good sense* or *common sense* its shibboleth, is also the age which invariably approached it in this minimising spirit. For Locke, as we have seen, it is merely the opposite of imbecility. When Boileau says that the works of Scudéri are formed *en dépit du bon sens*,[1] or that *il faut, mesme en chansons, du bon sens*,[2] he means mere 'reasonableness'. 'A general trader of good sense is pleasanter company than a good scholar,' says Addison.[3] Something homely and unspectacular is suggested. 'If we suppose him vexed', says Johnson, 'it would be hard to deny him sense enough to conceal his uneasiness.'[4] All that was needed was the most elementary prudence; not to be a fool. Pope says

> But, as the slightest sketch, if justly traced,
> Is by ill colouring but the more disgraced,
> So by false learning is good sense defaced.[5]

Sense is a 'slight sketch'. It may be spoiled by false learning, but it will need a lot done to it before it becomes wit or wisdom.

[1] *Satire* II, 80. [2] *L'Art Poétique*, 181. [3] *Spectator*, 2.
[4] *Life of Prior*. [5] *E.C.* I, 23.

At first it seems strange that the age which so constantly demanded *sense* should never speak of it with enthusiastic admiration. But presently one sees. The word has stooped to conquer. The implication of the whole Augustan attitude is 'We're not asking much. We're not asking that poets should be learned, or that divines should be saints, or courtiers heroes, or that statesmen should bring in a heaven on earth. Our fathers tried that, and look what came of it. We ask only for rationality. A good many who tried to go beyond it never got as far. They became Enthusiasts. We are more modest. We ask for plain sense, but that we do insist on.' The implication that if we really aim at this plain *sense* most of us will find that we have quite enough to do—for *le sens commun* (whoever said it first) *n'est pas si commun*—is never far below the surface. The demands of Augustanism (in reality, pretty exacting) are made to seem more obligatory by their apparent modesty. The less grandiose the name you give to your favourite virtue, the more you disgrace those who fail to practise it; they can't do 'even that'.

There is possibly a parallel to this in the (now perhaps obsolescent) use of *decent* and *decency* with reference to conduct which the speaker believed to be, and which perhaps was, altruistic, generous, or even heroic. Was there a double implication? (*a*) The standards in our class and nation are so high that what would elsewhere be praised as splendid ranks among us as 'merely' *decent*, or 'common' *decency*. (*b*) This behaviour is so completely obligatory that if you fail in it we must class you with people who spit in the dining-room.

4. What are we to make of Roscommon's statement (he is advising us not to use 'immodest words') that 'want of Decency is want of Sense'?[1] A great many immodest words have plenty of *sense* (meaning) and most of them refer us to objects of *sense* (*aesthesis*). Some fairly vague idea of *sense* as judgement was probably in his mind. But I suspect that we here see the injuries the word has undergone by becoming the popular vogue-word; and that Roscommon, wishing strongly to censure obscenity, calls it 'lack of *sense*' chiefly because *sense* is the favourite term of eulogy and 'lack' of it therefore the strongest accusation. His usage is in fact mainly tactical. Just so one can imagine one of the 'weaker brethren' today saying that a man or a book lacked 'percipience' or 'integration', not because at that moment (or ever) he had a very clear notion what he meant by the words, but because, from going to many sherry parties and reading many reviews, he had discovered they meant something everybody ought to have.

XII. 'SENSIBLE' AND 'SENSIBILITY'

As with the verb *amare* we have the adjective *amabilis* (lovable, capable of being loved), so of course with *sentire* we have *sensibilis*. Perhaps its most usual meaning is 'apprehensible by the *senses*'; thus in Seneca 'Those who give pleasure the highest place regard the good as something apprehensible by the senses (*sensibile*); we, on the other hand, as something apprehensible by the intellect (*intelligibile*)'.[2] This of course descends into

---

[1] *Essay on Translated Verse*, 115.   [2] *Epistle* 124.

English: 'Heat, Cold, Soft, Hard, Bitter, Sweet, and all those which we call sensible qualities'.[1] That comes from what we have called in section IV the *B*-meaning of *sentire*. But English *sensible* sometimes derives from *sentire* (*A*). It then means 'capable of being emotionally experienced'— usually strengthened by some word like *very*; as when Shakespeare's Lucrece complains that her husband's 'passion' makes her own woe 'too sensible'.[2]

But Latin adjectives of this type were subject to a peculiar semantic infirmity. One would expect *penetrabilis* to mean 'penetrable, able to be pierced'. And so it does; Ovid can speak of a body penetrable by no dart, *nullo penetrabile telo*.[3] But it can also mean 'penetrating, able to pierce'; *penetrabile frigus* in Virgil means the piercing cold.[4] Similarly one would expect *comfortabilis* and its derivatives to mean 'capable of being strengthened'; but *comfortable*, when the Prayer Book speaks of 'the most comfortable sacrament' means 'able to strengthen, strength-giving'. Conversely *unexpressive* in *Lycidas* (l. 176) means inexpressible. *Sensibilis*, by the same law, besides meaning 'apprehensible' (by the senses or otherwise) can mean 'able to feel, able to be aware'. Thus in Lactantius' *Divine Institutions* the creation of man is described in the words 'Then God made for Himself a sentient (*sensibile*) and intelligent image' (II, xi).

This is exactly the meaning of *sensible* when in the *Midsummer Night's Dream*, hearing the wall cursed by Pyramus and Thisbe, Theseus says 'The wall, methinks,

---

[1] Locke, *Essay* II, i, 3.   [2] *Rape of Lucrece*, 1678.
[3] *Metamorphoses* XII, 166.   [4] *Georgics* I, 93.

being sensible, should curse again' (v, i, 181); or when Hooker writes 'Beasts are in sensible capacity as ripe even as men themselves' (I, vi, 2), they see, smell and feel at least as well as we do.

Sometimes we may doubt whether *sensible* is intended to mean 'able to feel' 'or 'able to be felt'. When Claudio in *Measure for Measure* (III, i, 120) speaks of 'this sensible, warm motion', does he mean that organic movement in him which can be felt, or that movement of nerves and brains whereby he is capable of feeling other things? When Milton's Mammon hopefully suggests that habituation to the climate of Hell will in due course 'remove the sensible of pain',[1] will it remove that within him and the other fiends which is capable of feeling pain or that in the pain which is perceptible? (In the facts, no doubt, there would be no difference between these two alternatives; linguistically, I think there is.)

From the meaning 'able to feel', *sensible* proceeds to that of 'actually feeling', as in Johnson's 'I am not wholly insensible of the provocations'.[2] There is often an overcharge of meaning so that the word signifies 'fully, or vividly, or excessively, aware of'. This may be present in the example I have just quoted. When Dalila exhorts Samson with the words 'What remains past cure Bear not too sensibly',[3] she certainly means 'Let your consciousness of it be as little acute, as unemphatic, as possible'. But the idea of a superfluity to be avoided is of course partly contributed by the *too*. In the following from Dryden, however, though *too* is present, it qualifies not

[1] *P.L.* II, 278.   [2] *Rambler*, 200.   [3] *Agonistes*, 912.

sensible but the succeeding words: 'The gloomy sire, too sensible of wrong to vent his rage in words',[1] so that *sensible of* must mean 'deeply or violently responsive to'. So too in *Tom Jones* (v, vi) 'His backwardness...and his silence...wrought violently on her sensible and tender heart'. A modern would have used 'sensitive'.

The state of being (with whatever meaning) *sensible* is of course *sensibility* (with the corresponding meaning). Hence in scientific or philosophical texts *sensibility* is sentience; the opposite of that *insensibility* in which, say, a faint or an anaesthetic may plunge us. The popular and colloquial use is of more interest.

Sensibility, so used, always means a more than ordinary degree of responsiveness or reaction; whether this is regarded with approval (as a sort of fineness) or with disapproval (as excess). Addison approvingly defines modesty as a 'quick and delicate feeling' in the soul, 'such an exquisite sensibility as warns her to shun the first appearance of anything which is hurtful'.[2] Burke, while maintaining that 'a rectitude of judgment in the arts does in a great measure depend upon sensibility', warns us that 'a good judgment does not necessarily arise from a quick sensibility of pleasure'.[3] Johnson speaks of it a little contemptuously but shows in doing so that it began to be generally admired: 'the ambition of superior sensibility and superior eloquence dispose the lovers of arts to receive rapture at one time and communicate it at another'.[4]

The more than normal responsiveness which *sensibility*

---

[1] *Sigismonda and Guiscardo*, 270.   [2] *Spectator*, 231.
[3] *On the Sublime* etc., Introduction.   [4] *Idler*, 50.

connotes need not be responsiveness to beauty. Often it is tenderness towards the sufferings of others, so that it covers most of what would once have been described as pity or even charity. The important difference is that the idea of a merely temperamental vulnerability has replaced that of a habit in the will, achieved by practice and under Grace, as the thing admired in the merciful. 'Dear Sensibility,' exclaims Sterne, '*Sensorium* of the world', and cites as an instance of it a peasant whose 'gentle heart bleeds' at the sight of an injured lamb.[1] Cowper writes lines 'Addressed to Miss —' which combat Mrs Greville's *Prayer for Indifference*. Heaven has decreed that all our 'true delights' should 'flow from sympathy'. He prays to be granted, as long as he lives, 'sweet sensibility'. I think vulnerability to pity is still the main idea. But in Mrs Radcliffe *sensibility* perhaps implies a more universal *morbidezza*, though pity still makes an important part of it. Her heroine had 'uncommon delicacy of mind, warm affections, and ready benevolence; but with these was observable a degree of susceptibility too exquisite to admit of lasting peace. As she advanced in youth this sensibility gave a pensive tone to her spirits and a softness to her manner, which added grace to beauty and rendered her a very interesting object to persons of a congenial disposition'.[2]

The admired quality could not be better described. Mrs Radcliffe still remembers that it can be regarded as an excess (are not the virtues of Fielding's heroes 'the vices

---

[1] *Sentimental Journey*, 'The Bourbonnais'.
[2] *Mysteries of Udolpho*, I, i.

of really good men'?) and mentions it with a pretty pretence of censure—'too exquisite for lasting peace'. It is the very tone in which people ostensibly *confess* what they actually *boast* ('I know it's very silly of me but I can't bear to see anything suffer'). Notice too that the pains inflicted on the young lady by her *sensibility* are amply recompensed by the fact that they make her 'a very interesting object'. But not to everyone. Only to the only people she would want to attract, 'persons of a congenial disposition'. For of course she would not have wished, any more than Marianne Dashwood, to interest a Colonel Brandon.

XIII. 'SENSIBLE (D.S.)'

When *sense* (gumption, reasonableness) becomes the quality universally demanded, the need for an adjective to describe those who have it will inevitably be felt. On etymological and logical grounds *sensate* had the strongest claims to this post. But the language rejected it. Perhaps it sounded too technical and scholastic. *Sensible*, despite the meanings it already had, was given this new one. Thus it acquires its *dangerous sense*: 'having ordinary intelligence, the opposite of silly or foolish'. It is in some ways a strange usage. To call a man *sensible* because he has *sense* is at first sight as odd as to call him 'memorable' because he has memory or 'regrettable' because he feels regret. (A 'barkable dog', I am told, occurs in legal language.) Perhaps this is why Johnson, who seems freely to have used *sensible* (*d.s.*) in conversation, stigmatises it as 'merely colloquial' in the *Dictionary*.

How long before his time *sensible* (*d.s.*) had been in use is not easy to determine. Some think they find it when Falstaff says to the Chief Justice, 'For the box of the ear that the prince gave you, he gave it like a rude prince, and you took it like a sensible lord'.[1] But there are surely great difficulties in taking *sensible* here to mean prudent or intelligent. For one thing, rudeness and good sense are a strange antithesis. For another, the Chief Justice (as Shakespeare well knew from Holinshed) had reacted to his box on the ear by sending the Prince to jail. And neither the Chief Justice himself nor anyone else thought this a prudent thing to do.[2] Two other meanings for '*sensible* lord' both seem to me to fit the context better. It might mean sensitive, thin-skinned, over-susceptible. Falstaff may, probably would, take the view that a mere Chief Justice, insulted by royalty, would have been wise to pocket the insult. He may be saying in effect 'You made far too much fuss, stood excessively on your dignity'. This will give us a sort of antithesis to 'rude'. What it was admittedly rowdy and 'boisteous' of the Prince to do, it was none the less over nice, over refined, of the Justice to resent. Alternatively, *sensible* could mean perceptible, noticeable, palpable. On that view 'like a sensible lord' would mean 'very (excessively) perceptibly a lord'; that is, 'making your status as a lord too noticeable', 'flinging your official weight about'. The Justice's action had been, in Falstaff's opinion, too (and too blatantly) lordly. A different Shakespearian passage is much stronger evidence for the existence of the *dangerous sense* in his

[1] *Hen. IV*, Pt 2, I, ii, 191. [2] See *ibid*. v, ii, 6–13.

time. When Ford calls Pistol 'a good sensible fellow' I think he means he is no fool.[1]

XIV. TRIUMPH OF 'SENSIBLE (D.S.)'

Whatever the early history may have been, *sensible*, by the time we reach the late eighteenth century, is over-burdened with meanings. It can mean (1) perceptible to the senses, (2) sentient, not unconscious, (3) having such *sensibility* as Marianne Dashwood's, or (4) having (good or common) *sense*, being no fool.

The first two of these, being scientific and philoso-phical, can live safely with each other and with the remaining two; with each other, because the sort of writers who use them will know precisely what they mean and make it clear to their readers, and with the other two because these seldom compete with them by entering the same contexts. But the third and fourth meanings have every chance of being used by the same speakers in the same conversation. Johnson in his Club and Mrs Thrale at her tea table will both want to talk about people who have *sense* and also about people who suffer from or enjoy 'sweet *sensibility*'. But *sensible* is now the adjective for both. This is a semantic situation which is almost bound to end by destroying one or other of the two meanings.

Fortunately for the language the possible confusion was one that could not (as confusion between different senses of *nature* or *simple* can) long escape notice. It was revealed by the obvious fact that those who qualify for the

[1] *Merry Wives* II, i, 148.

adjective *sensible* in the one sense seldom do so in the other. It would be hard to maintain that Sophia, by being 'sensible and tender' where Tom Jones was concerned, showed her *good sense*. Indeed the two classes of '*sensible*' people designated by the two meanings of the word hardly overlap at all. The paradox, unlike many similar semantic paradoxes, is felt because all three words (*sense*, *sensible* and *sensibility*) are fully alive. The awareness of it, embodied in the half-punning antithesis of *sense* and *sensibility* has been preserved in the title of Jane Austen's novel.

The upshot of the whole affair was that, for nearly all purposes, the *dangerous sense* achieved undisputed possession of the word *sensible*. Once, Marianne Dashwood and her sister would have had equal, though quite different, claims to it; it now belongs solely to people like Elinor. The settlement was a good one. *Sensible* (*d.s.*) was needed, and we have replaced *sensible* in its other meaning. People of *sensibility* are now sensitive or percipient when we approve them, sentimental or gushing when we do not. All has been for the best.

7
SIMPLE

It has been the curious fate of this word to achieve enormous popularity (now, I think, on the decline) without acquiring a *dangerous sense*. In many people's usage it has, indeed, rather an atmosphere than anything that can be called a meaning.

We must start of course with Latin *simplex*; its first element related to *semel* (once) and its second to *plicare* (to fold). Originally, we must suppose, a thing was *simplex* when it was like a sheet of paper. Fold the sheet in two and it becomes *duplex*. We had a word somewhat like it in Anglo-Saxon; *anfeald*, as you might say, 'onefold'. 'You've heard my *anfeald* thought', says someone in Beowulf (l. 256); the single, uncomplicated, unqualified, unambiguous thing I have to say. He is poising a spear in his hand while he speaks (l. 235) and is explaining to some strangers that they'd better—and the sooner the better (l. 256)—explain who they are before they go a step further. You couldn't have a more 'one-fold' thought. The word appears again (*afaild*) in Gavin Douglas, there applied to God.[1] But we have lost it. And the (presumably) original idea of folding in the Latin word has no influence on the meanings we shall have to consider.

1. The *simplex* is the opposite of the compound or composite: 'The nature of the animating principle', says

[1] *Prologue to Aeneid.*

165

Cicero, 'must either be *simplex*...or else compounded (*concreta*) of diverse natures'.[1] Just so in English. 'A foote of two sillables is either simple or mixt', says William Webbe.[2] Locke tells us 'one thing is to be observed concerning ideas...that some are simple and some complex'.[3]

2. Every compound, or so we hope, can in principle be resolved into *simple* ingredients, ingredients which are internally homogeneous. And as the compound is a compound, so these ultimate ingredients are *simples*. Thus in older medical language the ultimate herbal ingredients of a medicine are *simples*, and a medicine which consists of one single herb (or what not) is a *simple*. Thus Amarillis in *The Faithful Shepherdess* (II, iii, 72) speaks of 'all simples good for medicine'. We had a verb from this once. To go looking for such ingredients was to *simple*. 'I know most of the plants of my country,' says Browne, 'yet methinks I do not know so many as when I...had scarcely ever simpled further than Cheap-side.'[4]

3. Anything that is not added to, anything operating by itself, is *simple*. In this sense the word is almost synonymous with 'mere'. In *All's Well* we read of a remedy 'whose simple touch Is powerful to araise King Pepin' (II, i, 78). Its mere touch; nothing more is needed. We get the same in French: 'En la justice...tout ce qui est au delà de la mort simple, me semble pure cruauté'; mere death, not aggravated by tortures.[5] Examples of this

---

[1] *De Natura Deorum* III, xiv.
[2] *Discourse of English Poetrie*, 1586. Ed. E. Arber (1895), p. 69.
[3] *Essay* II, ii, 1.   [4] *Religio Medici* II, 8.   [5] Montaigne II, xi.

usage are no doubt plentiful in Latin and in all languages
that owe it the word, but they are not easy to identify.
So often other ideas may come in as well. The sort of
difficulty I have in mind can be shown by a glance at
Pope's *Essay on Man* I, 103 f.—the Poor Indian passage.
'Proud science' has never taught his soul this or that but
'simple nature' has given him the hope of immortality.
Does this mean 'mere' nature, nature unaided, or does it
mean 'Nature, who (as we all know) is unsophisticated,
free from artificiality'?

So far all has been plain enough. But we must now
divide. This semantic trunk throws out three branches of
meaning, which may be distinguished as the logical, the
ethical, and the popular.

I. THE LOGICAL BRANCH

Simply, and Latin *simpliciter*, take over the function of the
Greek adverb *haplôs*. What that function was, a good
formal logician would define for us accurately in a very
few words, but readers who are not themselves formal
logicians might not be greatly enlightened. We had
better take the slower way of learning its meaning from
live examples.[1] They are all from Aristotle's *Ethics*.

'The best critic in each subject is the man educated in
that subject; but the best critic *haplôs* is the [generally]
educated man' (1094 b).

'If one pursues *B* for the sake of *A*, he pursues *A* in

---

[1] My translations are very free because Aristotle's style is so tele-
graphic that fragments torn from their context and rendered at all
literally would be hardly intelligible. I hope and believe I have not
misrepresented his thought.

itself, but *B* incidentally. To pursue anything "in itself" means the same as to pursue it *haplôs'* (1151 b).

'Some define the virtues as absences of passion or states of tranquillity. But this is wrong. For they say this *haplôs*, without the necessary *addenda* such as "in the right way" or "on the right occasion"' (1104 b).

'Things which are always good *haplôs* but not always good for a particular person' (1129 b).

'That habit of the soul which, *haplôs*, is virtue, when exercised towards our neighbour is "justice"' (1130 a).

'A similar problem arises about jettison, when men throw goods overboard in a storm to lighten ship. This act would not be voluntary *haplôs*, though any man in his senses would do it to save himself and his shipmates. Such acts are, then, mixed. They are voluntary [in the circumstances] but perhaps involuntary *haplôs'* (1110 a).

The use of *simpliciter* to translate *haplôs* is conveniently illustrated by Aquinas when he is discussing the same problem, and arrives at a different conclusion. Such acts are 'voluntary *simpliciter*, but involuntary *secundum quid*'.[1]

For purely logical purposes it is best to use in English the Latin word. For our own purpose, the meaning of it, and of *haplôs*, is now, I hope tolerably clear. What is good or true (or anything else) *haplôs* is so 'in itself', intrinsically, unconditionally, not in relation to special circumstances; can be called good or true (or whatever) without qualification. The opposites of *haplôs* would be expressed by reservations: 'in a way', 'in a sense', 'for some people', 'under certain conditions', 'up to a point', 'with

[1] *Summa Theologiae* 1, 2ae, Q. VI, Art. 6.

the necessary qualifications', 'relatively', 'in the circumstances'.

Our older writers use *simply* in precisely this way. As in
Hooker's 'under man no creature is capable of felicity
and bliss...because their chiefest perfection consisteth in
that which is best for them, but not in that which is
simply best, as ours doth' (ɪ, xi, 3). For our good is God,
who is best *simpliciter*. A bone is a good for a dog but a
bone is not good *simply*. (While it was still in a live animal
the bone was a good for that animal, and there might
come a day when it was a good for a palaeontologist.
But never good *simply*.)

'Other retentions and evacuations there are, not simply
necessary but at some times', says Burton (ɪ, ii, 2, 4).

The words which I have italicised in the following
(from Taylor) perhaps show that in his time the logical
use of *simply* was already becoming a little less familiar.
He seems to feel it needs expansion: 'Elias, that he might
bring the people from idolatry, caused a sacrifice to Baal
to be made...which *of itself* was simply *and absolutely*
evil'.[1] The word 'considered' in Johnson's (Boswell,
12 June 1784) 'If you admit any degree of punishment,
there is an end of your argument from infinite goodness
simply considered', may have the same cause.

Now to say that a thing is *simply* good (like charity)
and not merely good for someone (like insulin for
diabetics), or that it is *simply* bad (like envy) and not
merely bad under certain conditions (as eight is a bad
hour for breakfast if you're catching a train at 8.15) is to

---

[1] *Ductor Dubit*. ɪ, v, Rule 8. Heber, vol. xɪɪ, p. 159.

say more about the thing—to exalt it higher or damn it deeper—than we should do if we admitted qualifications. Hence, by a degradation of the logical use, *simply* and *absolutely* (which we have already seen Taylor using to explicate *simply*) become merely intensifying adverbs. By prefixing them to an adjective ordinary speakers will soon feel that they are merely underlining the adjective or asserting a strong claim to it. Hence, in our own day, '*simply* delicious', '*simply* marvellous', 'absolutely frightful'. (One could even have, though I am not sure I have yet heard it, 'it's all absolutely relative'.) This is a kind of gush which many suppose to be specifically modern, but it was already beginning in the sixteenth century. 'He hath simply the best wit of any handy craft man in Athens', says someone in *Midsummer Night's Dream* (IV, ii, 9); and Sir Andrew claims to 'have the back-trick simply as strong as any man in Illyria'.[1] Thus we may—in such studies as this we must—trace the noble dust of Alexander stopping a bung-hole and see how a homespun's *schwärmerei* or a gull's vanity makes its own momentary use of tools inherited from the great masters of all occidental thought.

II. THE ETHICAL BRANCH

Simplicity here is the opposite of duplicity. A man is *simplex* when there is 'only one of him' in the sense that the character he shows you and that which he bears within are one not two; especially, of course, when his words and his thought, his professed and his real motives, are

[1] *Twelfth Night* I, iii, 124.

identical. 'You and I are speaking to-day *simplicissime*', says someone in Tacitus[1]—frankly, sincerely, as we really think and feel. With an immeasurable deepening the idea can then be internalised so that it refers to an inner single-ness or *simplicity* which makes a man sincere with himself, seeing what he sees and playing no tricks with his own knowledge or purpose. 'If your eye is *haplous*', says the Greek—*haplous* being of course the adjective of the adverb *haplôs*;[2] and the Vulgate, *si oculus tuus fuerit simplex* (A.V. 'single').

Sincere people are guileless, and those who have no guile themselves are not quick to suspect it in others. (It has been said that no one ever meets anyone but himself.) It is here that the degradation of *simplex* begins. To be guileless, unsuspicious—is it not next door to being credulous, gullible? Accordingly Apuleius, explaining why Psyche believed the cock-and-bull story of her jealous sisters, says 'she was seized by the terror of such alarming words, for poor little (*misella*) Psyche was *simplex* and of a tender wit, *animi tenella*'.[3] An Elizabethan would here have rendered *simplex* by 'seelie'. Apuleius does not yet mean quite *silly* in the modern sense, but he certainly means she was no Solomon. Ingenuous Psyche? *Naïve* Psyche? At any rate, a Psyche quite incapable of looking after herself, anyone's prey.

The *simple*, being guileless and credulous, are of course not dangerous. They are harmless or—notice how all these words have a flavour of patronage or disparagement —'innocuous'. The apostles are told in St Matthew (x. 16)

[1] *Hist.* I, xv.   [2] Matth. vi. 22.   [3] *Met.* v, xviii.

to be as *akeraioi* as doves. The word, so far as I can
make out, meant 'guileless', and the Vulgate's *simplices*
would be a good translation. Tyndale, Cranmer, and
Geneva render it 'innocent', and A.V., 'harmless';
presumably, for them, synonymous with *simple*. And
the idea of harmlessness is probably uppermost when
Fraunchise in the *Romance of the Rose* is said (l. 1198) to be
'simple come uns colons' (English version, 'simple as
dowve on tree', l. 1219).

But in the same poem we can find the word at a further
stage of its decline. Frend is advising the lover to ignore
infidelities in his mistress; even when they are flagrant he
should pretend that he is blind or *plus simples que n'est uns
bugles* (l. 9700)—pretend, in fact, that he has no more
sense than a buffalo. *Simples* has got beyond the senses
'credulous' or 'naïf'; it means downright stupid. It is not
far from this when Claudius accuses Hamlet of 'An understanding simple and unschooled' (I, ii, 97) or when,
centuries later Mrs Morland says 'You are fretting over
General Tilney and that is very simple of you'.[1] Often
the defect implied is one of learning, skill and subtlety—
a defect felt to be rather charming and put forward as a
claim for pity, as in *Henry VIII*, 'I am a simple woman
much too weak To oppose your cunning' (II, iv, 106).
So Desdemona asks the Duke 'let me find a charter in
your voice to assist my simpleness'.[2]

The word takes a much sharper downward turn in the
sense which has given us *simpleton*. *Simple* can still—in
Ireland anyway—mean 'mentally deficient'. In Grim-

---

[1] *Northanger Abbey*, ch. xv.   [2] *Othello* I, iii, 247.

stone's *Siege of Ostend* (1604) we read of one who was 'lame of his body and half simple'—half an imbecile. When the exasperated Friar in *Romeo* asks 'what simpleness is this?' (III, iii, 77) *simpleness* probably means idiocy, and I think 'Simple Simon' in the Rhyme was a *fatuus*. Significantly 'innocent'—and *simple*, as we have seen, can mean that—is used in the same way, so that there is a section in Taylor's *Worthy Communicant* headed 'Whether Innocents, Fools, and Madmen, may be admitted'.[1] For *innocent, simple, silly, ingenuous,* and Greek *euethes,* all illustrate the same thing—the remarkable tendency of adjectives which originally imputed great goodness, to become terms of disparagement. Give a good quality a name and that name will soon be the name of a defect. *Pious* and *respectable* are among the comparatively modern casualties, and *sanctimonious* was once a term of praise.

As far as *simple* is concerned, Taylor comments on the process: 'Simplicity is grown into contempt...unwary fools and defenceless people were called simple.'[2] And Shakespeare exploits it to good effect in the line 'And simple truth miscall'd simplicity',[3] where *simple*, I take it, is not 'mere' but 'guileless, single-minded'.

III. THE POPULAR BRANCH

We have already had *simple* or *simplex* as 'mere', not added to. The meaning I now want to consider is perhaps

[1] III, 3. Heber, vol. XV, p. 508.
[2] *Fourteen Sermons* XXIII. Heber, vol. VI, p. 140.
[3] Sonnet LXVI.

just budding out of this when Horace, deprecating 'Persian'—Thackeray took 'Frenchified' as our equivalent—luxury in the arrangements for a dinner, says 'Don't bother to add anything to the *simplici myrto*', 'the mere or plain myrtle'.[1]

The word 'plain', which itself well deserves study, is the best translation for *simplex* in this sense; 'elaborate' or 'ornate' are the opposites. Thus Milton rightly turns Horace's *simplex munditiis*[2] as 'plain in thy neatness'. (Why, in heaven's name, did Monsignor Knox think his version of that ode was 'modelled on the Authorised Version'?)

Examples of this sense could be had by the armful. Addison says the opening lines of *Paradise Lost* are 'as plain, simple, and unadorned as any in the whole poem'.[3] Gulliver's 'style is very plain and simple'.[4]

This sense again divides into two.

1. What is *simple* or plain is the reverse of complicated. A complicated process is hard to learn and a complicated argument hard to follow. Therefore *simple* comes to mean 'easy'. The idea that it is within the capacity of those who are *simple* (in the sense 'unskilled') may perhaps have helped this development.

'God never does that by difficult ways which may be done by ways that are simple and easy', says John Norris in his *Essay towards the Theory of the Ideal World* (1701). F. H. Bradley in the Preface to his *Logic* (1922) says 'if I saw further I should be simpler'.

---

[1] *Carm.* I, xxxviii. [2] *Ibid.* I, vi.
[3] *Spectator*, 303. [4] *The Publisher to the Reader.*

2. There is a general feeling that what is unelaborate is modest or unostentatious. *Simple* thus acquires a sense which I might find it hard enough to define if a useful piece of modern slang did not help me out; the *simple* is the opposite of the 'posh'. Frugal and homely ways are *simple* ways; Lenten fare, *simple* fare. In *Gawain and the Green Knight* we read of 'the crabbed Lenten That fraystes the flesch with the fysche and fode more simple' (l. 502)—is a trial to our flesh 'with fish and *simpler* diet'. Virgil speaks of one whose health was never impaired by a *recherché* table, *non epulae nocuere repostae*.[1] Dryden renders it 'simple his beverage, homely was his food'.

In this usage, which is still very current, we often have good examples of the insulating power of the context. When we are warned that we shall get only 'a very *simple* meal' we may expect a shepherd's pie or a dish of hash. These are certainly not *simpler* than a pheasant or a haunch of venison in the sense of being less complicated, containing fewer heterogeneous elements. And to cook these well is not a *simpler* (in the sense 'easier') operation. Indeed it is everyone's experience that when we are hard up and start economising, our lives become *simpler* in the sense that they become homelier and less 'posh' while at the same time they become less *simple* (more complicated). Rags tacked together, and braces supplemented with string, and sleeves where you can hardly find the fairway —torn linings leading to so many dead-ends—make a man's toilet marvellously complicated.

[1] *Georgics* III, 527.

But *simple* as the opposite of 'posh', elaborate, or ostentatious, bifurcates again. It can be either derogatory or laudatory.

In its derogatory use it means, in one sense of that word, 'poor'; 'not up to much', second-rate, trumpery, slight. Thus, again from *Gawain*: 'Now forsake ye this silke, sayde the burde thenne, For hit is simple in hitself?' (l. 1846)—because it doesn't look much of a thing? Of course this is mock modesty; quite apart from its magical properties it was far from *simple*. But the lady uses the language of real modesty. So in Malory we learn that knights who use paramours will be unlucky and 'shal be overcome with a simpler knight than they be hemself' (VI, x)—a knight whose form or skill is below their own. In the same text (II, v) 'your quarrel is ful simple' might mean that it is foolish; more probably, I think, that it is trivial. Finally, *simple* can mean low-born, not of the gentry; as when the old fisherman says in *Waverley* (ch. XXXII) 'gentle or simple shall not darken my door'.

As a term of praise it covers several shades of meaning. When Shame in the *Romance of the Rose* (l. 3563) *si fu umeliant e simple*, the English version gives 'Humble of hir porte and made it simple' (l. 3863); *simple* is almost exactly a synonym for 'humble'. In Zechariah ix. 9, where A.V. reads 'lowly', Coverdale had 'lowly and simple', a doublet of synonyms. So in the *Romance* where we are told that Beauty was *simple comme une esposee* (l. 1000), 'simple as byrde in bour',[1] something

[1] English version, l. 1014.

like 'modest' or 'bashful' might do. And so also for Chaucer's Prioress who 'of her smiling was ful simple and coy' (A. 119), demure, unobtrusive. *Coy*, ultimately from *quietus*, is not far removed from it in meaning. Both adjectives paint a character who was far from being 'loud'.

IV. THE SEMANTIC SEDIMENT

The logical branch of this word's meanings has little effect on the others. But nearly all those others are bound together and (as Donne might say) 'interinanimate' one another in an unusual way, so that it is often impossible to decide which is intended or, if there are many intended, which is uppermost.

Dante writes: 'From the hand of Him who loves her before she is, like a young girl who prattles, with laughter and tears, forth comes *l'anima semplicetta*.'[1] We notice that Dante is using a diminutive. The feeling which prompted Apuleius to his *misella* and *tenella* for 'simple Psyche' is at work. The new-created *anima* or *psyche* is a touching or disarming thing, viewed with tenderness and not without pity. But if we try to go beyond the emotional content of the word, I do not know what definable sense we could fix upon it. Is the soul *simple* because she is uncomplicated? or innocent? or gullible? or unskilled? or humble? or foolish? or for all these reasons? Could Dante himself have told us?

Simple, as we have seen, can impute either defects (lack of intelligence, of rationality even, of skill, of nobility) or virtues (sincerity, humility). But none of these defects is

[1] *Purgatorio* XVI, 85.

such as to produce hatred. Good reason why; they leave our self-love secure. We feel superior when we impute them. Even if they irritate us, there is some pity, often some amusement and indulgence, mixed with our irritation. The idiot (one thing that *simple* can mean) may indeed raise uneasiness or disgust in a modern; but he does not seem to have done so in our ancestors. They loved 'fools' and kept them as pets. Again, the *simple* are the harmless; we feel safe in their presence as well as superior. But, oddly enough, the virtues which this word can impute have the same effect. Humility disarms us, and we seldom acknowledge a man's moral superiority to us in guilelessness and truth without reimbursing our self-esteem by a feeling that we are at least equally superior to him in acuteness and knowledge of the world. (The humour of Chesterton's Father Brown stories depends on the continual pricking of this bubble.) Hence, over a very wide range of its senses, *simple* either imputes virtues and defects which can equally be contemplated *de haut en bas*, or else, when the speaker uses it of himself (more often perhaps herself) is placatory—claims our indulgence, deprecates our severity, and flatters us a little. Yes, and even while it assumes the form of self-depreciation, it gently insinuates that the thing confessed is really almost a virtue; is at least very touching and endearing. 'I'm afraid you'll find we live very *simply*' may in fact be an appeal that we should regard dirty plates and tepid food, not as the results of laziness, but as somehow homely, unostentatious, modest, *simple* with the laudable *simplicité des anciens mœurs*.

This is why I describe the final state of the word as a semantic sediment. What effectively remains is not this or that precise sense but a general appealingness or disarmingness.

'They prefer the simplicity of faith before that knowledge which, curiously sifting and disputing too boldly...chilleth...all warmth of zeal'.[1] Faith un-added to and 'mere'? Unskilled? Easy? Humble?

'Never anything can be amiss when simpleness and duty tender it.'[2] Sincerity? Unskilfulness? *Simple* as against gentle? Silliness?

'His place of birth a solemn Angel tells to simple shepherds.'[3]

'A general simplicity in our dress, our discourse, and our behaviour.'[4] Sincerity (not affectation)? Plainness (not 'poshness')? The easy (not the hard)? The modest (not the ostentatious)?

Finally, in A. C. Benson's *From a College Window*: 'Simple, silent, deferential people such as station-masters, butlers, gardeners' (pp. 2–3). 'Quiet lives of study and meditation led here' (i.e. in Cambridge colleges) 'by wise and simple men' (pp. 8–9). 'The University is a place where a poor man, if he be virtuous, may live a life of dignity and simplicity' (p. 9). 'How seldom does a perfectly simple, human relationship exist between a boy and his father' (p. 10). 'To have leisure and a degree of simple stateliness assured' (p. 12). 'I have grown to feel that the ambitions which we preach and the successes for

[1] Hooker, v, lxxvii, 12. [2] *Midsummer Night's Dream* v, i, 82.
[3] *P.L.* xii, 364. [4] Steele, Dedication of *Tatler*, vol. I.

which we prepare are very often nothing but a missing of the simple road...I have grown to believe that the one thing worth aiming at is simplicity of heart and life' (p. 14).

The *simplicity* often lacking between father and son might be sincerity, but I think Benson would have used *sincerity* if he meant exactly that. In what sense either butlers or fellows of colleges are usually *simple* is hard to say. In two of the instances the word has, I fancy, almost an exclusively placatory function. You might grudge us 'dignity' or 'stateliness'; yet surely not 'dignity *and* simplicity' or 'simple stateliness'. Yet the continual recurrence of the word is undoubtedly necessary to the tone of the whole essay.

Though I do not myself much care for this word when it is in this condition—it is a soft, frilly, pouting, question-begging, almost a sly and sneaking, word—I would not say it is now meaningless. It indicates an (emotionally) specific area; like *supernatural*. We cannot say it serves none of the purposes of language.

8

CONSCIENCE AND CONSCIOUS

I. PRELIMINARIES

GREEK *oida* and Latin *scio* mean 'I know'. The Greek verb can be compounded with the prefix *sun* or *xun* (*sunoida*), the Latin with *cum* which in composition becomes *con-*, giving us *conscio*. *Sun* and *cum* in isolation mean 'with'. And sometimes they retain this meaning when they become prefixes, so that *sunoida* and *conscio* can mean 'I know together with, I share (with someone) the knowledge that'. But sometimes they had a vaguely intensive force, so that the compound verbs would mean merely 'I know well', and perhaps finally little more than 'I know'. Each verb has a train of related words. With *sunoida* goes the noun *suneidesis* and (its synonym) the neuter participle *to suneidos*, and the masculine participle *suneidôs*; with *conscio*, the noun *conscientia* and the adjective *conscius*. It will be seen at once that the double value of the prefixes may affect all these, so that *suneidesis* and *conscientia* could be either the state (or act) of sharing knowledge or else simply knowledge, awareness, apprehension—even something like mind or thought.

Our word therefore has two branches of meaning; that which uses the full sense ('together') of the prefix and that in which the prefix is—or may be treated for our purpose as being—almost inoperative. Let us for convenience call them the together branch and the weakened branch.

The richest and most useful developments of the weakened branch are in English comparatively modern, but some of its earlier and obsolete senses need to be noticed at once. I shall therefore begin with a brief glance at the weakened branch; then turn to the together branch; and in conclusion turn back to the weakened in its later condition.

II. THE WEAKENED BRANCH

We read in Diogenes Laertius (VII, 85) 'Chrysippus says that the first property of every animal is its structure and the *suneidesis* of this'. *Suneidesis* here can hardly mean anything other than 'awareness'. The Greek Lexicon quotes from Plutarch '*to suneidos* of the affairs', presumably the knowledge of them. The Septuagint version gives us 'curse not the king in your *suneidesis*'[1] where A.V. has 'curse not the king, no not in thy thought'.

Latin usages of the same sort are numerous, but usually post-classical. Macrobius mentions one Vettius as '*unice conscius* of all sacred matters'—uniquely knowledgeable about or learned in.[2] Where the Septuagint has merely 'we don't know' (*ouk oidamen*) in Genesis xliii. 22, the Vulgate reads 'it is not in our *conscientia*'. When Tertullian speaks of convictions lodged in our 'innate *conscientia*'[3] or Lactantius of what is 'clear to our *conscientia*'[4] some sense like 'mind' or 'understanding' is required.

It will at once be obvious that the French *la conscience*

---

[1] Eccles. x. 20.
[2] *Saturnalia* I, viii, 17.
[3] *De Testimonio Animae* v.
[4] *Inst.* VII, xxvii, 3.

descends from the weakened branch; a Frenchman could
perhaps use it to translate the *conscientia* of Tertullian and
Lactantius. In Modern English the specialisation of *consciousness* for this purpose has left *conscience* free to develop
almost exclusively the 'together' senses; a notable example
of desynonymisation. But it is a comparatively recent
achievement. When Gawain saw his hostess steal into his
bedroom and tried to figure out 'in his conscience' what
this might portend, the word must mean 'mind' or
'thought'.[1] In Shakespeare's 'Canst thou the conscience
lack to think I shall lack friends?'[2] it seems to mean
'sense' or 'gumption'. And this meaning, though finally
defeated by those of the together branch, may have had
subtle effects upon its conquerors.

One late Middle English usage is hard to account for.
Chaucer apostrophises Dido as the 'sely' (guileless)
woman, full of innocence, pity, truth, and *conscience*.[3]
His prioress sheds tears at the sight of a mouse in a trap
because of her 'conscience and tendre herte',[4] and that
whole passage is ushered in by the words 'for to speken
of her conscience' (l. 142). In Gower, Pompey 'tok pite
with conscience' on the captive Armenian king (vii,
3230). In all these some such meaning as 'tenderness'
(vulnerability, even excessive sensibility) seems to be
required. The influence of the 'together' branch may
have had something to do with it. There might also be a
progression from 'awareness' to 'extreme awareness',
thence to 'perceptiveness', the opposite of callousness.

[1] *Gawain and the Green Knight*, 1197.   [2] *Timon* ii, ii, 184.
[3] *L.G.W.* 1254-5.   [4] *C.T. A.* 150.

III. THE EXTERNAL WITNESS

To the 'together' branch, to usages where *sun-* and *con-*
have their full meaning, I now turn.

The man who shares the knowledge of anything with
So-and-so can say '*Sunoida* (or *conscio*) this to So-and-so'.
In order to avoid many cumbrous circumlocutions I am
going to describe this state of affairs as 'consciring'. But
of course when everyone is consciring about a piece of
knowledge (e.g. that the Sun rises in the east) it will
never be mentioned. Consciring is worth talking about
only when two, or a few, men share some knowledge
which most men do not possess; in fact, when they are in
a secret. The man who conscires anything with me is
conscius (or *suneidos*) to me. The fact of his consciring is
his *conscientia* (or *suneidesis*), his shared knowledge.

When Teiresias tries to evade the questions put him by
Oedipus about the origin of the curse that has fallen on
the city, Oedipus says 'What? *suneidos* (though you are
in the secret) you won't tell?' [1] In the *Antigone* the soldier,
questioned about the burial of Polyneices, says he will
take any oath that he has neither done it himself nor *tô
xuneidenai*—been privy to, been in the confidence of,
anyone who did it (l. 266). Tacitus says that Sallustius
had been *interficiendi Agrippae conscius*, privy to, in the
secret of, Agrippa's murder;[2] or again, that when
Tiberius practised astrology he 'used the *conscientia* of a
single freedman', took only that one into his confidence,
admitted no other witness of his proceedings.[3] By meta-

---

[1] *O.T.* 330.   [2] *Annals* III, 30.   [3] *Ibid.* VI, 21.

phor, an inanimate object or an abstraction can be *conscius*, can have *conscientia*. In Ovid, Ajax, competing with Ulysses for the reward of having done best service in the Trojan War, says that his own deeds were all done in public while his rival produces 'feats he performed without witness, feats of which only Night is *conscia*'—to which only Night was privy.[1]

Hobbes, in a curious passage which is perhaps not very true to the idiomatic English of his own day, gives English *conscious* exactly the classical meaning of *conscius*: 'When two or more men know of one and the same fact [i.e. deed] they are said to be conscious of it one to another.'[2]

Since secrets often are, and are always suspected of being, guilty secrets, the normal implications of *conscius* and *conscientia* are bad. My *conscius*, the man who is *conscius mihi*, who shares my secret, who can give evidence about something I have done, is usually the fellow-conspirator; therefore the possible witness against me, the possible blackmailer, or at least the man who can taunt me with my deed and make me ashamed.

It was principally, I believe, a desire to imitate the Latin classics rather than a native English tendency that gave this sense of *conscious* (privy to) a great vogue in literature from the Restoration period down to the early nineteenth century. Thus in Denham the hunted stag flies through 'the conscious groves, the scenes of his past triumphs and his loves'.[3] The usage here is of course very

[1] *Metamorphoses* XIII, 15. [2] *Leviathan* I, vii, 31.
[3] *Cooper's Hill*, 277.

flaccid; only the tiniest shade of mingled archness and pathos is gained by reminding us that these groves had witnessed his youthful battlings and ruttings. There is more point in Milton's 'So all ere day-spring under conscious night Secret they finished'.[1] What they finished— the manufacture of the first artillery—was really secret and, in Milton's view, abominable; personified Night was privy to their crime. The most interesting and most often misunderstood examples are in Jane Austen. In *Northanger Abbey* (ch. xxx) Henry Tilney is introduced to Mrs Morland 'by her conscious daughter'. She was *conscious* in exactly the classical sense; knowing much which her mother did not know about Henry and her own relations to him, she was in a secret, shared a knowledge with him. This is '*being conscious*'; but you can also '*look conscious*', look like a conspirator or accomplice. Mrs Jennings is sure that Colonel Brandon's letter had something to do with Miss Williams 'because he looked so conscious when I mentioned her'.[2] He looked as if he had a secret on his mind. So in the same book (ch. xviii) 'he coloured very deeply...Elinor had met his eye and looked conscious likewise'. Many students whom I have asked to explain these passages were content with the theory that, somehow or other, *conscious* meant 'self-conscious'. But this seems, without further explanation, an impossible bit of semantic history. No doubt when one is *conscious*, when one has a secret, one tends to be, and to look, 'self-conscious'. Thus, if you like, the speaker's meaning *is* 'self-conscious' in the sense that the mental

[1] *P.L.* vi, 521.   [2] *Sense and Sensibility*, ch. xiv.

state and facial expression she refers to would in fact be what we call 'self-conscious'. But that is not the word's meaning.

IV. THE INTERNAL WITNESS

Man might be defined as a reflexive animal. A person cannot help thinking and speaking of himself as, and even feeling himself to be (for certain purposes), two people, one of whom can act upon and observe the other. Thus he pities, loves, admires, hates, despises, rebukes, comforts, examines, masters or is mastered by, 'himself'. Above all he can be to himself in the relation I have called consciring. He is privy to his own acts, is his own *conscius* or accomplice. And of course this shadowy inner accomplice has all the same properties as an external one; he too is a witness against you, a potential blackmailer, one who inflicts shame and fear.

Linguistically, the construction which represents this experience in the simplest form is 'I conscire (this or that) to myself'. Thus in Aristophanes '*xunoida*, I conscire, many dreadful deeds to myself'[1]—I know a lot against myself. Or in St Paul: 'I conscire (*sunoida*) nothing to myself.'[2] The A.V. rendering, 'I know nothing by myself', not very good even when it was made, now completely obscures the meaning. The proper translation is 'I know nothing against myself'. In Latin it is the same. Horace says that the 'brazen rampart' round a happy life should be *nil conscire sibi*,[3] to know nothing against oneself, to have nothing 'on one's mind'. It will be noticed that the things conscired in the passage from

[1] *Thesmophoriazusae*, 477.   [2] I Cor. iv. 4.   [3] *Epistles* I, i, 61.

Aristophanes and the things of which there are none to be conscired in those from St Paul and Horace, are evil. In the situation within a man, as in the situation between man and man, consciring is presumed to be of evil unless the reverse is explicitly stated.

Now the state of thus consciring to (or with) oneself is in Greek *suneidesis* (or, more rarely *sunesis*), and in Latin of course *conscientia*. 'What is your malady?' Menelaus asks the haunted matricide Orestes. '*Sunesis*', he replies, 'for I have done a dreadful deed and conscire it'.[1] The Septuagint version of Wisdom reads 'Wickedness condemned by an internal witness is a cowardly thing and expects the worst, being hard pressed by *suneidesis*' (xviii. 11). Close to this is Menander's statement that if even the toughest man is aware of guilt, *sunesis* makes him a very coward.[2] The same experience finds expression centuries later when the murderer in *Richard III* says that conscience 'makes a man a coward' (I, iv, 132) or Richard apostrophises 'Coward Conscience' (v, iii, 180). When you have a clean bill of moral health, that is, when you conscire no evil to yourself, you are *eusuneidetos*, have a good *suneidesis*.[3] So in Latin, when what you conscire to yourself is good, or when at least you conscire to yourself nothing bad, you have a 'good' *conscientia*. 'All wish to hide their sins,' says Seneca, 'but a good *conscientia* loves the light.'[4]

One who conscires something to himself is of course *conscius sibi*, privy to himself, in his own secret; or

[1] Euripides, *Orestes*, 395–6.   [2] *Fragment*, 632.
[3] Marcus Aurelius VI, 30.   [4] *Epistles*, 97.

suneidos heautô in Greek. It would be prudish not to quote
the passage, worthy of Walt Disney, where Juvenal
describes the mysteries of the Bona Dea (which excluded
all men) as a ceremony *testiculi sibi conscius unde fugit mus*
(VI, 339)—whence a (male) mouse hurries away, laden
with the secret of its own virility. Exactly the same construction was current in older English. 'If he be an
impudent flatterer,' says Bacon, 'look, wherein a man is
most conscious to himself that he is most defective...that
will the flatterer entitle him to.'[1] So in Bunyan: 'I am
conscious to myself of many failings.' A modern reader,
carelessly ignoring the *to himself* and *to myself*, will think
he has met *conscious* (*d.s.*) (in its *dangerous sense* of
'aware'). He will have missed a shade of the real
meaning.

As I have already said, consciring, whether to oneself
or to another, is usually of evil, usually conspiratorial.
It may, however, be of good, as in Sophocles:[2] 'being
valiant, he is conscious (of it) to himself' (*hautô sunoide*).
When *conscious* or *conscience* are of qualities, not defects,
a neglect of their precise meaning may be disastrous.
Milton's Eve drew back a little from Adam's suit, so
impelled by 'her virtue and the conscience of her worth,
That would be wooed, and not unsought be won'.[3] We
rub the bloom off the passage if we give *conscience* simply
the meaning of modern 'consciousness' and take Milton
to be telling us simply that Eve knew she was eminently
desirable. It is far more delicate than that. It is (transferred to a woman) what Sidney attributes to a heroic

[1] *Of Praise.*   [2] Fragment, 669.   [3] *P.L.* VIII, 502–3.

189

king, the 'secreat assurance of his owne worthines which (although it bee never so well cloathed in modestie) yet alwaies lives in the worthyest mindes'.[1] A secret assurance. You must bring in the consciring. Eve's beauty was a secret between Eve and herself, 'worthy of sacred silence' even within, neither Eve mentioning to the other what both Eves could not but know, her *conscientia* of it thus resembling a conspiracy in all but guilt.

V. SUMMARY

This inner witness, one's own *conscientia*, or privity, to oneself, is already a sufficiently formidable idea. Quintilian (v, xi) quotes as a proverb *conscientia mille testes*; one's own consciring is (as bad as) a thousand (external) witnesses. But we must also notice what *conscientia*, in the examples hitherto quoted, is not. It bears witness to the fact, say, that we committed a murder. It does not tell us that murder is wrong; we are supposed to know that in some other way. In this respect it is exactly like an external witness who gives evidence about matter of fact; the criminality or innocence of the fact has been fixed by the legislator and will be declared by the judge. Hence according to the usages we have considered it would make no sense to say 'My *conscientia* tells me this is wrong'; it tells me simply that I have done this—for of course what we conscire is always in the past. Again, *conscientia*, so far as we have seen, issues no commands or permissions. Those can come from the law or the bench, but not from the witness box. To talk of 'obeying' or 'disobeying'

[1] *Arcadia* v, ed. Feuillerat, p. 155.

your *conscience*, so long as that word remains in the semantic stage we have been observing, would be non-sensical. I cannot by any present action 'obey' my future privity to the fact of having done that action itself. Nor is there yet any idea of *conscience* as a separate faculty of the soul. The only faculty involved is knowing by memory. *Suneidesis* or *conscientia* is rather 'a state of affairs'; knowing about your own past actions what others, or most others, do not know.[1]

VI. THE INTERNAL LAWGIVER

The remarkable development of meaning whereby *conscience*, so to speak, passed from the witness-box to the bench and even to the legislator's throne, must now be considered. Some such process is already foreshadowed

---

[1] There is room for debate about the meaning of the word in a passage from Tacitus. 'We have read that when Rusticus praised Thrasea, and Senecio praised Helvidius, it cost them their lives, and that the rage of government, not satisfied with the authors, extended to the books; three commissioners being appointed to have those monuments of high genius publicly burned. Our masters thought, it seems, that in that fire the voice of the Roman people, the liberty of the senate, and the *conscientia* of mankind, could be annihilated' (*Agricola* II). It is tempting here to say 'conscience', and to give that word its full, later, sense. Einar Löfstedt almost seems to favour that interpretation when he speaks of Tacitus as 'the man who first formulated this proud concept' (*Roman Literary Portraits*, trans. P. M. Fraser, p. 153, Oxford, 1958). But surely—and this is probably what Löfstedt meant—*conscientia* contains 'conscience' only because it is *conscientia* in Lactantius' sense; the *communis sensus*, the universal 'feeling' or 'outlook' of mankind? It might mean less. It might be the consciring of humanity to those truths the books contained. Of course consciring, as I have said, is normally the activity of a few. To make all men conscire would thus be a bitter and magnificent oxymoron; Domitian's government had turned humanity itself into a sort of underground movement.

in a fragment of Menander quoted by Mr Pierce:[1] 'to all
mortals *suneidesis* is *theos*'—which might be rendered 'is
a god' or 'is divine', but hardly 'is God'. More important
is the influence of the New Testament.

Some of its usages quite clearly conform to the pattern
we have already studied; *suneidesis* means consciring and
sunoida means 'I conscire'. Such are the passages from
I Cor. iv. 4, noted above, 'I conscire nothing (that is,
nothing bad) to myself'; 'from a pure heart and good
suneidesis';[2] 'a good *suneidesis*';[3] 'with all good *suneidesis*'.[4]
But other passages are harder. 'With *suneidesis* of the
idol' in I Cor. viii. 7 is possibly corrupt. There is a similar
use of *suneidesis* with the genitive in I Pet. ii. 19, 'It is
meritorious if a man who is unjustly punished patiently
bears his sufferings through *suneidesis* of God'. What this
means, or how A.V. could get out of it 'for conscience
toward God', I am uncertain.

I now turn to passages which may probably have contributed to the great semantic shift. In I Cor. viii. 10,
St Paul says that if a 'weak brother', a scrupulous person,
sees you eating meat which has been offered to idols—a
thing, in St Paul's view, innocent in itself—his *suneidesis*
will be emboldened or 'built up' to do likewise. (This is
a bad thing because, being scrupulous, he will probably
be worried about it in retrospect.) What St Paul really
meant is a question for theologians; we, busied about the
history of a word, are concerned with what he would
possibly, or probably, or almost inevitably, be taken to

[1] C. A. Pierce, *Conscience in the New Testament* (1955).
[2] I Tim. i. 5.   [3] *Ibid.* 19.   [4] Acts xxiii. 1; cf. xxiv. 16.

mean by succeeding generations. I believe this passage would have suggested to them (as to most of us) the idea that *suneidesis* here means, not consciring, but 'judgement as to what is right and wrong'. The weak brother's scale of values, or standard of good and evil, originally classified the eating of sacrificed flesh as a sin; under your influence, encouraged by your example, he alters his scale or standard, modifies his moral judgement. Again, in Rom. xiii. 5, we are told to obey magistrates 'not only because of the wrath' (because it is dangerous not to) but also 'because of *suneidesis*' (A.V. 'for conscience sake'). Now it may be true in fact that St Paul only meant 'Obey, not only for safety's sake, but also because, later on, you will not like consciring to yourself that you have not'; it being assumed that we all know we ought to be law-abiding, and that the *conscience* or consciring of a failure in this duty will be a 'bad' conscience. But the passage very easily, indeed more easily, suggests that *suneidesis* here means our actual moral judgement (that men should be law-abiding). Similarly in II Cor. iv. 2, 'commending ourselves to all men's *suneidesis*' may in fact mean only 'showing ourselves respectable to all men's knowledge', *sun-* being of the weakened branch; but it can easily be taken to mean 'behaving in a way which everyone's moral judgement will approve'.

Whether the word is already taking on a new meaning in the New Testament or whether a new meaning, arising from different causes, led to a misreading of these passages and was then, by that very misreading, greatly strengthened, the change was certainly effected and the new sense remains current today. To trace it through the earlier Christian centuries would be beyond my learning and beyond our present needs.

In its new sense *conscience* is the inner lawgiver: a man's judgement of good and evil. It speaks in the imperative, commanding and forbidding. But, as so often, the new sense does not replace the old. The old lives on and the new is added to it, so that *conscience* now has more than one meaning.

Theologians and scholars are aware of this and draw the necessary distinctions. Aquinas, who claims to be conforming to the 'common use of language', says that *conscientia* is an application of our knowledge to our own acts, and that this application occurs in three ways. (1) We judge that we have done this or that. (2) We judge that something ought, or ought not to be done. (3) We judge that our past act was good or bad. The first is *conscire* in the classical sense. The second, which really includes the third (*synteresis* or *synderesis*) is something quite different; something which will be named, according to the system we employ, practical reason, moral sense, reflection, the Categorical Imperative, or the super-ego. *Conscientia* in this second sense can be said to 'bind' and 'impel' (*instigare*), and can of course be obeyed or disobeyed.[1] Our own Burton follows Aquinas in substance, but will not stretch the word *conscience* to cover synteresis. For him there are: (1) synteresis, which is knowledge of good and evil; (2) a *dictamen rationis*, a precept or injunction of reason which 'admonishes' to do the one and

[1] *S.T.* I[a], LXIX, art. 13.

forbear from the other; (3) the *conscience* which then justifies or condemns what we have done.[1] Jeremy Taylor makes the semantic situation unusually clear by noting the ancient meaning of *conscientia*—Horace's *conscire sibi*—and saying that while this is correct so far as it goes it is not 'full and adequate; for it only signifies conscience as it is a witness, not as a guide'. Under the name *conscience* we must also include 'that which is called *synteresis*, or the general repository of moral principles'.[2]

If popular language had followed these distinctions, much confusion, and perhaps not a little bloodshed, would have been avoided. But that is not the way of common language. It would have nothing to do with the word *synteresis* though it was ready to talk abundantly about the thing. It therefore used the single word *conscience*, sometimes to mean the consciring of what we have done, sometimes the Inner Lawgiver who tells us what we should or should not do, sometimes the inner nagger or prompter that urges us to obey the Lawgiver here and now, and sometimes other things as well. All the senses work upon, and in and out through, one another, and often, no doubt, men did not know themselves, much less make clear to others, exactly what they meant. There are, it is true, passages where we find *synderesis* in more or less popular texts. Deguileville in his *Pilgrimage of the Life of Man* defines it as the higher part of reason whereby a man can learn how to govern his conscience.[3] This is intelligible

---

[1] Pt. 1, Sec. 1, Mem. 2, Subs. 10.
[2] *Ductor Dubitantium* 1, i, 1, para. 24. *Works*, ed. Heber, vol. XI, p. 382.　　　　　　　　　[3] Lydgate's version, 4963–8.

but would not much help a reader who had never met the word before. In the *Assembly of Gods* (ll. 932–8) we learn no more, and perhaps the poet knew no more, than that synderesis and conscience are somehow connected. Nothing was likely to come of either passage. The word had no future and does not occur in Johnson's Dictionary. Todd's supplemented edition of Johnson (1818) gives it with an erroneous definition and quotes only one example.

Conscience is thus left with a maze—or, better, a simmering pot—of meanings which we must now try to investigate.

VII. SURVIVAL OF THE SENSE 'CONSCIRING'

This continues to flourish unimpaired to the present day. We can still have a 'guilty conscience', that is a consciring of guilt; for it is certainly not the inner lawgiver who is guilty. Thus we find a 'coumbred conscience';[1] 'clearness of conscience';[2] a 'grieved conscience'.[3] The Prayer Book urges us to 'examine our own consciences' and suggests confession for any who cannot 'quiet his own conscience'. *Conscience* is still the witness, though with added reference to the judge-before-whom, when Taylor says it 'doth excuse or accuse a man before God'.[4] A slight and not unnatural confusion is perhaps creeping in when Cranmer talks of feeling 'our conscience at peace with God'.[5] Why is it our *conscience* (whether as witness or lawgiver) rather than we who are at peace? Here, as throughout, we

[1] More, *Dialogue of Comfort*, I, xviii.
[2] Roper, *Life of More*. [3] Spenser, *F.Q.* I, x, 23.
[4] *Op. cit.* p. 376. [5] *Homily, Rogation Week*, Pt 3.

must remember the intense emotional pressure of the experience the words refer to; in this circumambient emotion the separate semantic rights, so to speak, of the culprit soul and the witness get confused.

VIII. THE LAWGIVER

We have seen that already for Menander *suneidesis* was *theos*. When synteresis (whether distinguished in name from *conscience* or not) is being thought about within a Christian frame of reference, the tendency to regard it as a separate, and special, and specially divine, faculty in man, will be increased. For the inner lawgiver must now be conceived either as God himself or as his specially appointed lieutenant in the soul. Who else could claim such legislative rights? 'Conscience (*suneidesis*) is God', says Tatian. 'It is the whiteness of eternal light, the spotless mirror of God's majesty and the image of his goodness', says St Bernard; 'the corrector and *paedagogus* of the soul', says Origen; God 'rules in us by his substitute, our conscience', says Taylor, from whom I take these quotations.[1] So in Milton, where God says 'I will place within them as a guide My umpire conscience'.[2] 'I feel not this deity in my bosom', says the conscienceless Antonio, scoffing, but none the less showing how those who did not scoff regarded the matter.[3] Even hardier— for he spoke not 'rapt above the Pole' but standing on the floor of an Elizabethan House of Commons—are the words of Edward Aglionby: 'the conscience of man is

[1] *Op. cit.* pp. 369, 370, 376.   [2] *P.L.* III, 194–5.
[3] *Tempest* II, i, 278.

eternal, invisible, and not in the power of the greatest monarchy in the world in any limits to be straitened, in any bounds to be constrained'.[1] Less exalted in language but, well weighed, no narrower in its claim, is Butler's assertion that 'Conscience does not only offer itself to show us the way we should walk in, but it likewise carries its own authority with it that it is our natural guide; the guide assigned to us by the Author of our nature'.[2]

Expressions of this sort are not, I think, to be found in the New Testament. They neither arise from it nor lead back to it. The claims made for *conscience* as something beyond 'the power of the greatest monarchy in the world' because it was God's vicegerent will be repeated in later times by 'conscientious objectors' of all kinds; including those who claimed (in my opinion rightly) freedom to obey their conscience by maintaining that God does not exist.

One whimsical result of making *conscience* a name for synteresis is that the adjective 'good' when applied to it may now have a quite new sense. Immemorially—and still in the commonest usage—a 'good conscience', Seneca's *bona conscientia*—means a good consciring, that is, a consciring of good or, more usually, a consciring of no evil. This is what it means in the Prayer Book when the compilers claim that it 'doth not contain any thing which a godly man may not with a good conscience use' —anything which he would conscire to himself that he had sinned in using. But it means something totally

[1] See S. T. Bindoff, *Tudor England*, ch. VII.
[2] *Sermons upon Human Nature* III, 6.

different when Hall (1649) says 'A good conscience will tell you...you are bound to make restitution';[1] if your synteresis or inner lawgiver is a good or sound one—if it is functioning properly—it will tell you this. The ambiguity is prettily seized by George MacDonald: 'she was sorely troubled with what is, by huge discourtesy, called a bad conscience—being in reality a conscience doing its duty so well that it makes the whole house uncomfortable'.[2]

IX. DIVERSITY OF CONSCIENCES

I must here, for a moment, adopt what I know to be a false simplicity.

The more boldly men claim that *conscience* is, directly or vicariously, a divine lawgiver and the 'spotless mirror of God's majesty', the more troublesomely aware they must become that this lawgiver gives different laws to different men; this mirror reflects different faces. Hence we have *consciences* in the plural, not meaning those different conscirings which different men must obviously have but those different inner laws they acknowledge. Thus Whitgift writes that such an alteration of the Church as the Puritans demand would cause 'offence to many consciences'[3]—many men have a *synteresis* which will forbid them to accept it. Butler complains that the Presbyterians force all people to become 'Saints', though 'against their consciences'.[4] The preface to the Prayer Book mentions 'such alterations...as should be thought

---

[1] *Cases of Conscience* I, ii, 24.   [2] *Sir Gibbie*, ch. 37.
[3] *Apud* J. B. Black, *Reign of Elizabeth* (1936), p. 161.
[4] *Hudibras* I, iii, 1141–2.

requisite for the ease of tender consciences', for some men have a synteresis so 'tender', so sensitive, that it forbids what others with a less exacting inner lawgiver would feel free to do. Hence, inconveniently, almost any man can claim exemption from the laws of the state on the ground that his own peculiar synteresis (is it not a far higher law?) forbids him to obey them, so that 'nothing is more usual than to pretend conscience to all the actions of man which are public'.[1] *Pretend* does not mean 'simulate', but 'put forward' or 'plead'. On Taylor's view such men are right in obeying their synteresis even when their synteresis itself is wrong; for it is man's lawful sovereign and in such cases 'the king is misinformed, but the inferiors are bound to obey'.[2]

Hence arise the conceptions of 'forcing' or 'freedom' of consciences. Thus in *Hudibras* (I, i, 765) 'Liberty of consciences'. Thus Robinson Crusoe, shortly before his departure from the island, finds himself absolute sovereign over a Protestant, a Pagan, and a Papist, but adds 'I allowed liberty of conscience throughout my dominions'. Everyone will remember Milton's 'New Forcers of Conscience' in the sonnet. Language does not always make quite clear whether the liberty in question is that of having a certain synteresis, or of endeavouring by persuasion to make the synteresis of other men more like your own, or of obeying your own synteresis in overt action, or all three.

But this, as I have warned the reader, is an over-simplification.

[1] Taylor, *op. cit.* p. 410.   [2] *Ibid.* p. 411.

X. PRECARIOUSNESS OF THE SENSE 'LAWGIVER'

The over-simplification lies in the attempt to isolate the inner lawgiver from the intellectual context in which he speaks. No lawgiver, inner or outer, gives laws in a vacuum; he always has real or supposed facts in mind, an idea of what is, which influences his rulings about what ought to be. Thus the outer lawgiver ceases to make new statutes against witchcraft when he ceases to believe in it, and does not make vaccination compulsory till he thinks it will prevent smallpox. It is the same with the inner lawgiver. If you believe in the Christian God, synteresis will lay upon you many duties towards him, and if you disbelieve, it will not. If you believe in transubstantiation it will tell you to risk Tyburn by attending Mass, and if you believe the Mass to be idolatry it will tell you to risk Smithfield by abstaining from it. It is indeed extremely difficult to find a *pure* difference of synteresis, one that does not flow from different beliefs about matter of fact. Perhaps the belief that it is in any possible circumstances wrong to kill a man, or that non-Aryans have no rights against the *Herrenvolk*, or that justice is the will of the people, might rank as 'pure'. But for the most part the imperatives of the lawgiving synteresis are conditioned by the indicatives of each man's belief or 'convictions'. The two together make up what would now perhaps be called an 'ideology'.

Philosophers and theologians, no doubt, will usually draw the distinction and will see that the high claims which can plausibly be made for the imperatives cannot

with equal plausibility be made for the indicatives. 'Since
you think A, do B' might conceivably be a 'divine' voice.
But the opinion that A is true—which may involve
answers to all sorts of problems in ecclesiastical history,
Greek and Hebrew scholarship, textual criticism, the
nature of authority, international law, or the interpretation of Karl Marx—is clearly in a different position.
Ordinary language, however, makes no distinctions. In
it, your reasons for thinking the Mass holy or idolatrous
and your consequent duty to go, or not to go, to it are
both equally *conscience*. Side by side with this confusion,
we have (I think) a faint influence from the Middle
English usage mentioned above in section II—*conscience*
as 'mind' or 'thought'. As a result, we shall find the
word sliding from the full sense of synteresis into that of
profound conviction about truth and thence into that of
mere opinion (about comparatively trivial matters), yet
often carrying with it overtones from the idea of consciring. That is why I spoke about a simmering pot of
meanings; any ingredient may be flavoured by any other.

XI. MIXED USAGES

We should all agree it was for *conscience*' sake that Sir
Thomas More refused to take the Oath of Supremacy.
But in how many different senses? Urged by the Lord
Chancellor to observe that all the bishops, universities,
and scholars in England had agreed to the Act, More
replied that he did not see 'why that thing in my con-
science should make any change', for by going outside
England and back into the past he could find a greater

weight of authority on his side; 'therefore I am not bound, my lord, to conform my conscience to the council of one realm against the general council of Christendom'.[1] Here neither the Chancellor's claim nor More's answer has any bearing on the law given by synteresis that you must not swear what is false. The question at issue is whether the thing he is asked to swear to is false or not. If More had been an obscure private person, not called upon to swear but merely forming an opinion on Henry's supremacy, the formation of that opinion would hardly have been a matter of *conscience* in the sense of synteresis. When he says that the decision of the English authorities will not alter his *conscience*, does he mean 'will not alter my conception of my duty' or 'will not alter my view' (on which, of course, the duty is based)? Probably both, but language does not of itself make this plain.

In this passage the indicative (Henry is not the head of the Church in England) and the imperative (Thou shalt not forswear thyself) are so closely linked both in logic and in emotion that the double meaning is almost inevitable. We come a little further when More, earlier in the same book, says it was not likely he would disclose to the government Tool (Mr Rich) 'the secrets of my conscience touching the King's Supremacy'. I think this means principally 'my private opinion', perhaps with some notion of consciring—'the opinion to which I alone am privy'. Another passage from Roper carries us further still. The Chancellor asks Lord Fitzjames whether the indictment against More is 'sufficient' and gets the cautious

[1] Roper, *Life of More*.

reply 'If the act of parliament be not unlawful, then is the indictment in my conscience not insufficient'. Fitzjames is giving a judge's reply; *conscience* must mean 'opinion'.

But I would not say it means *simply* 'opinion'. The word has not completely lost touch either with the sense 'synteresis' nor with the sense 'consciring'. This will perhaps become clearer if we add two other examples. Pepys writes, 'The Duke did, to my Lord's dishonour, often say that he did in his conscience know the contrary to what he then said' (in a dispute about a game of cards).[1] The disguised King in *Henry V* says 'By my troth, I will speak my conscience of the King' (IV, i, 119). In these, as in Fitzjames's reply, *conscience* does indeed mean 'what I think' (or, in Pepys, 'know'). But to get the exact shade of meaning I believe we should translate it 'what I really think', or 'my honest opinion', or (in Pepys) 'he really knew very well'. That is how this usage is still flavoured by the other meanings of *conscience*. In all three examples we may infer some motive for evading or lying. If, despite this, you say what you really think or know, you are (*a*) uttering your *conscience* in the Middle English sense, declaring your actual mind; (*b*) obeying your *conscience* (synteresis) one of whose laws is 'Tell the truth'; (*c*) revealing what you conscire to yourself as your secret opinion or knowledge. In the Pepysian passage there may lurk also the idea that my Lord will, after lying, have an unpleasant consciring (*mala conscientia*) of the fact.

The word may seem to have lost all trace of an ethical meaning when, as Taylor says, 'some men suspect their

[1] *Diary*, 7 February 1660–61.

brother of a crime and are persuaded, as they say, in conscience that he did it'.[1] But even here there is probably some muddy-minded assertion that the suspicion is sincerely held and was honestly come by; combined, no doubt, with a monstrous, though only half-conscious, attempt to dignify it by all the lofty associations which the word *conscience* derives from the meaning 'synteresis'.

XII. CONSCIENCE AS FEAR

Even in ancient times, as we have seen, a 'bad conscience', that is, the consciring evil deeds to oneself, was associated with fear; fear of possible detection and punishment by men, or of punishment by the gods whose detection was certain. The Christian doctrine of certain judgement and (highly probable) damnation naturally linked *conscience* and fear even more tightly together. From the consciring 'I have sinned' to the fear 'I may be damned' the transition became instantaneous and invariable, so that it was not felt to be a transition at all. When this process is complete, the word *conscience* itself may come to mean simply 'fear of hell'.

The process has not gone so far in Milton when Adam says 'O conscience, into what abyss of fears And horrors hast thou driven me!'[2] *Conscience* is still the driver into that abyss, not the abyss itself. A slightly further stage has been reached in Book IV (ll. 23 f.) where *conscience* 'wakes' in Satan, not the memory of guilt, but 'despair', the 'memory' of past bliss, present misery, and greater misery to be expected in the future. *Conscience* here is

[1] *Op. cit.* p. 410.   [2] *P.L.* x, 842–3.

'of' punishment, not of sin. So in Taylor 'conscience is present with a message from God and the men feel inward causes of fear'.[1] In Bunyan's *Holy War* it is Mr Conscience who explains that Emanuel's last messenger 'was a messenger of death'. Similarly in Johnson, 'he that feels himself alarmed by his conscience',[2] the fact that *conscience*, strictly speaking, testifies and thus is the occasion rather than the source of the alarm, disappears.

But some usages go beyond this. Latimer says 'when with the eye of his conscience...he beheld the horror of death and hell'.[3] Punishment has completely replaced sin as the object or content of *conscience*. Taylor, here again, is instructive. He says that, on 'viewing' the legislation of synteresis, *conscience* 'binds to duty', but on viewing 'the act' (our own past act) 'it binds to punishment or consigns to comfort'.[4] Surely he unwittingly uses the verb *bind* in two quite different senses, of which the first (obliging) is clearly proper to the inner lawgiver but the second (condemning to) is not, or not in the same way; it is an executive act and, if a command at all, a command to the hangman not the culprit. And indeed *bind* in this sense is barely English. I suspect that Taylor is trying to find room for 'fear of punishment' as one of the senses of *conscience* without admitting to himself that it has, historically, very little claim to that position and may even be regarded as a semantic degradation. The furthest stage of all is reached by Henry More—the last author in whom I expected to find it—who embodies this sense in a

[1] *Op. cit.* p. 371.   [2] *Rambler*, 110.
[3] Seventh Sermon before Edward VI.   [4] *Op. cit.* p. 390.

definition: 'And first, of natural conscience, it is plain that it is a fear and confusion of mind arising from the presage of some mischief that may befall a man beside the ordinary course of Nature or the usuall occurrences or affairs because he hath done thus or thus.' To be sure, it is only 'natural' *conscience*, pagan conscience, that he is defining. But he is ignoring the element of synteresis, the judgement of good and evil, even in it. His conscience would cover the merely prudential avoidance of 'un-lucky' actions (*Antidote*, I, 10).

I feel almost certain that we here have the clue to Hamlet's use of *conscience* at the end of the famous soliloquy (III, i, 83), where I believe it means nothing more or less than 'fear of Hell'. I see that a case can be made for taking it to mean 'reflection, thought'—an instance of the Middle English sense, belonging to the weakened branch. And this is even supported by the 'pale cast of thought' two lines later. But when we remember the passages already quoted from *Richard III* ('conscience...makes a man a coward', 'O coward conscience'); and the close linking, which finally leads to the actual identification, of *conscience* with fear of punish-ment; and the fact that fears of 'what dreams may come' and 'ills we know not of' are the very reflections which have 'sicklied o'er' the native hue of Hamlet's resolution; I think we must interpret the passage otherwise. In Latimer and Henry More we see the consciring of sin confused or equated with the fear of future suffering. Hamlet goes a step further. He says nothing at all about sins to be conscired; he fears future suffering, and he calls

that fear *conscience*. It must of course be remembered that
sins to be conscired, in every man, would be taken for
granted. When once fear of the next world had been
mentioned they would be understood.

XIII. RAMIFICATIONS OF THE SENSE 'SYNTERESIS'

'I will make a Star Chamber matter of it', says Shallow.[1]
You may or may not bring Falstaff's poaching before
that tribunal; similarly, a man may or may not bring this
or that of his actions before the inner tribunal of *conscience*;
for most people think that at least some choices—say,
having a boiled or a buttered egg—are 'morally indif-
ferent' and do not fall under *conscience*' jurisdiction.
When we bring an act before the tribunal we make it a
'matter' (or 'case') of *conscience* just as Shallow would
make poaching a Star Chamber 'matter'. Thus Burton
says of religious melancholics, 'I see them make matters
of conscience of such toys and trifles'.[2] 'Some think it a
great matter of conscience to depart from a piece of the
least of their ceremonies', says the Prayer Book (*Of
Ceremonies*). In these cases it is scrupulosity that burdens
the court of *conscience* with unnecessary business. But
moral laxity, eager for loopholes and hence fruitful in fine
distinctions, may do the same; 'when men have no love
to God, and desire but just to save their souls, and weigh
grains and scruples, and give to God no more than they
must needs, they shall multiply cases of conscience to a
number which no books will contain'.[3]

---

[1] *M.W.W.* I, i, I.   [2] Pt 3, sec. 4, memb. I, subs. 3.
[3] Taylor, *op. cit.* p. 366.

Very often, where the thought to be expressed is exactly the same, the words 'matter of' or 'case of' are omitted, so that Burton can write 'we make a conscience of every toy';[1] or in Bunyan's *Mr Badman* we read 'a family where the governors...made conscience of the worship and service of God' (thought it their duty to have family prayers). So Taylor: 'He is a good man, and makes conscience of his ways'[2]—brings before the inner tribunal all that should be brought.

Some more difficult usages remain. 'My conscience will serve me to run away from this Jew my master', says Gobbo.[3] *Conscience* here means, I think, not the faculty but the content of *synteresis*, not the lawgiver but the law he gives. There is nothing (or nothing that can't be got round) in Gobbo's internal Statute Book which rules out running away. To be sure, the rest of his soliloquy shows this claim to be far from true, but we are concerned with its meaning. Something of the same process possibly accounts for Hamlet's 'Is't not perfect conscience To quit with this arm?' (v, ii, 67). As we say 'it's the law', meaning 'it is what the law permits (or enjoins)', Hamlet describes, perhaps, as 'perfect conscience' what any sound synteresis would approve. Along the same line we may reach Iago's generalisation about the ladies of Venice, that 'their best conscience Is not to leave't undone, but keep't unknown'.[4] This might mean that the only (and therefore the best) precept contained in their synteresis is 'Thou shalt not be found out'.

---

[1] Pt 3, sec. 4, memb. 1, subs. 4.   [2] *Op. cit.* p. 372.
[3] *Merchant* II, ii, 1.   [4] *Othello* III, iii, 204.

All such semantic bridges are, however, conjectural, and it is most improbable that the authors I quote could have enlightened us on the semantic history of their own expressions.

The words of the money-lender in Wilson's *Usury* give rise to more than one problem. 'It may bee', he says, 'there is some shifte to save a man's conscience wyth all'.[1] If *save* means 'salve',[2] 'heal', or 'soothe', *conscience* will here be principally consciring; the usurer wants something which will silence the internal witness and make him feel comfortable. But he may speak of 'saving' his synteresis —as one 'saves' one's credit or 'face'—in the sense of enabling it without disgrace, without loss of all its high pretensions, to issue more lenient laws.

XIV. RETURN TO THE WEAKENED BRANCH

We have already observed that English *conscious* retained even to the nineteenth century the together sense and was therefore a synonym for Latin *conscius*. But a weakened sense was growing up at the same time. The noun *consciousness* had a similar history, for though it was formed later than *conscience* it was not formed in order to express a new meaning, but was at first a useless synonym.

[1] *Discourse upon Usury*, ed. R. H. Tawney (1925), p. 234.
[2] *Save* and *salve*, and even *solve*, may replace one another rather oddly. Milton reproduces the Greek scientific canon *sozein ta phainomena* (to preserve, 'get in', do justice to, all the observed phenomena in any hypothesis you frame) correctly as 'to save appearances' (*P.L.* VIII, 82: cf. 'to save the phenomenon', *Doctrine and Discipline* I, i, *Prose Wks.* ed. Bohn, vol. III, p. 186). But Burton has 'to salve all appearances' (Pt 3, sec. 4, memb. 1, subs. 3) and even 'to solve all appearances' (Pt 2, sec. 2, memb. 3).

The gradations between the original (together) sense of both words and that which both now bear are very fine. The extremes are clear. When they are used absolutely ('the patient is conscious', 'the injection removed all consciousness') the modern—and dangerous—sense is fully present. When either is followed by *to* the drift towards the *dangerous sense* (so far as concerns that author and that context) has not yet begun; thus the *N.E.D.* quotes from a seventeenth-century author 'their consciousness to themselves of their ignorance', and, more strikingly, from Berkeley 'God is conscious to our innermost thoughts' (*Principles*). Here the idea of consciring is obviously at work. In between these two extremes come the doubtful cases.

Of large and irregular assemblies Hobbes says 'he that cannot render a particular and good account of his being amongst them is to be judged conscious of an unlawfull and tumultuous designe'.[1] This is almost certainly the together sense; if *conscious of* meant merely 'aware of' it would imply no complicity; a government spy might be so aware. When Locke says 'To be happy or miserable without being conscious of it seems...impossible'[2] the *dangerous sense* ('aware') is almost full-blown. Almost, but perhaps not quite. Locke may be saying something more than that an un-felt misery is not a misery. What that something more could be is apparent from Clarke's definition, 'Consciousness in the most strict and exact sense of the word signifies...the Reflex act by which I know that I think and that my thoughts ... are my own

[1] *Leviathan*, Pt 2, XXII, *ad fin.*   [2] *Essay*, II, i, II.

and not another's'.[1] *Consciousness* is here something very like the medieval common sense, something distinguishable from mere sentience,[2] and something whose absence would be not quite identical with what most speakers today call 'unconsciousness'. There would still be a slight together sense—myself consciring my thoughts as mine. But notice that Clarke has to qualify this as 'the most strict and exact sense'; a looser, and more weakened, sense was presumably current. I think Locke is using it, if not in the passage I have quoted yet in the very next paragraph, when he says the soul 'must necessarily be conscious of its own perceptions'.

I am very puzzled as to what Pope meant when he wrote

> The forests wondered at th'unusual grain
> And secret transport touch'd the conscious swain.[3]

If *conscious* here bears the *dangerous sense*, one wonders why we need be told that the swain who felt transport was neither fainting, asleep nor anaesthetised. If it means 'consciring', what was this mystery to which he was privy? Why, if it comes to that, was his transport so 'secret'? What 'touched' him was the sight of 'yellow harvests', approved by 'monarchs'. Or is it, as the following lines perhaps suggest, that the swain was in a secret because, in all this, he saw—and monarchs did not—'fair Liberty' beginning to rear 'her cheerful head'? We are on firmer ground when Cowper speaks of having

[1] *Second Defence* (1707).
[2] Even now this distinction can sometimes be made and can use the words *consciousness* and *sentience*; but only in learned works.
[3] *Windsor Forest*, 90.

'borne the ruffling wind, scarce conscious that it blew'.[1]
This is the weakened sense, though not yet in its absolute
use.

While these senses obviously belong to the weakened
branch, there is no evidence so far as I know that they
descend from that language in which the weakened
branch flourished without rival; in other words that they
were influenced by French. They are an independent
effort of our own language to provide itself with necessary tools of thought.

[1] *Task* 1, 156.

9

WORLD

IN the earliest recorded period of our language this noun has two senses which we may call *World A* and *World B*.

(*A*.) In Alfred's version of Boethius we read that children die and the parents 'mourn for it all their *woruld*'.[1] This clearly means 'all their life'. But to cover all the shades of the *A*-sense we had better say that *World A* means something like age or *durée*. In Ælfric's homily on the Assumption of St John we find[2] 'through endless *worulda*' (plural), through ages without end. In Alfred again[3] 'will stand to *worulda*', will last forever. The *A*-sense long survived the Anglo-Saxon period. In the thirteenth-century *Sawles Warde* comes 'praise thee from worlde into worlde',[4] from age to age, representing *in saecula saeculorum*. By an unusual archaism, the *A*-sense is preserved in the Prayer Book, where it probably mystifies many church-goers. 'World without end' means 'age without end', forever. As a boy I thought that 'before all worlds' in the Nicene Creed meant 'before any of the planets'. It really means 'before all ages', outside time, *ab aeterno*.

[1] Ed. Sedgefield (1899), p. 24, l. 14.
[2] Sweet, *Reader* (1922), p. 72, l. 322.
[3] Sedgefield, *op. cit.* p. 48, l. 30.
[4] Ed. R. M. Wilson (1938), p. 36, l. 344 (Royal MS).

(*B.*) The *B*-sense is that which the word most naturally suggests to a modern speaker. The poet who did the Metres of Boethius into Anglo-Saxon writes 'in those days there were no great houses in the *weorulde*'.[1] Here we could translate it 'earth'. But whenever the distinction between the earth and the universe is present to the mind, *World B* can mean either, and the context usually shows which. Thus Gower writes

> Tofore the creacion
> Of eny worldes stacion,
> Of hevene, of erthe, or eke of helle   (VII, 203)

—'before the creation of any place in the universe, e.g. of heaven, earth or hell'. *World B* may loosely be defined as the region that contains all regions; if all absolutely, then it means universe; if 'all that usually concern us humans', then it means earth.

Since *World A* is something in time and *World B* something in space, it is not at once easy to see the semantic trunk out of which two such different branches have grown. But the very form of the word provides a probable clue. *Worold*, like its Old Norse equivalent *veroldr*, appears to be built out of two elements. The first is *wer* (a man), related to Latin *vir* and Irish *fir*, and fossilised in *wer-wolf*, the man-wolf. The second is something like *ald*, age or period. But what would 'man-age' mean? Something, I believe, which all our attempts at translation will make too precise. The generations of men? Human history? The common lot of men, the sort

[1] Metr. 8, l. 8 (Sedgefield, *Boethius*, p. 160).

of life they have? Anyway, 'all this' in which we find ourselves embedded. Perhaps 'human life' will serve us best.

Now when we turn from considering words in isolation
and look at them in concrete sentences, we discover that
'human life' is not nearly so distinguishable from *World B*
(the region of regions) as we had supposed. In *Beowulf*
'parting from *worulde*' (3068) means death; to enjoy or
share in or have *worolde* (1061-2) means to be alive; 'they
woke into *worold*' (60) means 'they were born'. Whether
we translate *woruld* by 'human life' or 'earth' or 'universe', we shall make equally good sense, and very nearly
the same sense, of all three. And good reason why. To be
alive and to be in the region of regions are the same thing;
we seem to enter both when we are born and perhaps
leave both simultaneously when we die. Sense *A* and
Sense *B* were not before the poet's mind as alternatives at
all; just as, if we say 'He left the College in 1930', we do
not always know whether we mean primarily that he re-
linquished his status as a member of it or that he moved his
belongings out of his rooms and went away by a taxi.
Here, as not seldom, we begin by thinking that we have
met a semantic chasm which has to be bridged and then
discover that we were digging the chasm.

A glance at Old Norse will here prove helpful. Besides
veroldr (their form of *world*) the Norsemen had the word
heimr. This sometimes means no more than a limited
region or 'land'. *Jotunheimar* are the giant-lands. But it
certainly also came to mean the region of regions. In the
Prose Edda (49) the death-goddess says that Balder may
return from the dead if he is wept for by all things *i hei-*

minum. Here both the tenor of the story and the form *heiminum* (which contains the definite article) make it certain that we must translate it 'all things in the World' (Sense *B*). And *heimr* clearly has the same meaning when Snovri begins his great saga with the word that has become its title: *heimskring'a*, the 'world-disc'. Here, then, we have the linguistic outfit for a clear and fixed distinction. If the Norsemen had chosen, they could have kept *veroldr* for *World A* and *heimr* for *World B*. In fact, however, the two words can become almost synonyms. In *Volsungasaga* (XIX) we read 'as long as the *veroldr* stands' (or 'lasts'); and in XXX, ii 'while the *heimr* stands' (or 'lasts'). Both mean the same and, save by a difficult abstraction, must inevitably do so; for both refer to the same event. Ragnarök will put an end to 'human life' as we know it and to this universe simultaneously. The same catastrophe will end the play and destroy the theatre.

II. 'WORLD A' AS STATE OR PERIOD

A man's *woruld*, as we have seen, can be his life. And *worulda* in the plural can be ages. By keeping these two shades of meaning together in our minds we shall best understand the sense I now have to investigate.

A man's 'life' can be considered in three ways. First, simply as his being alive; e.g. 'this will cost you your life'. Secondly, as a subject of moral approval in the reverse; 'what sort of life has he led?' means, pretty well, 'how has he behaved?' Thirdly, 'what sort of life has he had?' will mean 'what were his circumstances, his fortunes?' It is the third way that here concerns us.

Again, an age (or epoch, or period) can be considered in two ways. It can be a tract of time distinguished solely by position; as it would be if we said 'the period between his accession and the Transylvanian campaign is not well documented'. But also, and much more often, it can come before the mind as a tract of time with a character of its own; a period qualitatively, as well as positionally, distinguished from others. This is what happens when we speak of the Stone Age, the Middle Ages, or the Age of Enlightenment.

Now 'life', taken not as the life 'led' but as the life 'had', so that it is almost synonymous with lot or future, and 'age' or 'epoch', taken qualitatively, blend to give *world* the sense I am talking of. It may be defined either as 'A condition or State of Affairs (which lasted for a certain period)' or as 'A period (during which there was a certain State of Affairs)'. The difference is one of emphasis. Sometimes the qualitative, sometimes the chronological, aspect is uppermost.

In the following examples the emphasis is on the qualitative. We are told that when the rebel angels were hurled into Hell, 'their *worold* was changed'; their 'case was altered'.[1] In *Beowulf* we read of a man so fortunate that 'for him all *woruld* turns out agreeably' (1738-9). The state of his affairs is exactly as he would wish. In Alfred's version Wisdom asks Boethius 'was all your *woruld* ever to your pleasure?'[2]—were 'things' ever exactly as you liked? Centuries later Thomas More[3] after

[1] *Genesis*, 318.   [2] Sedgefield, *Boethius*, p. 58, l. 28.
[3] *Apologye*, ed. A. I. Taft (1930), E.E.T.S. p. 78.

painting a picture of hypothetically total corruption concludes, 'But that worlde is not I thanke god in Englande yet'. The lover in Gower says that once 'mi world stod on an other whiel'.[1]

When *world* in this sense is accompanied, as in the last example, by a personal pronoun, it is hardly at all distinguishable from 'future' or 'interests'. Thus Gower elsewhere[2] says that nowadays every clerk is determined to 'kepe his world'; almost to keep his 'position'. Twice[3] he speaks of someone achieving 'his goode world'; getting what he wants. To the same class belongs the Wife of Bath's gratitude 'that I have had my world as in my tyme';[4] something like 'I've had my good times in my day'.

Wolsey in Cavendish's *Life* prays Mr Kingston 'to have me most humbly recommended unto his Royall majestie, beseeching him in my behalf to call to his most gracious remembraunce all matters proceeding bytween him and me from the beginning of the world unto this day'.[5] Here 'the world' may be a mistake for 'this world'; but, either way, the *world* referred to is the association between Wolsey and the King, the State of Affairs which is now so lamentably ending.

Some doubt may be felt about Marvell's 'Had we but world enough, and time'.[6] Since he goes on to speak of Ganges and Humber, we might at first suppose that he means *World B*, that he is saying 'If the region of regions

[1] I, 178.
[2] *Prol.* 383–4.
[3] I, 1257; VII, 2521.
[4] D. 473.
[5] Ed. R. S. Sylvester (1959), E.E.T.S. p. 179, l. 8.
[6] 'To his coy mistress.'

were large enough'. But, on a closer view, he does not seem to be complaining that the two rivers are insufficiently far apart or that there are too few places in which the lovers could wander separately. The implied complaint is that they lack opportunity to utilise them. I should paraphrase the first line as 'if our circumstances and our time were less restricted'. This is *World*-as-Condition almost at its vaguest.

For examples of *World* with the more chronological emphasis we may turn once more to Gower. The golden head of the image in Nebuchadnezzar's dream symbolises

> A worthi world, a noble, a riche
> To which non after schal be liche[1]

—in other words, the Golden Age. He also speaks[2] of comparing 'these olde worldes with the newe', comparing former ages, former States of Affairs, with one's own. The banished duke and his followers in Arden 'fleet the time carelessly, as they did in the golden world',[3] the *bell'età de l'oro*. The virtues of the same 'antique world' live again in Adam.[4] John Holland, Jack Cade's follower, says 'It was never merry world in England since gentlemen came up',[5] and his companion echoes the sentiment with 'O miserable age'. 'Your father', says Johnson, 'is a judge in a remote part of the island, and all his notions are taken from the old world'.[6] Scott speaks of 'an auld-world party who made themselves happy in the auld fashion'.[7]

[1] *Prol.* 633.
[2] VII, 2702.
[3] *A.Y.L.I.* I, i, 126–7.
[4] *Ibid.* II, iii, 57.
[5] *Hen. VI*, Pt 2, IV, ii, 10–11.
[6] Boswell, 14 July 1763.
[7] Journal, 20 January 1826.

I am not sure how to classify the place in *Huon*[1] where Lord Berners says of an army 'the noise and bruit that they made seemed to be a new world'. It can hardly mean that the noise was like a new *heimr* or universe. More probably 'it was like nothing on earth' and thus was a wholly new State of Affairs. But we must remember that colloquial hyperbole reduces words to the vaguest semantic status.

III. 'WORLD A' AS THE COMMON LOT OR 'THINGS'

'Alas,' says Alfred, 'in how bottomless a pit the mind lies suffering when the mutabilities of this *worulde* beset it!'[2] He does not mean the mutabilities of *World B*, such as changes of climate or landslides. These would be only one instance, and rather a rare instance, of the changeableness he has in view. Nor does he use 'this *woruld*' to mean 'this (i.e. the present) period or state of affairs'. On the contrary the mutability he complains of consists in the very fact that neither 'this' period nor any other is permanent. It would be truer to say that 'this *woruld*' means 'human life' or 'life'. We have already seen that *woruld* can be so translated when *Beowulf* says 'they woke into *woruld*', meaning 'they were born'. But Alfred's use, closely considered, is not exactly the same. In our Beowulfian examples *woruld* meant by 'human life' simply the being alive; the biological fact and, as bound up with this, one's presence in *World B*, the region of regions.

---

[1] *Huon of Bordeuxe*, ed. S. L. Lee, E.E.T.S. vol. II (1883), p. 498.
[2] Sedgefield, *Boethius*, p. 9, l. 11.

Alfred's 'this *woruld*' emphasises the qualitative aspect—what it is like to be a man, the sort of things that happen to you while you are alive. The characteristic of *woruld* in this sense is that it constantly changes men's *worulda*, their states of affairs. Another way of putting it would be that, just as *World B* is the Region which includes all other regions, so *World A* in the sense we are now considering is the State of Affairs which includes all other states of affairs; the over-all human situation, hence the common lot, the way things go. *Things* or *Life* would often translate it.

Thus (again from Alfred), 'You thought fate ordered this *woruld*'[1]—'arranged things' would mean the same. Chaucer's Egeus 'knew this worldes transmutacioun';[2] knew the ups and downs of things. As a result he had concluded that 'this world'—he could equally have said 'this life' or simply 'life'—'nys but a thurghfare ful of wo'.[3]

We read a still vaguer reference when we read in *Piers Plowman* of 'the mene and the riche worching and wondring as the world asketh',[4] or in *Gawain*[5] how 'wynter wyndes agayn' (comes rolling back) 'as the world askes'. You can, if you insist, render *world* by something like 'nature' or 'necessity'. But it may be doubted whether we have made any advance in clarity by saying that anything is necessitated by necessity or that nature prescribes the course of nature. Even if we had, I believe

---

[1] Sedgefield, *Boethius*, p. 11, l. 6.
[2] A. 2839.   [3] *Ibid.* 2847.
[4] B. Prol. 18.   [5] 530.

we should be foisting upon the poets an abstraction that was not in their minds. 'As the world asks' means no more than 'as must be'. Similarly, when Chaucer's monk repels the suggestion that he should live according to his Rule by asking 'How shal the world be served?',[1] I do not think we should translate *world* by some abstraction such as 'society'. He only meant 'How are things to go on?' So in *As You Like It*,

> 'It is ten o'clock;
> Thus we may see', quoth he, 'how the world wags.'
>
> (II, vii, 22)

Centuries later Johnson in a letter to Boswell, recalling their jaunt to the Hebrides, observes 'Such an effort annually would give the world a little diversification'.[2] If he had said 'would be a diversification' or even 'would make a change', he would have conveyed just as much.

It might be thought that a sense, if you call it a sense, so vague as this was useless. But this is not so. A word may continue to have a syntactical function when it has lost all precise reference; witness the *it* in 'it's raining'.

IV. 'WORLD' IN BIBLICAL TRANSLATION

The developments I have mentioned so far were all in my opinion purely native; we must now turn our attention to meanings which *World* acquired as a result of its use in translations of the Bible. It acquired them all during the period when our translators were still working from the Vulgate Latin, and they were hardly at all altered when, in the sixteenth century, the new scholars went behind the

---

[1] A. 187.   [2] Boswell, 16 November 1776.

Latin and began to produce translations directly from the Hebrew of the Old Testament and the Greek of the New.

For Biblical purposes *World* was seriously over-worked. In the New Testament it was made to do duty for no less than four Latin words (which in their turn do duty for four Greek words). In the Old it represents ultimately five words in Hebrew but, since for our present purpose the New Testament alone is of any real importance, we may leave the Hebrew words out of account, merely noticing that two of them (*cheled* and *olam*) contain the idea of time and are in that way very close to our English *World A*. But we cannot quite so summarily dismiss the Greek words; for though they affected English only indirectly through their Latin renderings, we shall not fully understand those renderings unless we know what they were meant to represent.

First, then, *world* may stand for Latin *terra* which in its turn stands for Greek *ge*, the earth. It does so, for example, in Rev. xiii. 3 ('all the world wondered').

Secondly, it may stand for *orbis* or *orbis terrae* in Latin. This represents Greek *he oikoumene* which is an ellipsis for *he oikoumene ge*, 'the inhabited earth'. So in Matt. xxiv. 14 ('preached in all the world') or Luke ii. 1 ('that all the world should be taxed').

It will be noticed that only in my quotation from St Matthew is either word used in its perfectly literal sense. In the others the earth means the inhabitants of earth, the human race; just as when we say the baby was a nuisance to the whole street, 'street' means its inhabitants. Usually this idiom involves hyperbole. The author of the Apocalypse might perhaps mean that every single human being felt wonder, but the Evangelist certainly did not think that the whole human race was being 'taxed'— or registered—by Augustus. He knew well enough that there were people outside the Roman Empire.

This usage presents no difficulties and is probably to be found in nearly all languages.

Thirdly, *world* represents Latin *saeculum*, as in 'the care of this world' (Matt. xiii. 22), 'the children of this world' (Luke xvi. 8), 'wise in this world' (I Cor. iii. 18), 'not only in this world but in that which is to come' (Eph. i. 21).

The central meaning of *saeculum* seems to have been something like 'generation'. Venus causes all animals to procreate their *saecula*.[1] According to Cicero the Platonic 'Great Year' includes 'I hardly dare to say how many *saecula* of men'.[2] The oak outlives many human *saecula*.[3] And, like *world*, it can mean an age or period; 'the age (*saeculum*) of Romulus coincided with the time (*aetas*) when Greece was full of poets'.[4] Augustus will inaugurate *aurea saecula*, Ages of Gold.[5] Here we have the qualitative aspect of an age. We have it even more emphatically when Tacitus, trying to shame the Romans of his own day, says that among those noble savages, the Germani, 'mutual conception is not called the *saeculum*'.[6] (Obviously there were those at Rome who excused immorality by saying 'It's the *saeculum*', the mode, the way

[1] Lucretius I, 20. [2] *De Republica* VI, 22.
[3] Virgil, *Georgics* II, 295. [4] Cicero, *De Republica* II, 10.
[5] *Aen.* VI, 792. [6] *Germania* XIX.

we live now; compare the modern equivalent, 'It isn't as if we were Victorians'.)

Saeculum regularly translates Greek *aion*. *Aion* can mean simply life; to be 'robbed of one's dear *aion*' is to be killed.[1] It can also mean 'the sort of life one has', one's lot or fortune; not even such lucky people as Peleus and Cadmus had an *aion* free from all disasters.[2] In a passage from Aeschylus it seems to mean a generation.[3] Out of this trunk two strangely different branches grow.

On the one hand, like *World*, *aion* can come to mean 'indefinite time' or 'ages and ages'. As Aristotle says, 'the totality that includes all the time there is...is called *aion*'.[4] He connects it with *aei* (always). Chronologically earlier, but logically a further step, is Plato's use of *aion*. For him it means 'eternity' in the strictest sense; not indefinite nor even infinite time but the timeless. The Creator, he says,[5] made a 'movable model' of *aion* and this model is what we call time. Time is a model of *aion* because it attempts, by incessantly replacing its transitory 'present moments', to compensate for this transience and symbolise, or parody, the actual plenitude of the changeless reality—like trying to imitate omnipresence by visiting as many places as possible in rapid succession. Hence in Shakespeare time is 'thou ceaseless lackey to eternity'.[6]

On the other hand, *aion*, especially among those who had a Jewish background and used Greek only as their

[1] *Iliad* XXII, 58.   [2] Pindar, *Pyth.* III, 152.
[3] *Septem*, 745.   [4] *De Caelo*, 279 a.
[5] *Timaeus*, 37 d.   [6] *Lucrece*, 967.

second language, developed the sense of epoch or period with the fullest possible change of meaning. In many cultures we find the idea that the course of history once was, or some day will be, or at any moment might be, interrupted by catastrophic change, ushering in a wholly, or at least overwhelmingly, new state of affairs and even of the natural universe. Such an event constitutes the end of one *aion* and the beginning of another. *Aiones* differ from the 'periods' used by our historians because their diversity from one another is far greater, and also (more importantly) because the later *aion* does not grow out of the earlier by any natural development. Continuity has been broken. The new *aion* is not so much a new act as a new play. If any survive the change they will find themselves playing new parts against new scenery; she who was a star in the old play may find herself a super in the new.

Ragnarök, which I had to mention some pages ago, would thus mark a change of *aiones*. Still more would the terrible moment imagined by Plato, when the universe starts revolving backwards and all natural processes go into reverse.[1] But no people were more haunted by the conception of *aiones* than the Jews; and the Jews never more haunted than during the two centuries that preceded the Christian era. These are the age of Apocalyptic, of popular works prophesying the imminence of the new *aion*. Christianity itself in some sense—we must leave it to theologians to define—reaffirmed this prophecy. Whatever else the first Christian teaching was, it was certainly a statement that the old (and bad) *aion* was ending or

[1] *Politicus*, 269 d–270 e.

ended and that the new *aion* was about to begin or had begun already.

Rather unfortunately both these senses of *aion* are used in New Testament Greek. Thus *es ton aiona* 'into the *aion*' (I John ii. 17) means 'forever', 'eternally', and the adjective *aionios* means 'eternal' or 'everlasting' (as in Matt. xxv. 46). But side by side with these we find dozens of passages where 'this *aion*' or 'this present *aion*' is the very reverse of eternal, being contrasted with an *aion* that is 'to come' (e.g. Matt. xii. 32; Gal. i. 4). English *world*, however, was never used to translate *aion* where *aion* means eternity.

This being so, we may feel that *world–saeculum–aion* are in an excellent relationship, for the Latin and Greek words, and the English word in one of its senses, coincide surprisingly in their ranges of meaning. All indeed would have been well if *world* had had only this sense and had been used to translate only *saeculum*.

In fact, however, it also translates *mundus*, which translates *kosmos*. With these words, in their classical usage, we at last escape from all those ideas of time, or life, or generation, which, in one language or another, have surrounded us ever since this chapter began. They mean, quite unambiguously, the universe, the *heimr*, the region of regions. But we should get nearer to the ancient point of view if we said rather 'the pattern of patterns' or 'the arrangement of arrangements'.

Mundus in Latin is both an adjective and a noun. The adjective's range of meaning is something like clean, neat, tidy, spruce, well turned-out. People who are *mundi* are *elegantes.*[1] Horace will have the furniture *munda* if a visitor is coming.[2] In Christian Latin the *cor mundum* is the (morally) clean heart (Matt. v. 8). The noun *mundus* is a collective, roughly translatable as 'means of adorn-ment'. The delightful things Pope puts on Belinda's dressing-table were her *mundus*. *Mundus muliebris*, says the Digest, includes lotions, face-cream, mirrors and 'things by which a woman becomes *mundior*'. And that, says the elder Pliny,[3] 'is why what the Greeks [using their word for adornment] call the *kosmos*, we call the *mundus*, because of its perfect and flawless *elegantia*'. (I despair of translating the last word, but shall have something to say in another section about the attitude to Nature which underlies it.)

The semantic parallel between the developments of *mundus* and *kosmos* which Pliny here suggests is suspi-ciously neat. It may be doubted whether the Latin word, on its own steam, would have reached just that meaning by just that process. Perhaps it was coaxed in that direc-tion, under Greek influence, for the very purpose of making it a synonym to *kosmos*. But this makes little difference. The force and flavour of a word may depend as much on its imagined history as on its real history; sometimes more. So with the Greek word. The Greeks thought they were calling the universe *kosmos* because it was the adornment, the arranging,[4] the embellishment of what had originally been ugliness, disorder, chaos. If in reality they had reached the name *kosmos* by some different route—say, because the stars twinkled like

---

[1] Cicero, *De Finibus* II, 8.   [2] *Epist.* I, v, 3.
[3] II, iv, 3.   [4] Plato, *Gorgias*, 508 a.

jewellery—this would make no difference to what they thought and felt about it.

Like *he oikoumene*, both *kosmos* and *mundus* can be used to mean the inhabitants of the *world* (B), 'everybody', *tout le monde*; of course, with hyperbole. When the Pharisees said 'All the *kosmos* (Vulgate, *mundus*) has gone after him' (John xii. 19), they did not think the whole human race was proceeding up that street. Again, both can be used vaguely to mean no more than a vast area; as when the Gospel says 'I suppose the whole *kosmos* (Vulgate, *mundus*) wouldn't hold the books that would be written'. This is a *façon de parler*. The Evangelist was not really picturing a universe packed tight up to the highest heaven with rolls of manuscript; no more than we, if we said 'I wouldn't for the world distress the archdeacon', have a picture of being offered the galaxies as a bribe and refusing the offer.

V. THE CONFUSION OF 'KOSMOS' AND 'AION'

The distinction between *aion* or *saeculum* on the one hand and *kosmos* or *mundus* on the other clearly provides the instrument by which a consistent and lucid way of talking might have been achieved. And this would have been of immense value. We should then have had no confusion between (1) the natural universe which, on the Christian view, must be good, since its Creator pronounced it to be so; (2) the present evil *aion*, under which that universe has long been labouring, and which, as the Christians assert, is to be succeeded by a better *aion*. But powerful forces prevented this.

(1) The universe as we know it, the *heimr*, must no doubt be good. True. But the final goal of every human person is the enjoyment of God, not of this *heimr*. Therefore nothing that the *heimr* can offer, not even its most innocent blessings (daily bread, health, natural affection, or friendship) must be allowed to engage the whole heart. If it were, we should be treating as our home what was meant to be only a wayside inn. Unless we practise detachment, the *heimr* (however good in itself) becomes for us a danger.

(2) This evil *aion*, this present *veroldr*, is essentially evil. Evil is its specific characteristic; it is to it what stone implements are to the Stone Age or enlightenment to the Age of Enlightenment. Whereas the *heimr* can become a danger to us accidentally, through our infirmity, the *aion* is always and necessarily a danger. It is not enough to be merely 'detached' about it; we must defy, resist, and utterly renounce it.

(3) But this distinction, however important philosophically, dwindles into something merely academic in the daily practice of the spiritual life. The *heimr*, no doubt, is merely to be dispraised in comparison with a higher object, as something, though good, not rearly good enough; and the *aion* is to be utterly condemned. But surrender to either is fatal. For as Law says, 'If you are not wheat, if the heavenly life is not grown up in you, it signifies nothing what you have chosen in the stead of it, or why you have chosen it'.[1] One man may die by drinking poison and another by drinking good liquor in

[1] *An Appeal to all that Doubt* (1742), p. 86.

excess, but both will be equally dead. As a result, in all that concerns the will, the emotions, and the imagination, the (good) universe and the (evil) *aion* become extremely close neighbours. To most people at most times, for all practical purposes, both have to be treated, though not for exactly the same reason, as enemies.

(4) We have seen in Old Norse how the destruction of the *heimr* and the end of the *veroldr* become interchangeable; for the very good reason that the same catastrophe will destroy the one and conclude the other simultaneously. For a similar reason the end of the *kosmos* and the end of the present *aion* will coalesce in thought. In Matt. xiii. 39 we read of 'the end of the *aion*'. It is probably useless to ask whether this means the cessation of the existing, evil regime, or the abolition of the material universe as we know it. The curtain, and the theatre, will both fall.

These then, quite apart from language, are pressures tending to confusion. But—

(5) Language aggravates them. The New Testament writers themselves do not consistently use *kosmos* for the one conception and *aion* for the other. They were not consciously collaborating in the production of a work. They worked far apart in place and time and there was no question of meeting to hammer out an agreed terminology. And none was writing his native language. They wrote the sort of Greek which scholars have called the *koinè*, a deracinated and internationalised Greek used all over the Levant for business and government. It was not a barbarous corruption like Pidgin nor a contrived language

like Basic. It was more like the sort of English in which two educated Indians who had no mother-tongue in common might converse today; grammatical but un-idiomatic, lacking both in *nuance* and in precision, cut off from the associations of the nursery, the hearth, and also the library. The *koinè* is the speech of people who are living linguistically from hand to mouth; grabbing at 'any old word' which, however roughly, will, at a particular moment and for a particular audience, serve the wholly practical purpose they have in view.

As a result we find *kosmos* used where *aion* (the present evil 'set-up') must be meant. Examples are 'The world (*kosmos*) cannot hate you, but it hates me because I give evidence that its behaviour is evil' (John vii. 7); 'the spirit of the world (*kosmos*)' in I Cor. ii. 12; or 'unspotted from the *kosmos*' (Jas. i. 27). In this last passage the Latin translator significantly renders *kosmos* by *saeculum* and not, according to his usual practice, by *mundus*.

(6) Finally, the English translators always use simply *world* for both *kosmos* and *aion*, except where *aion* means eternity.

The consequent semantic situation is most strikingly illustrated by the occurrence within a work attributed to a single author of 'God so loved the world' (John iii. 16) and 'Love not the world' (I John ii. 15). The Greek uses *kosmos* in both passages. In the first the *kosmos* must be either the universe, the whole creation, or else, by the idiom already noticed, its inhabitants, the human race. In the second it cannot mean the human race. But it could mean either the evil *aion* with whose *ethos* we must make no truce, or the perishable universe which we must not love as if it were our true home. Or both.

It is therefore not surprising that English *world* has acquired, or retained, certain meanings and indeed certain antiquities from the multiple functions it had in Biblical translation. The next few sections will be devoted to these.

VI. 'THE OTHER WORLD'

'Neither in this *aion* nor in the *aion* to come' (Matt. xii. 32). Let us suppose that *aion* is here used in the strictest sense, so that the whole contrast is between one epoch and the next. And let us also suppose that the English translators understood this perfectly well. It is clear that if they had done so they could with perfect propriety have translated *aion* by *world*, since age or epoch or state of affairs is one of the things *world* could mean.[1] And since in fact they did translate it by *world*, it would seem only fair to conclude that they understood the verse.

On the other hand, I believe I should be safe in betting fifty pounds that for several centuries only the smallest minority of those who have read or heard the text have got out of it any idea of *aiones* whatever. The 'world to come' has meant to them not a new state of affairs but a region or *heimr*, the land of the dead. Whether this is conceived naïvely as somewhere in remote space, or more ambitiously as 'a different plane of being', makes little linguistic difference. Either way it is 'future' or 'to come' only in the sense that the speaker has not yet been there; as America might be 'my future home' to one contem-

[1] See above, p. 218.

plating emigration. It is contemporary with this earth. It has always been there. Innumerable generations have already entered it.

The idea of *aiones*, with other apocalyptic ideas, has sometimes re-emerged in particular sects. It comes every now and then before the minds of ordinary believers in special contexts. Theologians sometimes deal with it. But the picture common to popular Christian feeling and imagination, the normal object of fears and hopes, the consolation of the bereaved, the subject of play and poem, has been the one I have just described. We need not bother about the mind of the translators themselves. Whatever they intended, this is how their version has usually been read. And that is what mattered to our language.

The popular conception is partly—in the French sense of this word—a *vulgarisation* of something far more elusive and less familiar. The whole tenor of the New Testament implies that the life of the new *aion* will be immortal. But, except in parables, there seems to be very little suggestion of any realm of the dead to which all souls at all times have passed in virtue of their intrinsic indestructibility. If they believed in any such Hades, the first Christians seem, as Christians, to take no interest in it. What gives entry to the new *aion* is not natural immortality but miraculous resurrection (Luke xx. 35). The fact that such resurrection will occur and that men will thus enter such a life is one of the novelties of the new *aion*. For this very Semitic conception popular belief unconsciously substitutes something with which it can feel more at home—the old idea of 'life after death' in some 'other place', as it has been believed, surmised, hoped, feared, denied, fondled, or debated by nearly the whole human race.

The process was greatly facilitated by the ambiguity of the noun *world*; and another linguistic factor co-operated.

In the New Testament the *basileia*, the reign or kingship, of God is frequently mentioned (Mark i. 15; iv. 11, *et passim*). No one doubts that this conception is closely connected—it is not for me to say just how—with that of the new *aion*. Sometimes, instead of 'the *basileia* of God', we find 'the *basileia* of heaven' (Matt. iii. 2; v. 10). These two phrases meant exactly the same, *heaven* being merely a reverential Hebrew euphemism for *God*. But it did not sound like that to people who were preoccupied with imaginations of 'the land of the dead'. It sounded like a place—the very same place, up in the sky, once occupied by Olympus or Asgard. As if this were not enough, the word *basileia* took on a new colour when it was turned into Latin or English. *Regnum* and *Kingdom*, perhaps from the first, and increasingly as time went on, carried a territorial implication. The '*basileia* of God' had meant 'the *aion*, the State of Affairs, in which God's monarchy is undisputed'. The 'kingdom of God' comes more and more to mean 'the region or *heimr* in which God is king'. Now substitute *heaven* for *God*, and the territorial aspect almost extrudes every other. Heaven is a 'kingdom' almost in the same sense as Wessex. The idea of living under the direct kingship of God sinks into the idea of 'going to heaven when you die'. On top of all this, you have the passage where Peter is given 'the keys of the kingdom of heaven' (Matt. xvi. 19). The picture is now

complete. Heaven is the land of the happy dead, surrounded by a wall, with a gate and a gate-keeper.

The result of this is to give *world* one more meaning.
The land of the dead is a *world*: 'the other world'. Scott,
in bereavement, consoles himself with the reflection,
'well, there is another world'.[1] Blougram says

> As this world prizes action, life and talk;
> No prejudice to what next world may prove.[2]

But there is no need to parade examples. You may hear it
from simple lips tomorrow.

VII. 'WORLD' AND 'WORLDLY' (PEJORATIVE, DEPRECIATIVE OR IMPURE)

From the many passages where *world* translated *aion*, and
aion meant 'the present evil age', it contracted a pejorative
sense. From passages where the *kosmos* was belittled as
transitory it contracted a sense which is depreciative
without being fully condemnatory. Thirdly, from the
mere necessity of distinguishing the known and temporal
universe for the believed-in and eternal, where no evalua-
tion was being made, it acquired a neutral sense. Between
the first two, the fully pejorative and the merely depreciative, confusion can arise. The adjective *worldly* shares the
fortunes of its noun.

I will begin with the fully pejorative.

The most precise and useful development of this sense is
seen in the triad familiar to Anglicans from their litany,

[1] Journal, 8 June 1826.
[2] Browning, *Bishop Blougram's Apology*, l. 770.

'the world, the flesh, and the devil'. Here the *world* is no longer synonymous with all the evils of the present *aion*. It refers to a particular set of evils, distinguishable from, others. The firm establishment of this restriction was largely the work of the Middle Ages.

There are, however, passages in scripture which may contain the germ of the later meaning; those where the *aion* is conceived not as mere moral disorder but as an order—a systematic *ethos* in rivalry to the Christian *ethos*. It has its own sort of 'wisdom' (I Cor. i. 20; iii. 19). Its 'children' may, in terms of their own system, behave more sensibly than the 'children of light' (Luke xvi. 8). It has its own appropriate *merimna* (Matt. xiii. 22) and *lupè* (II Cor. vii. 10)—its own anxiety and misery. It is this systematic, and even arduous, character that distinguishes the *world* in its most precise sense. Mere drift—planless lechery or idleness—is not 'worldly'. The *world* rebukes the flesh in Clough's *Decalogue*—

> Do not adultery commit;
> Advantage rarely comes of it. (13–14)

To pass from the spiritual to the *worldly* life is not to become masterless but to accept a new master. And not a soft one. Who does not close Chesterfield's *Letters* with the feeling that to become a fine gentleman is as costly as to become a saint; young Stanhope is always being told, in effect, to 'seek not yet repose'.

The *Castle of Perseverance* characterises the three members of the triad very clearly. They are 'the Worlde, the Fende, the foul Flesche' (29). The Fiend tempts to Anger,

Envy and Detraction; the Flesh to Sloth, Lechery, and Gluttony; the World to Pride and Covetousness (31 *sq.*). Its baits are fine clothes, kneeling flatterers, house and lands (588). The Anglican catechism assigns (unspecified) 'works' to the devil, 'sinful lusts' to the flesh, 'pomps and vanity' to 'this wicked world'. Spenser's Mammon, whose realm contains both the house of riches and the court of Philotima (Ambition) proclaims himself 'God of the world and worldlings'.[1] Chaucer's Clerk, that devoted student, 'ne was so worldly for to have office'.[2] Long before Bunyan's Mr Worldly Wiseman we have 'world-liche wyse' in *Piers Plowman*.[3] Bunyan's Madam Bubble, 'one in very pleasant attire, but old', offers to make Mr Stand-Fast not merely happy but 'great and happy'; she is marginally glossed as 'this vain world'.

All these I class as pure examples. But there are also what I would call impure examples; passages where we cannot be quite sure, and where the author was perhaps not quite sure whether *world* means this wicked *aion*— the whole set-up of *arrivisme* and 'enlightened self-interest'—or this transitory universe where solid satisfactions are not to be had. This was an almost inevitable result of the multiple burden which the noun *world* had laid upon it in Biblical translation.

The thirteenth-century *Poema Morale* says that if we don't take care 'this world will drown us' (328). Does he mean that we shall be reduced into accepting the standards of this evil *aion* by becoming snobbish and ambitious and fixing our eye on the main chance, or only

[1] F.Q. II, vii, 8.   [2] A. 292.   [3] C. xi, 90.

that, if we lose our detachment, all earthly goods, even
the most innocent, being perishable, will break our hearts
in the end? When Quarles says

> O what a crocodilian world is this,
> Composed of treacheries and ensnaring wiles
>
> *(Emblems,* I, iv, 6)

World could bear either sense or both. The following, also
from Quarles, is interesting:

> Worldlings, whose whimp'ring folly holds the losses
> Of honour, pleasure, health, and wealth such crosses.
>
> *(Emblems,* I, vi, Epigr. 6)

There is, to be sure, a very reasonable sense, in which
health, like all the other items, is a 'worldly' good; that
is, a temporal good, belonging to this transitory *kosmos.*
But honour and wealth are, in addition, 'worldly' in the
different and narrower sense.

In one passage from Baxter I think we see the mind
sliding unconsciously from one sense to the other. He
begins by asking his reader 'Hath not the world from thee
that which God hath from the heavenly believer?'
World here need only mean—should mean, if the question
is to be as searching as Baxter intended—the *kosmos,* the
temporary. Natural happiness, of however humble and
innocent a sort, could be absorbing your whole heart to
the exclusion of a higher object. But when Baxter goes
on to probe our conscience in more detail he talks solely
about 'worldliness' in the narrower sense: 'thou beginnest
to feel a sweetness in gain and to aspire to a fuller and
higher estate...the rising of thy house or the obeisance of

thy inferiors'.[1] The result is somewhat unfortunate. An idle, frivolous, feckless reader might be pulled up by the initial question and say 'that's me'; reading the subsequent diagnosis he could, truthfully, say, 'Thank goodness. It wasn't me after, all. I never saved a penny in my life'.

In all these examples, both 'pure' and 'impure', the context is definitely theological. But *world* was far too useful a pejorative to be abandoned by speakers when they abandoned the theology it presupposes. The attitude of the devout or 'elect' to 'the world' is after all sometimes very like that of the aesthetic or intellectual *élite* to the 'bourgeois' or 'philistines'. The *élite* take the word over, and so we find it used in sub-Christian, un-Christian and anti-Christian passages; always in a sense which is indebted, but not always equally indebted, to the Christian use.

In Wordsworth's sonnet 'The world is too much with us' *world* is still very close to its source, for it means primarily our economic life ('getting and spending'). The opposite to the *world*, what stands to him for the 'unworldly', is however neither divine contemplation nor works of charity; it is the enjoyment of external nature. But he would have felt this to be contemplation. In two poems of Arnold's the *world* is envisaged in very nearly Christian terms, as an organised and powerful system with its own kind of wisdom. In the sonnet 'Written in Emerson's Essays' it consists of those who draw back from Transcendentalism in 'wistful incredu-

[1] *Saints' Everlasting Rest* IV, iv.

lity' being 'sorrowful and full of bitter knowledge'. In 'The World's Triumphs' he forearms himself against it. He is afraid of becoming—as St Paul would say—'conformed' to that sorrowful wisdom; he must throttle that *world* or it will throttle him. This is very close to the *Poema Morale*'s warning that the *world* will 'drown' us if we don't watch. Arnold himself, I fancy, would have maintained that he was, in essence, saying much the same as the Middle English poet, but I think he would have been mistaken. The opposite of the *world*, for the older writer, was the spiritual life as conceived by Christianity; and with this, however 'demythologised', Arnold's ideal of urbanity and sweet reasonableness would never coincide.

Shelley provides some piquant examples. In the notes to *Queen Mab* (v, 189) resort to prostitutes destroys those 'delicate sensibilities' whose existence is denied by 'worldlings'. More strikingly still in the same notes we have an obvious, though probably unconscious, echo of the New Testament (Jas. i. 27) when he presses vegetarianism (for its 'abstract truth, its beauty, its simplicity') on the 'pure and passionate moralist' who is 'yet unvitiated by the contagion of the world'. Finally the 'broad way' (Matt. vii. 13) in *Epipsychidion* (155–6) is appropriated for a very unexpected purpose. The 'poor slaves' who tread 'the broad highway of the world' are the monogamists.

Despite the use of the religious word 'martyr' (in a secularised sense) I think the following, from Yeats, shows a further stage:

> the noisy set
> Of bankers, schoolmasters, and clergymen
> The martyrs call the world.[1]

The difference is in the tone. In the three earlier poets the *world* is still 'trailing clouds' of seriousness from its theological use. Wordsworth meets it with grave rebuke; Arnold with (not unpitying) defiance; Shelley with indignation. All, in one way or another, hold up their hands. Yeats lifts his eyebrows. If one disliked all four (I don't dislike any of them myself) one would say there was more of the prig in the others: more of the snob in him. *World* (*pejorative*) is cooling. It may soon be a mere cinder.

Unworldly is now in some danger of acquiring a new, and useless, meaning. I have had pupils who take it as a synonym for *unearthly*. They would say there was 'an unworldly atmosphere' in *Christabel*. This is a natural enough linguistic result of their unfamiliarity with the Christian background, but I am surprised it has come so quickly. I should have expected it would take a century or so more.

In his Journal Scott, then ruined, speaks of a friend; submission 'under circumstances more painful than mine—for the loss of world's wealth was aggravated by the death of his youngest and darling son' (20 January 1826). The sentence goes down easily enough and we all feel we know why bereavement should be thus distinguished from loss of *world*'s wealth. But often such a feeling shows only that we are familiar with a way of talking, not that we fully understand it. The expression is in reality not quite easy to analyse. Both losses are equally temporal, things of this

[1] 'Adam's Curse', 12-14.

243

kosmos. Neither wealth, nor one's son, is being condemned by Scott as being *worldly* (*pejorative*), as elements only prized. by the 'children' of the wicked *aion.* Wealth could be so regarded, but Scott is not so regarding it. The process of thought which, unconsciously, underlies his language is perhaps something like this. Wealth (along with fame, rank, and power), wrongly or excessively pursued, is a feature of the wicked *aion.* Therefore the whole economic side of life (remember Wordsworth's sonnet) is closely associated with the *aion,* is *worldly.* And the *worldly,* originally contrasted with the spiritual, was in the nineteenth century equally, if not more, contrasted with 'the domestic affections'. (Ambition and *arrivisme* can be rivals to the simple pleasures of the fireside.) Economic wealth is therefore *world*'s wealth; not condemned, but despised in comparison with something felt to be 'higher'. But this analysis is doubtful, and it is arguable that we ought to place Scott's sentence under our next heading.

VIII. 'WORLD' AND 'WORLDLY' (NEUTRAL)

Side by side with the pejorative use a merely descriptive use of *world* continued to flourish. It is equally Christian in origin, for it always implies a contrast between this *kosmos* and the eternal; but the contrast is not drawn for the purpose of condemning the former. The speaker is not evaluating but merely distinguishing.

We can say that a man cast away all *woruldcara,* all 'worldly cares'.[1] These cares need not have been Baxter's 'the rising of his house and the obeisance of his inferiors'.

---

[1] Ælfric, *Oswald,* 55.

They could have included political or agricultural activities not only innocent but, for some men, obligatory. They are 'worldly' only because they aim at objects that are temporal, that belong to this *kosmos*. Similarly, one can speak of *woruldlicra aehta*,[1] 'worldly possessions'; not passing any judgement on them, but simply making clear that one is not referring to goods of a different kind, such as 'the means of grace and the hope of glory'. So with *worolde wynne* (*Beowulf* 1080). They need not be 'worldly joys' in the bad sense (pomps and vanity of this wicked *aion*); they are *merely* worldly, merely of this natural and transitory life. A lover can address his mistress as 'min worldly joy'.[2] The adjective in no way reprobates either her or his love for her. She is to him what lands and social status and health and sunlight and fame are to other men— the principal happiness of this present life, what he most cares for this side of heaven.

But even when *world* is neutral it can take over from its pejorative use a curious restriction. In *As You Like It* (I, ii, 36–40) Celia complains that Fortune makes fair women 'scarce honest' and honest women 'very ill-favouredly'. Rosalind replies, 'Nay, now thou goest from Fortune's office to Nature's; Fortune reigns in gifts of the world, not in the lineaments of Nature'. We may leave on one side as irrelevant to our present inquiry the rather odd view that 'honesty' is in Fortune's gift. What concerns us is that natural goods, such as beauty, should be contrasted

---

[1] Ælfric, *Assumption of St John*, 57–8.
[2] 'A Sovereign Mistress', R. H. Robbins, *Secular Lyrics of the XIVth and XVth Centuries* (1955), p. 142.

with 'gifts of the world'. Beauty is obviously in one sense a 'worldly' gift; temporal, of this *kosmos*. The explanation I take to be this. Fortune, apart from Celia's comical view about 'honesty', and in serious discourse, is primarily the dispense of wealth and status. Even modern usage, when we speak of making one's *fortune*, bears this out; and in Dante, it may be remembered, *Fortuna* disposes and guides *li splendor mondani*,[1] the brilliancies of earthly life (for *mondo* here is *earth*, not *universe*). But *World* (*pejorative*) in its full medieval development had come to mean, not evil in general, but the evils particularly incident to social and economic life. The spheres of Fortune and of 'the world' are therefore identified in Rosalind's mind and distinct from natural advantages. Her use is not pejorative, but it depends on associations which the pejorative use of *world* had created. Exactly the same thing happens when the ruined Scott reminds himself[2] of a friend's fortitude 'under circumstances more painful than mine— for the loss of world's wealth was to him aggravated by the death of his...son'. *World's* here means 'economic'. This usage, for Scott but perhaps less for Rosalind, though not pejorative, carries a relative depreciation. In a theological context, the *kosmos*, if not to be condemned like the evil *aion*, has to be kept in its proper place, to be rated low in comparison with something infinitely more important. Scott's use of *world* retains the implication; but the more important something has ceased to be the eternal and become natural affection. Quite possibly he would have felt—I do not say 'thought'—his usage to be

[1] *Inferno* VII, 77.   [2] Journal, 20 January 1826.

much closer to the religious than it actually is. For it would hardly be going too far to say that for many nineteenth-century people, at many moments, the home, its 'domestic affections', tended to be a religion.

To some it may appear that I am making a great pother about a very simple sentence and explaining what everyone understood better without explanation. 'We all know exactly what Scott means.' I, on the other hand, have come to distrust the feeling—with which I am very familiar—that we 'know exactly' what something 'means'. I think this feeling often proves not that we have understood but that we have met a familiar turn of expression and therefore feel no shock. I believe we can think we know the meaning of a word when we know only, through imitation and practice, where and when to use it. 'Security'—the *feeling* of safety—as we know, is 'mortals' greatest enemy'. This is as true of semantic security as of other kinds.

Worldly in its neutral sense is now almost an archaism, kept alive by its occurrence in the Anglican marriage service ('With all my worldly goods I thee endow') and by the jocular echo of that phrase when Lear enumerates 'all the worldly goods' of the Yonghy-Bonghy-Bò. It has become archaic because Latin *saecularis*, from *saeculum* for *aion*, has given us the useful word *secular*. Ælfric's *woruldcara* would now be 'secular affairs'. The penitent Launcelot says to the penitent Guinevere 'God defend (i.e. forbid) but that I should forsake the world as ye have done'.[1] She has entered a convent: by 'the world' he

---

[1] Malory XXI, ix.

means 'secular life'. So, by archaism, the Abbot in Browning says 'So, boy, you're minded...to quit this very miserable world':[1] that is, to become a monk.

Most readers will not need to be reminded that *secular* has, however, two meanings. The one we have just been considering descends from the medieval and Christian use of *saeculum* to translate *aion*. The other is a learned word which goes back to the classical meaning of *saeculum*, an age or generation. What lasts for many ages or generations is therefore *secular*. Milton's phoenix[2] is 'secular' not because it is less ecclesiastical than other birds but because it lives much longer—'ages of lives'.

IX. 'WORLD B' AND 'EARTH'

World B, as we have seen, has two senses. It can mean either the region of all regions, or else that far smaller region of accessible and practically important regions which we call the Earth. We must now define a little.

It will be noticed that the Earth is seldom called *world* when we are thinking astronomically. It would sound odd to say 'the orbit of the world is between those of Mars and Venus'. When we call Earth the *world* we are usually considering her not as a globe in space but as our habitation, the scene of the human story, the area we travel in. Hence 'I wish to see the world'[3] or 'cost Ceres all that pain To seek her through the world',[4] or 'I still bear on the conquering Tartar ensigns through the world'.[5]

---

[1] *Fra Lippo Lippi*, 93.
[2] *Samson*, 1707.
[3] Shaw, *Man and Superman* IV, i.
[4] Milton, *P.L.* IV, 271.
[5] Arnold, *Sohrab*, 46.

The same restriction usually applies nowadays—it did not always—to the plural *worlds*. Eddington considers 'the habitability of other worlds'.[1] But habitability is the point. If they were inhabited, then they would be to their inhabitants what 'the world' is to us. They are being called *worlds* by analogy. If there were no question of habitability we should not give them that name; I have never heard anyone call the Sun a world.

Wells's voyager, on his return journey from the Moon, first saw 'the earth' growing larger and larger. Then, a few lines later, 'it was no longer a planet in the sky but the world of man'.[2] The transition from *earth* to *world* exactly expresses a transition from the astronomical to the human point of view. Yet the Earth can be *world* even in an astronomical context if there is a good emotional reason. Thus Eddington can say 'the contemplation of the galaxy impresses us with the insignificance of our own little world'.[3] By calling it *world* he emphasises the contrast between its vastness for us and its paltriness by sidereal standards. By giving it the bigger name he makes it finally smaller.

On the other hand, *world* is decreasingly used to mean the absolute region of regions; *universe* tends to replace it. Partly, no doubt, this has happened because the ambiguity of *world* can cause inconvenience. But the change of name is also connected with a change in our conception of the thing.

[1] *The Nature of the Physical World*, p. 169.
[2] *First Men in the Moon* XXI.
[3] *The Nature of the Physical World*, p. 165.

For many centuries those who used *world* in the wider
sense had a very clear picture of what they meant. The
world (or *mundus* or *kosmos*) they had in mind was that
depicted by Greek and medieval science, with its unmoving spherical Earth, a tiny speck, at the centre and
the successively larger and swifter spheres or 'heavens'
revolving round it, and the *Primum Mobile* encircling the
whole. This *mundus* had its internal diversities: a realm of
air and change and chance which extended up to the
lowest sphere (that of the Moon), and beyond that the
immutable realm of ether and necessity. But these made
a pattern that could be easily grasped and the whole
system had the unity in multiplicity of a vast building.
When Marlowe spoke about 'the wondrous architecture
of the world',[1] the word *architecture* was hardly a metaphor. The world was the great work of art, matchless (as
we have seen) in its 'elegance'; perfect: neither needing
nor allowing any addition.

The language of some text-books carries the suggestion
that this model differed from its Newtonian successor
principally by being smaller. I think that misses the real
point. The important differences were two. First, it had
an absolute Up (away from Earth) and Down (towards
Earth). This meant that whereas to us the night sky
suggests the highly abstract conception of distance, it
suggested to our ancestors that very special, and far
more concrete, sort of distance we call height. It was a
vertiginous world. Secondly, it was both unimaginably
large and unambiguously finite. It therefore had shape.

[1] *Tamburlaine*, 873.

The emotional and imaginative difference between this and Newton's universe is accordingly very great. The old *kosmos* humbled you by its size, but exhilarated you by its symmetry; the mind could rest in it with full satisfaction. The Newtonian model is less like a building than a forest; illimitable, without horizons. It appeals to a romantic taste: its predecessor appealed to a classical taste. Hence the numerous sky-wanderings in Dante, Chaucer and others never once strike that note of lost bewilderment, loneliness, and agoraphobia which the idea of 'space' has aroused in Pascal and other moderns. The new attitude begins, I believe, with Bruno. It first reaches English poetry in Milton's lines about the Moon riding

> Like one that had been led astray
> Through the heaven's wide pathless way.[1]

The way had always been wide; only in the last few centuries has it become pathless.

The long use of *world* to mean an object so patterned and unified as the geocentric *kosmos* went far to disqualify it as a name for what we now call the 'universe'. When once the old model is broken, we become aware that a detailed knowledge of the Region of all regions will be forever unattainable. We now need a word not for some specific and imaginable object but for 'whatever the totality may be', and *universe* is such a word. Furthermore, the same process which broke the old model threw a new meaning on *world* which, while it lasted, made it impossible, without grave inconvenience, to call the totality the *world*.

[1] *Il Penseroso*, 69.

I have already quoted a passage where Eddington speaks about 'other worlds'. Our ancestors would have misunderstood him: not because they never discussed 'the plurality of worlds' but because that expression had for them a different sense. For them, the question about plurality of worlds meant the question whether 'the world'—the whole geocentric, patterned *kosmos*—was the only one that existed. Whether the planets which it contained were inhabitable was not the issue.

Plato and Aristotle[1] both maintained that there was only one *kosmos*. Their view prevailed for centuries and dissent from it finally arose, not from speculation as to what, if anything, might exist outside the mundane shell,[2] but as a by-product of emendments made in our map of its internal economy. Copernicus pointed out the great methodological advantages of treating the Sun, rather than the Earth, as the unmoving centre of the great arrangement. Then Galileo's telescope showed moons actually revolving round Jupiter just as Earth, on the Copernican hypothesis, was pictured as revolving round the Sun. The analogy was irresistible. *Satellite* became a key-conception. Other observations suggested that the 'fixed' stars, far from being all embedded in a single celestial sphere and therefore all equidistant from Earth, are at very different distances. If you were still to locate them in a sphere, that sphere would have to be of an immense, perhaps of an infinite, thickness. But, if so,

[1] *Timaeus*, 30 c–31 b; *De Caelo*, 276 a–279 b. They call it indifferently *kosmos* and *ouranos* (heaven), the Earth being such an inconsiderable part of it.

[2] Nothing spatial or temporal did; see *De Caelo*, 279 a.

there is no longer much point in regarding it as a sphere. What had been the wall of the *kosmos* turns out to be the indefinite, or possibly infinite, sea of space in which the *kosmos* floats. And the *kosmos* itself becomes merely the naked Sun with a few satellites. The question then naturally arises whether any of the stars has similar attendants. If any had, then that star, with its parasites, would be another instance of the same sort of thing as our own system: would in fact be 'another world'. When, therefore, the earlier natural philosophers talk about plurality of worlds, whatever language they are writing, whether they use *mundi* or *mondes* or *world*, they are really speculating about the plurality of solar systems. 'Why may we not', says Burton, 'suppose a plurality of worlds, those infinite stars visible in the firmament to be so many suns...to have likewise their subordinate planets as the sun hath his'; or again, 'if there be infinite planetary worlds'.[1] So in French. The (hypothetical) planets that circle another star are invisible, says Fontenelle, because their light is too weak to show *au-delà de leur Monde*, outside their own system; but the star itself must be, like our sun, *le centre et l'âme d'un monde*.[2] On the other hand, when he considers the Moon as inhabitable he does not call it a world, as Eddington in the like context probably would, but an earth: *que la lune est une terre habitée*.[3]

Obviously, while this language was current, *world* could hardly be used to mean also the region of all regions. Now that the old idea of the *kosmos* is forgotten

[1] 3, 2, 3; 3, 4, 1, 5.   [2] *Entretiens sur la Pluralité des Mondes* v.
[3] *Ibid.* title of *Soir* II.

by all but historians, we can if we wish, where it is stylistically desirable, once more call the universe the *world*. Thus in Tennyson: 'Look up thro' night: the world is wide'.[1] Or, from Eddington:

Not the stars this time but universes stretch one behind the other beyond sight.... But there is one feeble gleam of evidence that perhaps this time the summit of the hierarchy has been reached, and that the system of the spirals is actually the whole world.[2]

Neither is common form. Tennyson is writing poetry, in which the native and monosyllabic word usually hits harder and has a richer freight of associations. He is also alliterating; and initial *w* has always been an enchanter. Eddington obviously could not use *universe* for the whole just after he has used *universe* for the parts. But his choice of *world* also gives a bleaker and more paralysing finality. *Universe*, as I have said, means 'whatever the totality may be'. But the author is here suggesting that 'this time' we have grasped what it actually is, mentally got to the end of it, and can say, 'This is all there is'. It thus becomes once more, for the moment, a definite object as the geo-centric *mundus* had been, and like it the only object there is. As such it claims the old word.

Careless readers of *Paradise Lost* sometimes fail to notice Milton's careful and sensitive use of *world* and *earth*, and thereby miss some of the greatest achievements of his visual imagination. Milton felt a strong need to express the new sort of space-consciousness. But he also wanted

[1] *The Two Voices*, 24.
[2] *The Nature of the Physical World*, p. 166.

to retain a good deal from the old walled and elegant *kosmos* which is so much richer in plasticity, in asso-ciations, and indeed in everything except one particular (and romantic) species of sublimity. His solution was to enclose his *world* (*kosmos* or *mundus*) in an opaque spherical shell, hang this from the floor of his *Heaven* by a golden chain, and surround it with illimitable *Chaos*

> Without dimension, where length, breadth, and highth,
> And time, and place are lost.[1]

The *world* is an artifact; indeed Book VII describes the making of it. Inside it, safe inside the shell, he can still enjoy the old beauties, 'all this World beheld so fair',[2] Libra and Andromeda, 'innumerable stars', Earth among them 'not unconform to other shining globes',[3] and, supreme, 'the golden sun' that 'gently warms'[4] the whole enclosure. Outside, in the pathless, the waste infinity, he becomes the poet (our first poet) of space. Indeed, he probably first used the word *space* in that sense.[5]

X. 'WORLD B' AS A MEASURE OF VALUE

In the fifteenth-century *Assembly of Ladies* (539) we read 'It was a world to look on his visage'. There is no doubt at all about the meaning. Lady Anne Bacon, translating Jewel's *Apologia Ecclesiae Anglicanae* (1562) renders *operae pretium est videre* by 'it is a world to see'. And Lady Anne, as anyone can see by comparing her version with Jewel's original throughout, is an utterly reliable translator; quite as racy as the famous Elizabethan trans-

---

[1] *P.L.* II, 893.   [2] *Ibid.* III, 554.   [3] *Ibid.* V, 259.
[4] *Ibid.* III, 583.   [5] *Ibid.* I, 650.

lators and at the same time far closer than most of them. We may be certain that 'it is a world to see' meant 'it is very well worth seeing'.

How it could reach this meaning seems to me very easy to understand, and I should hardly have thought of spending many words on it if I had not met in the works of a scholar whom I respect what seems to me an immensely unlikely explanation. He has noticed that Chaucer says the Tartar king's music was 'lyk an hevene for to heere';[1] and he believes the formula 'it was a world' arose from substituting *world* for *heaven*. But if *world* were merely a substitution for *heaven* it would be pointless. 'Like heaven' meant (by hyperbole) 'as blissful as heaven'. No one could praise anything by saying it was as blissful as the world, for no one thinks the world blissful.

The truth, surely, is that *world* here becomes a term of value because it is first treated as a quantitative term. Whether *world* is taken for *mundus* or for earth, it is, by our standards, a very large object. If anyone could be supposed to own it, he would be immensely rich: if anyone could be supposed to give it away, he would be immensely generous. This idea, easy at any period, would suggest itself even more easily in an age when territorial ownership was the most obvious and frequent sort of riches: an age when cities, provinces, or kingdoms could be given as dowries.

From this point of view 'it was (or is) a world' falls naturally into place as the upward limit in an ascending series of hyperbole.

[1] Squire's Tale, F. 271.

On the lowest level you can assess the prized object by saying it is worth a city, or more than a city. If King Henry offered you *Paris, sa grand'ville* on condition that you abandoned your beloved, you could reply

> J'aime mieux ma mie, ô gué,
> J'aime mieux ma mie.[1]

If a city is not felt to be enough, you can step the price up and say with Du Bellay *ma pauvre maison qui m'est une province.* If a province is still too little you can, like Hugo, step it up to an empire: *enfant, si j'étais roi, je donnerais l'empire,* etc. Working along these lines, language is certain to reach the world in the end.

In fact, it reached it at the beginning; for I have been giving these examples in their crescendo of hyperbole, not in their chronological order. We get the usage in the New Testament: 'What good will it do a man to get the whole *kosmos* and lose his own psyche?' (Matt. xvi. 26). It flourishes still in more than one language; for all I know, in every language. Thus we have *je n'y manquerais pas pour un monde,*[2] or in Italian, *la domestica che la spassava un mondo quella mattina*[3] ('the housemaid, who was having a world of fun that morning'). In English we hear daily 'He thinks the world of her' or 'I wouldn't hurt it for the world'.

Such is the human passion for exaggeration that even the *world*, on occasion, will not satisfy it. Chaucer's Troilus says 'Me levere were than thise worldes tweyne'[4]

---

[1] Molière, *Le Misanthrope* I, ii.   [2] Musset, *Un Caprice* III.
[3] G. Vivante, *Il Nipote del Mago* (1960), p. 69.
[4] *Troilus* III, 1490.

—I'd like it better than this world twice over, than two such worlds.

Usually, as I have said, the idea of quantity is present only to supply the ground for an idea of value: *world* means 'as big as the world and therefore as valuable'; sometimes however it is merely quantitative, as in Milton's 'brought into this world a world of woe'.[1] 'A world of folk'[2] in Chaucer, and 'a world of ladies' in *The Flower and the Leaf* (136) are probably in the same class. Our colloquial 'a world of trouble' and 'a world of difference' certainly are.

I am in some doubt how to classify Gower's statement that someone 'couthe al the world of tricherie'.[3] This might be merely quantitative, like 'a world of woe'. It might mean, with more precision, 'he knew all there is to know of trickery', his store of trickery being, like the universe, something that could not be added to. But there is a third possibility. It might be an instance of the usage to which our next section is devoted.

XI. SUBORDINATE 'WORLDS'

Solar systems, we have seen, were *mundi* or *mondes* or *worlds*. This greatly facilitated—I do not say it caused—the usage I am now going to consider. Any region whatever can be called a *world* if it is being regarded, within a given context, as constituting a (relatively) closed system. The most obvious, and perhaps the earliest, instance of this usage is the geographical. Once America was dis-

---

[1] *P.L.* IX, II.   [2] *Troilus* III, 1721.
[3] IV, 2078.

covered, it became the 'new world', and the land-mass
which we already knew became 'the old world'. Pre-
historic America, says Bacon, had 'far greater rivers and
higher mountains than any part of the old world'.[1]
Thomas Browne quotes a line from a doggerel prophecy,
'When the new world shall the old invade';[2] i.e. when
America will invade Europe. By a very slight extension
Donne writes 'Let sea-discoverers to new worlds have
gone';[3] or Gibbon, 'Britain was viewed in the light of a
distinct and insulated world'.[4]

In these examples the area which is being dubbed a
world is an area in the literal sense: somewhere in space.
But it can also be an entirely notional area, an intellectual
or spiritual *milieu*. 'St Thomas Aquinas', says Chesterton,
'would have found himself limited in the world of
Confucius'[5]—if he had had to confine himself to the
range of conceptions and values which Confucius used.
'The author of the *Cloud* and Walter Hilton', says
Professor Knowles, 'move in the same world of ideas and
motives'.[6] We are told by another writer that nonsense,
for Edward Lear, 'became ultimately a world in itself'.[7]

The *world*, in this sense, which a man normally inhabits
may be called 'his' *world*. Thus in H. G. Wells we read,
'Why didn't I stick to my play? That's what I was equal
to. That was my world and the life I was made for.'[8]

[1] *New Atlantis.*   [2] *Miscellanies*, Tract XII.
[3] *The Good-morrow.*   [4] Ch. I.
[5] *The Everlasting Man* II, i.
[6] *The English Mystical Tradition* (1961), p. 42.
[7] H. Jackson, *The Complete Nonsense of Edward Lear* (1947), p. x.
[8] *First Men in the Moon* XIII.

In calling any such notional area a *world* we always suggest that it has some internal unity and a character that sets it apart from other areas. But the gravity of the suggestion varies with the context and with the style of the writer. When Wordsworth says 'all the mighty world Of eye, and ear'[1] the suggestion is strong. Sight and hearing stand together and apart from all other experiences, by being sensuous yet embracing distance. But when Keats speaks of 'Daffodils And the green world they live in,'[2] this sally of the esemplastic power frames and so unifies a merely momentary picture. Wordsworth's phrase would be possible in prose; Keats's, hardly.

Gower's 'al the world of trickerie' may obviously come in here. Trickery, jugglery, and the like can be a *world*, as there can be a *world* of finance or higher mathematics, and an expert could be master of all that *world*.

When the area or *milieu* in question has a position in time as well as a distinctive character, it becomes impossible to distinguish this sense from *World* (State or Period) which we considered in Section II. 'Christianity', says Arnold, 'was a new spirit in the Roman world.'[3] It is useless to ask whether he means 'The Roman period, state of affairs' or 'The system of thoughts and sentiments in which the Roman mind was at home'. Consciously, I take it, he meant the latter, for he was no *Anglist* and knew nothing about the medieval usage. But he is, willy-nilly, referring to what Gower would have called a *world* (period). Thus the exigencies of language which separate meanings also at times reunite them.

[1] *Tintern Abbey*, 105.   [2] Endymion I.   [3] *Marcus Aurelius*.

XII. 'WORLD' (PEOPLE)

We have already had to notice that, just as *street* can mean those who live in the street, so *world*—and, for the matter of that, *kosmos, mundus, saeculum,* and *monde*—can mean the inhabitants of the world, mankind. Examples will occur to everyone. The Lamb of God 'takes away the *hamartia* of the *kosmos*' (John i. 50). 'The hope of the *mundus* was frustrated.'[1] 'Blessed Cross on whose arms hung the ransom of the *saeculum*.'[2] '*Toz li monz [tout le monde]* lies in her power.'[3] 'The Queen that (i.e. to whom) all this worlde schal do honoure.'[4]

In some of these examples *world* may mean, quite literally, the whole human race; much more often it is, and is known by the speaker to be, a hyperbole. When the lady says 'Sir Wowen ye are that alle the worlde worshipes',[5] neither she nor the poet is ignorant that many people—benighted Saracens and ignorant villeins— have never heard of him. When Johnson 'undeceived the world'[6] about the ghost-story, this means he undeceived a few hundreds.

The importance of this (sufficiently obvious) fact is that the hyperbole is one source of the various different meanings which arise within *World* (*People*). The hyperbole talks of some men as if they were all men. But the 'some' selected for such treatment may vary according to the speaker's point of view.

[1] *Lucan* v, 469.　　　[2] Venantius Fortunatus, *Vexilla regis.*
[3] *Roman de la Rose*, 1033.　　[4] *Pearl*, 423–4.
[5] *Gawain and the Green Knight*, 1226.
[6] Boswell, 25 June 1763.

It may mean simply 'the majority': that is to say, the supposed majority, for there are seldom any statistics behind this usage. What the *world* thinks is 'common' or 'public' opinion: what it does is 'ordinary' or 'normal' behaviour. *Le monde ayt entrepris*, says Montaigne,[1] the world has agreed, to honour melancholy with its peculiar favour. 'Madness', said Johnson, 'frequently discovers itself by unnecessary deviation from the usual modes of the world.' He was thinking about Smart's habit of suddenly kneeling down to pray in the street or wherever he happened to be. Johnson adds that 'rationally speaking it is greater madness not to pray at all than to pray as Smart did', but it does not discover itself as madness because it involves no deviation from the modes of the *world*, the behaviour of the majority. Scott says of a lady 'In her case the world is good-natured, and perhaps it is more frequently so than is generally supposed'.[2] In other words 'most people are kinder than more people think'.

When we speak of the majority, one or other of two implications is often present. We may imply 'Most people, but of course not ourselves', or 'Most people, and therefore of course you and I'. The first is present in the passage just quoted from Montaigne; indeed his previous words have made it explicit. When this happens, *world* is slightly pejorative and may carry associations derived from the theologically pejorative use. It would be hard to say whether the fastidious and retired man's distaste for the majority or the Evangelical's reprobation of the 'worldly' is uppermost in Cowper's

[1] I, ii.   [2] Journal, 13 November 1826.

How various his employments whom the world
Calls idle; and who justly, in return,
Esteems that busy world an idler too !

(*Task* III, 352)

When the opposite implication ('and therefore of course
you and I') is at work, the *world* is contrasted with some
special circle or way of life which the speaker regards as
eccentric, uncouth, restrictive—a 'hole-and-corner' affair.
When looked at in this way, *world* is often buttressed with
some such adjective as *real, adult* or *actual*. Scott speaks of
'good sense and knowledge of the world picked up at one
of the great English schools'.[1] The school rubs off the
regionalisms and archaisms and corrects the peculiar
perspectives of a provincial home: makes a boy, as the
Americans would say, 'like folks'. Similarly he says
'One knows nothing of the world if you are absent from
it so long as I have been'.[2] As the context makes plain,
world here means London, conceived as the centre of
politics, fashion, and literary 'contacts'. A few pages
later it has what seems at first to be a startlingly different
sense: he 'knows the world, having been a good deal
attached both to the turf and the field'.[3] But the same
semantic principle is still at work. London was contrasted,
as *World* (*simpliciter*), with Edinburgh and Abbotsford
because the latter were felt to be special, departmental,
not exactly current or standard. Race-meetings and hunts,
with their rowdiness and mixture of classes, are similarly
contrasted with a more guarded, selective, refined life

[1] *Ibid.* 25 August 1826. [2] *Ibid.* 7 October 1826.
[3] *Ibid.* 27 March 1827.

which can in its turn be thought special or departmental.
In all these usages alike, the *World* is something you meet
if you go outside the enclosure in which, willingly or un-
willingly, you usually live.

This explains the curious fact that while it is derogatory
to call anyone *worldly* it is complimentary to call him 'a
man of the world'. Johnson would have hotly denied, or
(more likely) confessed with shame and trembling, that
he was *worldly*, but he says with some self-complacency
'I am a man of the world'.[1] That is 'I am no longer the
uncouth schoolmaster from Lichfield, nor the learned
Hottentot, nor even the drudging Lexicographer. I know
my way about. I know how to behave. I am a very
polite man. No one need make allowances for me. I can
meet anyone—even, on occasion, Wilkes.' Hence his
indignation at the suggestion that he is not, in this sense,
a man of the world: 'What do you mean, Sir? What do
you take me for? Do you think I am so ignorant of the
world, as to imagine that I am to prescribe to a gentleman
what company he is to have at his table?'[2]

The unwilling Nun in Browning's 'The Confessional'
says

> 'Lies', 'They lie', shall still be hurled
> Till spite of them I reach the world.

World here carries double weight. It is (obviously)
saeculum, the *world* in the sense of secular life. But it is also
emphatically the outside: the free, open, common world
of humanity.

[1] Boswell, 14 July 1763.
[2] Boswell, shortly before 15 May 1776.

In all these examples the *world* is contrasted with a minority (simply) or with some special and restricted circle. But there is also an almost opposite usage. *World*, with some specifying adjective, can itself mean a particular group of people, and therefore usually a minority. The examples, however, are ambiguous. Addison speaks of 'reforming the female world';[1] Arnold of 'the literary world'[2] or 'the Paris world of letters and society';[3] Johnson, of someone's behaviour 'when first he set his foot in the gay world'.[4] They are ambiguous because it is impossible to determine whether they are reached from *World* (*People*) or from *World* (*Subordinate Region*). My feeling, for what it's worth, is that Arnold is thinking of a *milieu*, a relatively closed system, but that Johnson means only gay people. Addison's 'female world' may be intended to reify and unify women somewhat as Keats did the daffodils by his 'green world'. On the other hand his phrase may have no deeper source than that curious horror of the word *woman* which has filled our eighteenth- and early nineteenth-century poetry with *nymphs* and *females*. These distinctions are admittedly tenuous.

World, without an adjective, can mean a particular set, but a set which regards itself as the norm, as the realisation of what all sets would be if they could: in a word, Society with a capital S. This is what Warton means when he says that Pope shows himself to be 'a man of gallantry and of a thorough knowledge of the world'.[5] I believe

---

[1] *Guardian*, 116.   [2] 'Joubert', *Essays in Criticism*.   [3] *Ibid.*
[4] Boswell, 8 December 1763.   [5] *Rape of the Lock:* end-note.

this usage is not a native English development but an attempt to render French *le beau monde* (or simply *le monde*). Often the French expression itself is borrowed, with the same sense: as when Pope writes

This the Beau monde shall from the Mall survey,[1]

or Chesterfield, 'A man who thinks of living in the great world must be...attentive to please the women...they absolutely stamp every man's character in the *Beau monde*'.[2] 'Great world' and *beau monde* are probably almost synonymous.

The French expression itself was, I suspect, facilitated by a development of *monde* to which I find no parallel in the history of English *world*. Both words, in so far as they mean (usually with hyperbole) the human race, can be said to mean people. But *monde* can mean, as *world* cannot, any collection of people however small or temporary, whether they have any unifying characteristic or not. In this sense *monde* could be defined merely as 'the opposite of solitude'; *company* is the nearest English equivalent. Thus we have *je ne compte pas sur grand monde aujourd'hui*,[3] 'I don't expect many people today'.

Granted this sense, it becomes natural to ask, say, whether at a given moment there is *beaucoup de monde* in Paris, just as an Englishman might ask 'Are there many people in town?' But the literally truthful answer (there are millions) would show a misunderstanding. The speaker wanted to know whether there were many

---

[1] *Rape* v, 133.   [2] Letter, 5 September O.S. 1748.
[3] Musset, *Il faut qu'une porte*.

people of a particular class, people he might call on or dine with. That *monde* should therefore come to mean that class is no stranger than that *society* should have come to mean *Society*. It is not even particularly arrogant. At the beginning of term an undergraduate who said 'There's hardly anyone up yet' would mean 'There are hardly any undergraduates', but a don who used the same words would mean 'There are hardly any fellows'. It is the most natural way of talking in the world; each gives as good as he gets back, neither has any reason to feel offended. It is perhaps by some such process that *monde* comes to mean 'fashionable people'. You can make it clearer by saying *beau monde*, but you needn't.

Since we have also adopted from French *demi-monde* and *demi-mondaine*, a word on these will not come amiss.[1] It is a curious, but by no means unparalleled, story of linguistic waste. *Demi-Monde* was the title of a play published by Dumas *fils* in 1855, and in the text he explains very clearly what he means by the expression. The *demi-monde* consists of women who all have 'a past' (*une faute dans leur passé, une tache sur leur nom*). What is common to them all is *l'absence de mari*. They are compromised, and therefore no longer members of *le monde*. They are not to be confused with prostitutes, not even with the 'top-drawer' prostitutes, the great *hetairai*. The whole purpose of Dumas' neologism was to name a shadowy region on the fringes of the *monde* which had had no name before. It is therefore with very pardonable chagrin that he reiterates

[1] For what follows I am gratefully indebted to the kindness of Professor G. Gougenheim of Vanves.

the correct meaning in his Preface of 1868. He complains that everyone takes *demi-monde* to mean *la cohue des courtisanes*; whereas in his intention *il commence où l'épouse légale finit et il finit où l'épouse vénale commence. Il est séparé des honnêtes femmes par le scandale public, des courtisanes par l'argent.* But all this availed nothing. Offered a word which would have supplied a linguistic need, the French, followed by the English, preferred to use it as the name for something which had several names already.

Aspiring neologists will draw the moral. Invent a word if you like. It may be adopted. It may even become popular. But don't reckon on its retaining the sense you gave it and perhaps explained with great care. Don't reckon on its being given a sense of the slightest utility. Smart little writers pick up words briskly; but only as a jackdaw picks up beads and glass.

10

LIFE

I. 'LIFE' (CONCRETE)

IT is for biologists and philosophers to discuss 'what life is'; we have the less ambitious task of examining what people mean by the word *life*, or, more strictly, some of the different things they may mean. If it were possible to identify the earliest sense of the word, we should naturally begin with that sense. But we cannot even be sure that there was anything which could be quite unambiguously called 'the earliest sense'. That very expression suggests that the word must have begun by having a single, rigidly homogeneous meaning. And some words—*triangle*, say, or *knee*—may have begun life with such an equipment. It can hardly be so with the greater words. I must therefore be content to start not with what can be shown to be oldest but with what seems to me the simplest and most immediate, the sense which practical and emotional pressures most fully force upon man's attention.

Life in this sense is the something which a man or any other organism loses at death. It is concrete and individual, the life 'of' someone or something. A man's life is 'his' as his beard is 'his' and can, like his beard, be removed. In Greek it is often *aion*. Achilles is afraid that flies and maggots will get at Patroclus now his *aion* is gone.[1] A man says 'Let *aion* leave me' (let me die).[2] To

---

[1] *Iliad* XIX, 24-7.   [2] *Ibid.* V, 685.

kill someone is to deprive him of *aion*.[1] Sometimes it is *zoe*; we read in Pindar of a 'death-and-*zoe* struggle'.[2] *Psuche* can be used in the same sense. When Achilles was pressing Hector, both on foot, it was a race (literally, 'they ran') for Hector's *psuche*.[3] But in general *psuche* has implications which the other two words lack. It can leave the man temporarily. When they drew the spear out of Sarpedon's wound, 'his *psuche* left him but was soon breathed back into him again'.[4] And even when it leaves him for good it apparently makes sense to ask—as it might not have made sense to ask about *aion* or *zoe*— where it has gone. It is then 'a *psuche* and phantasm (*eidolon*) in the house of Hades'.[5] But this *psuche* is not 'the man himself' or 'the real man'. The body is the real man. After a battle the *psuchai* of the slain go to Hades but 'the men themselves' are devoured by dogs and birds.[6] What is even stranger, a demi-god like Herakles is 'himself' alive among the gods while his phantasm is in Hades.[7] Such are the earlier usages. Later, the word *psuche* undergoes two far-reaching developments. By one it becomes *soul* in the full theological or pneumato-logical sense of immaterial, intelligent, immortal sub-stance. This, unlike the Homeric *psuche*, is emphatically the man himself, so that the body is regarded merely as its temporary prison.[8] By the other it achieves the highly technical and biological senses which Aristotle uses.

[1] Aeschylus, *P.V.* 862. [2] *Nem.* IX, 29.
[3] *Iliad* XXII, 161. [4] *Ibid.* V, 696.
[5] *Ibid.* XXIII, 104. [6] *Ibid.* I, 3–4.
[7] *Odyssey* XI, 601–4.
[8] The *Phaedo* gives perhaps the fullest statement of this theme.

In Latin, what a man loses at death can be *anima*, which is often identified with the breath or the blood. 'You could see the weary *anima* breathed out', says Ovid;[1] a wounded man 'vomited his *anima*'.[2] It can also be *vita*. When Turnus was killed his *vita* 'fled, full of resentment, to the shadows'.[3] Like *psuche*, *anima* and *vita* can be regarded as something that exists in separation, elsewhere, after the man is dead. Mercury conducts pious *animae* to the happy dwellings.[4] In another place *vitae* seem to be incorporeal beings which had never belonged to men.[5]

The Anglo-Saxons, being Christians, believed much more firmly than the ancients in an entity within each man which survived his death, but they did not call it *lif*: it was *gast* or *sawol*. *Lif* is a property of the body: 'when my *lif* goes from my body'[6]—'separating *lif* from body'.[7] Or you can put it the other way round; instead of *lif* leaving the body, the man may 'depart from *lif*'.[8] On a strict view this involves a slightly different sense of the word. It is no longer the attribute of an individual; it is a scene of which he has had his share and from which he now makes his exit. But Pope's larks which, when shot, 'fall and leave their little lives in air'[9] are not a true example of it, for their lives, being plural, are individual. The expression is fanciful and unidiomatic because Pope is imitating Virgil's line about the pigeon that was struck

[1] *Met.* xv, 528.
[2] *Aen.* IX, 349.
[3] *Ibid.* XII, 952.
[4] Horace, *Odes* I, x, 17.
[5] *Aen.* VI, 293.
[6] *Beow.* 2743.
[7] *Ibid.* 731–3.
[8] *Ibid.* 2471.
[9] *Windsor Forest*, 134.

by the arrow, *vitamque reliquit in astris*, 'and left its life in the sky',[1] where Virgil himself is using a kind of conceit.

In Middle English *a life* can mean 'a living one', hence simply a person. Thus Gower says about one of his heroines 'and every lif hire loveth wel',[2] everybody likes her very much. The Flood drowned all humanity except eight individuals 'outake lyves eyhte'.[3] At the beginning of *The Kingis Quair* the poet fancies for a moment that the bell has said to him 'Tell on, man quhat the befell'. Then he pulls himself up and says

> This is myn awin ymagynacioun;
> It is no lyf that spekis unto me.[4]

—nobody was really talking.

II. 'LIFE' (CHRONOLOGICAL)

The name for any state or condition inevitably becomes a name for the period during which that state or condition obtained. *Presidency* is the name of an office, but a man's presidency is also the period during which he was president. *Life* is something my body has, but my *life* is also the period during which my body had it. Thus 'he had reached the end of transient life',[5] or 'Ther loved no wight hotter in his lyve',[6] or 'nothing in his life became him like the leaving it'.[7] This quantitative sense is one of the easiest channels by which *life* passes from the particular to the generalised. It then means the normal span, the

---

[1] *Aen.* v, 517.
[2] II, 1225.
[3] VIII, 81.
[4] St. 11, 12.
[5] *Beow.* 2844–5.
[6] Chaucer, *Leg. Prol.* F. 59.
[7] *Macbeth*, I, iv, 7.

number of years for which an organism can be expected to remain alive. If we do not specify what kind of organism—e.g. 'the life of an oak, of a gnat'—it is assumed to be a human organism. Hence, in Greek, the Hippocratic maxim '*Bios* is short but *techne* is long', and the Latin *ars longa, vita brevis*, and Chaucer's 'The lyf so short, the craft so long to lerne'.[1]

III. 'LIFE' (QUALITATIVE)

Periods, as we noticed in the history of *world*, have not only length and position, but also quality. A man's *life*, meaning the period during which he was alive, can be considered qualitatively in more than one way.

(1) It can be considered ethically. After the death of Augustus, says Tacitus, 'his *vita* was diversely praised and censured'.[2] In a medieval *jeu d'esprit* a cardinal visits a convent *vitam inquirere*, to examine the *life* of the inmates.[3] Jeremy Taylor quotes from a Missal printed in 1626 a prayer that a dead man, even if his salvation is out of the question, 'may enjoy a *refrigerium* amidst the torments which now, perhaps, he suffers, for we have little confidence in the quality of his *vita*'.[4] The English Prayer Book has a petition that Bishops and Curates may set forth God's word 'both by their life and doctrine'. Traherne, wishing to suggest that example, rather than heredity, explains our corruption, says 'it is not so much our parents' loins as our parents' lives that enthralls and blinds us'.[5] A man's

[1] *Parlement* 1.　　　　　　　　[2] *Annals* I, ix.
[3] *Concilium in Monte Remarici*, 52.
[4] 'Christ's Advent', pt. 3, *Works*, ed. Heber (1822), vol. v, p. 45.
[5] *Centuries* III, 8.

life in this sense is the general tenor of his conduct or behaviour. Let us call it *Life* (*Ethical*).

(2) But a man's *life* can also mean his lot or fortunes. 'We desire a quiet life', says Latimer.[1] 'All men desire to lead in this world a happy life', says Hooker.[2] Masefield speaks of a girl in an unhappy home 'enduring life however bleak'.[3] For some reason I have found early and literary examples of this usage rather hard to come by, but we meet it every day in conversation—a miserable life, an easy life, a sheltered life. It comes out with sharp clarity if we contrast 'He lives the life of a beast' with 'he has a dog's life'. In the former we have *Life* (*Ethical*): he behaves like a beast. In the latter we are saying not that he behaves but that he is treated like a dog. We may call this *Life* (*Fortunes*).

(3) There is a third sense which, though it may shade off into one or other of these two, has a central area distinguishable from both. We use it whenever we speak of an open-air *life*, or of married, or professional, or civilian, or nomadic *life*. For any one of these could be either good or bad ethically and any of them could be miserable or happy. This is the sense required when Duke Senior asks 'Hath not old custom made this life more sweet Than that of painted pomp?'[4] It is often strengthened by 'way of', as in Johnson's 'we must think of some other way of life for you'.[5] We label this sense *Life* (*Routine*).

Latin *vita* was used in all three ways. In Tacitus, as

---

[1] *Lord's Prayer* v.   [2] I, I, X, 2.
[3] *Reynard.*   [4] *A.Y.L.I.* II, i, 2.
[5] Boswell, 27 March 1775.

already noticed, we have *Vita* (*Ethical*). In Ovid, *malae taedia vitae*,[1] the evils of my wretched life, we have *Life* (*Fortunes*). We have *Vita* (*Routine*) in Virgil's rustic life *nescia fallere*[2] (it never 'lets you down') or Horace's 'by-way of an unobtrusive life', *fallentis semita vitae*.[3]

In Greek, *aion* is perhaps the most usual word for *Life* (*Fortunes*). 'What sort of *aion* will you have after this?'[4] the Chorus ask Peleus in his bereavement. Even the most fortunate heroes, said Pindar, did not have an untroubled *aion*.[5]

When Odysseus says to Eumaeus 'you have a good *bios*'[6] he clearly means 'you have a good master and plenty to eat', so that *bios* is here *Life* (*Fortunes*); but I do not know any other passage where it does so. Most often *bios* is *Life* (*Routine*), so that we have in Aristotle the nomadic, the agricultural, the fisher's, or the huntsman's *bios*.[7] Herodotus uses *zoe* in the same sense,[8] reached perhaps through the intermediate use of *zoe* to mean 'livelihood'.

To some readers these distinctions will seem over-fine, but the truth is that they are not even now fine enough to accommodate all the shades in the meaning of *bios*. Side by side with the *bioi* of the nomad, the fisherman, etc., we meet a different classification. The three 'outstanding' *bioi*, according to Aristotle, are those of pleasure, of political activity, and of contemplation (or research).[9]

[1] *Pont.* I, ix, 31.   [2] *Georgics* II, 467.
[3] *Epist.* I, xviii, 103.   [4] Euripides, *Andr.* 1214.
[5] *Pyth.* III, 152 *sq.*   [6] *Od.* xv, 491.
[7] *Pol.* 1256 a *sq.*   [8] IV, 112.
[9] *Eth. Nic.* 1095 b.

They are partly differences of *Routine* but also, no doubt, of ethical quality. It would be difficult to assign ancient conceptions of the happy (*eudaimon*) life either to *Life* (*Fortunes*) or to *Life* (*Ethical*). The Stoic claim that virtue makes a man happy even on the rack is one extreme. Solon's warning ('Call no man happy till he's dead'), equating happiness with Fortunes, is the other. Aristotle says that a man's *bios* will be *eudaimon* if his activities conform to the standard of excellence[1] (*arete*). But this is not nearly so ethical as it looks. First, because Aristotle later admits that certain gifts of fortune are required for such a life: secondly, because *arete* itself is a far less narrowly moral term than English 'virtue'. *Arete* involves not simply 'being good' but being 'good *at*' a great many things (including morals), and Aristotle's conception of the happy life comes very close to our conception of the fully civilised life, in which the raw material (such as health, peace, and competence) provided by fortune is used by a master. Happiness is almost a *style*.

The emphasis of the word *bios* is nearly always, I think, on behaviour; we have only once found it used to mean Fortunes. This, taken in conjunction with the fact that the written record of a man's life was itself called a *bios*, throws some light on the practice of the earlier biographers. All of them, down to and including Walton (with the possible exception of Suetonius) seem to a modern reader somewhat niggardly. There is hardly any attempt to recreate the man's *milieu*; we are given no clue as to

[1] *Eth. Nic.* 1179 a.

what it must have felt like to be he. The explanation, I suggest, is that the authors are undertaking to tell us precisely his *bios*, his behaviour, and no more either of his *Routine* or of his *Fortunes* than is needed for that purpose. We are not expected to be much interested in what happened to him, for its own sake; the important thing is how he coped with it, the wise saws he uttered, the shocking or improving example he set—in a word, his style.

IV. 'LIFE' (THE 'COMMON LOT OF MAN')

As *Life* (*Chronological*) can be generalised to mean the normal span, so *Life* (*Qualitative*) can be generalised to mean the common character of men's experience between birth and death—the sort of thing every man must expect. This is nearly always a generalisation of *Life* (*Fortunes*) rather than of *Life* (*Ethical*). Thus pessimists say that disasters are probable, 'life being what it is', but cruelties and treacheries are probable, 'human nature being what it is'.

In Greek, *Life* (*Common Lot*) is *bios*. 'Tragedy', says Aristotle, 'is an imitation not of personalities but of action and *bios* and happiness.'[1] In Latin, *vita* is used in the same way. 'The fear of hell disturbs human *vita*'.[2] '*Vita* is neither a good nor an evil, but the field in which both good and evil occur.'[3] 'Menander delineated every image of *vita*.'[4]

The English word was so used at every period of our

---

[1] *Poet.* 1450 a.   [2] Lucretius II, 38.
[3] Seneca, *Ep.* XLIX.   [4] Quintilian x, i.

language. 'I can see no reason', says the Anglo-Saxon poet, 'why my mind should not grow dark when I consider the whole *lif* of men.'[1] Later examples come easily to mind. 'Life is a tale told by an idiot;[2]' 'when I consider life, 'tis all a cheat';[3] 'human life is every where a state in which much is to be endured and little to be enjoyed';[4] 'Life is real! Life is earnest!';[5] poetry is 'a criticism of life'.[6]

These are all plain sailing. But I must now turn to certain modern usages which seem to me difficult.

Henley writes 'Life! Life! Life! 'Tis the sole great thing this side of death'.[7]

'Our attitude to life', says Chesterton, 'can be better expressed in terms of a kind of military loyalty than in terms of criticism and approval': and again, suicide 'is the ultimate and absolute evil...the refusal to take the oath of loyalty to life'.[8]

An undergraduate periodical[9] praises an author's work because, 'like tragedy, it is ultimately for and not against life'.

A female correspondent tells me in a parenthesis that 'not to love life is blasphemy'.

Fr. Jarrett-Kerr says of Dr Leavis, 'he is explicit that life is above all to be affirmed'.[10]

---

[1] *Wanderer*, 59–60; cf. 89.   [2] *Macbeth* v, v, 24.
[3] Dryden, *Aureng-Zebe*, IV, i, 33.
[4] Johnson, *Rasselas* XI.   [5] Longfellow.
[6] Arnold, 'The Study of Poetry'.
[7] *Hawthorn and Lavender* XL.   [8] *Orthodoxy* v.
[9] *Delta*, 23 February 1961, p. 28.
[10] *Essays in Criticism* II, 4 October 1952, p. 358.

Dr Leavis himself says of Lawrence, 'It was not possible for him to be defeatist. The affirmation of life was always strong in him.'[1]

Mr R. Bolt, in the Magazine Section of the *Sunday Times*,[2] has the following: 'If Man destroys himself, it will be because his hatred of life is stronger than his love of life, because his greed, aggression, and fear are stronger than his self-denial, charity, and courage.'

The difficulty is to determine whether in these examples *life* means the Common Lot at all; and if at all, then with what precision and with what exclusion of other senses.

If Henley means the Common Lot his dictum would appear to be a perfect tautology. But I can think of no other meaning which would make it less tautological. Whether *life* means the Common Lot, or the Normal Span, or Conduct, or Fortunes, or Routine, or the mere state of being an organism, it is of course not only 'the sole great thing' this side of death, but the sole thing (until you die you will always be alive). You might as well tell us that morning is the sole great thing before afternoon or minority the sole great thing till your twenty-first birthday. Obviously Henley means by *life* some element or state within life (within our tale of years or our fortune or our conduct) on which he sets a high value; but his use of the noun *life* gives us no clue to what this element or state is.

Mr Bolt, on the other hand, makes it quite clear what he values. He values, as well he may, self-denial, charity,

[1] *D. H. Lawrence* (1957), p. 28.   [2] 29 January 1961, p. 25.

and courage. The problem is why he chooses to describe these virtues as 'love', and the opposite vices as 'hatred', of *Life*. To call fear 'hatred of life' when death is in fact what most men chiefly fear—to call courage 'love of life' when in reality it involves not setting one's life at a pin's fee—is surely a monstrous paradox. You may say, no doubt, that acts of courage and charity usually are, and always should be, motivated by love for my neighbour's life. But this only shows the inutility of talking about a love for *life* in the abstract. The lives both of individuals and of species are always in potential, and usually in actual, competition. The behaviour Mr Bolt approves and that which he condemns can equally, if you like, be called 'love of life', though I would much rather describe them as love of food, freedom, happiness, etc. But, either way, the real question is food (or freedom) for whom. Or does Mr Bolt mean that greed, aggression and the rest will in the long run destroy all (human) life, and therefore may be called 'inimical' or 'hostile' to it—and if they are hostile they can be called 'enemies', and if they are enemies they can be pictured as 'hating' it? But this would be to turn a metaphor into a mythology. A man does not at all necessarily hate a state of affairs which his own actions are in fact going to prevent, nor love a state of affairs which they are going to produce. Idleness is not a hatred of passing examinations: lechery is not a love of the pox.

It would, I think, be impossible to take *Life* in Mr Bolt's sentence as the Common Lot. Favourable and un-favourable estimates of that lot cannot at all plausibly be linked with degrees of selfishness and altruism. We may therefore eliminate both Henley and Mr Bolt from this list. Both use *life* as an evaluative term; Mr Bolt for moral virtue, and Henley for nobody knows what. But both, as we shall see, bear valuable witness to a remarkable linguistic situation.

The undergraduate who values work because it is 'for and not against life' appears to me to mean by *life* exactly the Common Lot. The somewhat defiant reference to tragedy—which might be thought by some to be 'against life'—makes that clear. Apparently good literature must not suggest the Johnsonian, still less the Sophoclean,[1] view of our destiny. *Life*, 'the sort of thing that happens', must be in some sense or other commended. Whether because it is really commendable or because we had better dream it to be so, does not appear.

Chesterton, writing in conscious reaction against *fin de siècle* pessimism, has raised that question. He means by *life* the Common Lot. His choice of the word *loyalty* makes his answer brilliantly clear. He is not expressing an opinion but calling for an attitude. We have no business to form opinions, whether favourable or otherwise, about life. We must plunge into it for all we are worth. We must fight the ship as long as we can keep her afloat.

Fr. Jarrett-Kerr and Dr Leavis use *life* in the same sense, and I think their view is really the same as Chesterton's. For of course *affirmation* cannot mean 'statement', and to affirm life cannot mean 'to state that organisms exist'.

[1] *Oed. Col.* 1222.

The opposite of this affirmation is significantly 'defeatism'; and the metaphor in that word, as in Chesterton's 'loyalty', calls up military and patriotic associations. The appeal in these two writers, as in Chesterton, is to what Plato would have called 'the spirited element' in us.

One step remains to be taken, and my correspondent takes it when she tells me that not to love *life* is 'blasphemy'. The Common Lot had been for Seneca the neutral field of good and evil. For Longfellow it was 'real' and 'earnest'. For Chesterton and Dr Leavis it is something like a banner or a 'cause'. For my correspondent it has become a deity.

All these modern examples alike, including those from Henley and Mr Bolt, bear witness to the steadily rising emotional temperature of the word *life*. Unless it had acquired a sort of halo, such usages as Henley's and Mr Bolt's could hardly have occurred. And even in the other writers, though I think the principal and fully conscious meaning of *life* is the Common Lot, the influence of the halo is possibly at work.

V. SEMANTIC HALO

What I mean by a semantic halo is well illustrated by the word *gentleman*. This was once a word without a halo, a designative term like *peasant*, *burgher*, or *nobleman*. It then acquired a quasi-ethical sense and for a while this and the old sense lived in uneasy symbiosis. But the ideal embodied in the ethical sense came to be almost the centre of the *mystique* by which a whole society lived. The incantatory power of the word when used in that sense was so great that it 'seeped' (as Professor Empson would say) into almost every sentence where the word, with whatever intention, was used. Yet at the same time the purely social meaning was never in fact—though often in profession—emptied out. Hence the bewildering nineteenth-century discussions in which speakers define *gentleman* in purely ethical terms but make it quite clear that at the same moment their idea of a gentleman involves membership of a social class. The emotion derived from one sense of the word can thus disastrously infect all its senses. The whole word is haloed, and finally there is nothing but halo. The word is then, for all accurate uses, dead. My suggestion is that something of this sort may at present be happening to the word *life*.

The enthusiastic utterances about *life* which occupied our attention in the last section are, let us note, a great novelty. The older writers know nothing of *life* as a flag, a cause, or a deity. Sober moralists like Seneca say, unanswerably, that the condition which makes all evil and all good possible can hardly be called good or evil itself (is a chess-board a good or bad move?). Imaginative writers, or their characters, describe *life* as something to be (at best) endured. Sages, far from exhorting us to 'affirm' or 'love' *life*, constantly warn us against a love of *life* which, they assume, will be excessive and in need of correction. Heroic death is praised by all; martyrdom by Christians; suicide by Stoics. Even the more moderate maxim is *summum nec metuas diem nec optes* ('nor dread thy last day nor desire it'[1]): 'nor love thy life nor hate'.[2]

[1] Martial x, 47.　　[2] Milton, *P.L.* xi, 549.

This does not mean that our ancestors had fewer or fainter enthusiasms than we. They were full of enthusiasms and desires: but not for mere *life*; rather for liberty, wealth, fame, virtue, pleasure, godliness or the like. These things were not valuable for the sake of *life*; *life* was valuable, when at all, for the sake of these things. We were specifically warned not 'to lose for life's sake what makes the reason for living', *propter vitam vivendi perdere causas.*[1]

We may well ask how so radical a change has come about, and two possible explanations will probably occur to everyone. It may be, on the one hand, that for all our talk of crisis and anxiety, the Common Lot has in modern times become very much more agreeable, and men speak better of *life* because it is really better. On the other hand, it might be that things have grown worse and we are now whistling to keep up our spirits; that the death-wish is now too insistent to be dallied with; that at all costs the cat must not be let out of the bag.

But to explore causes of that order would be to attempt, at the deepest level, the total history of our own time. That is no task for a mere philologist. And I believe that within our own discipline, within language itself, we may find causes which have at any rate contributed to the modern way of talking about *life*. If *Life* (*Common Lot*) now wears a halo this may be partly due to infection or 'seepage' from other senses of the word. To these, which of course demand attention for their own sakes as well as for their contribution to the halo, we must now turn.

[1] Juvenal VIII, 84.

VI. 'LIFE': WHAT I LIKE

When we think that something is a bad specimen of its class we often express this thought by saying that it is not a specimen of that class at all. We say 'This is not poetry (or tennis)' when we mean 'This is bad poetry (or tennis)'. And conversely, when we mean 'This is good poetry (or tennis)' we say 'This is real poetry (or tennis)'. In Greek a similar tendency sometimes changes *a-* from a negative into a pejorative prefix: *gamos agamos*,[1] literally 'marriage un-marriage', means a shockingly bad marriage. The German *un-* can be used in the same way. *Unwahr* means untrue; but *Unfall* and *Untier*, literally 'unchance' and 'unbeast', mean 'mischance' and 'monster'. Compare the Scots *unchancy*, for 'ominous', 'untoward', etc.

This treatment can be applied to *life*. The word may be used to mean the element or elements within life which the speaker values most highly. *Living* or *alive* may mean 'enjoying those experiences or performing those actions which are most worth while'. But people differ very widely as to which experiences and actions these are. Accordingly the word *life* when used in this evaluative sense has almost as many different contexts as there are speakers.

Life can be amorousness. Farquhar's Mr Sullen, on discovering that Dorinda 'can't think of the man without the bedfellow', observes, 'Why, child, you begin to live'.[2]

Life can be emotion in general, as against intellect. 'From the middle class one gets ideas, and from the

[1] Sophocles, *O. T.* 1214.   [2] *Beaux' Stratagem* IV, i.

common people—life itself, warmth. You feel their hates and loves.'[1]

Life can be intellectual activity and self-consciousness. '*Vivre, c'est penser et sentir son âme*, the essence of life lies in thinking and being conscious of one's soul.'[2]

Life can mean, as *nature* sometimes means,[3] whatever in our experience is not specifically human. 'The vast unexplained morality of life itself, what we call the immorality of nature, surrounds us in its eternal incomprehensibility, and in its midst goes on the little human morality play.'[4] (But possibly this should be listed below under *Life, Biological.*)

But what is *vital* can also be what is specifically human. 'Self-control...is nothing but a highly developed vital sense, dominating and regulating the mere appetites.'[5]

Life may apparently be, or be evidenced by, any moral virtue which is for the moment under consideration. In Shaw's play the two artificial hominoids whom the rash scientific adolescents have made, use lies. We are told, 'if they were alive they would speak the truth'.[6] A moment later there is a question of destroying the hominoids. The male one desperately pleads that only his mate should be destroyed. Their makers, disgusted at this, say 'Let us see whether we cannot put a little more life into them'. They do so, with the immediate result that the male hominoid

[1] Lawrence, *Sons and Lovers* x.
[2] Arnold, 'Joubert', *Essays in Criticism.*
[3] See above, pp. 48–50.
[4] Lawrence, *Selected Literary Criticism*, ed. A. Beal (1955), 'Study of Thomas Hardy', p. 177.
[5] Shaw, *Back to Methuselah*, p. iii.   [6] *Ibid.* p. 238.

changes his entreaty to 'Spare her and kill me'.[1] Thus *life* is willingness to die and an old paradox meets us in a new setting.

In all these examples the use of *life* to mean whatever the speaker values is serviceable language because, though the writers may value very different and even opposite things, they make it clear what those things are. *Life*, thus employed, is as useful a word as *good* or *nice*. The only danger is lest we should think it somehow more precise or scientific than they.

There are, however, other instances where *life* is thus approvingly used but the immediate context does not make clear what is being approved. Often a longer context—the tenor of the author's works as a whole or our knowledge of the sort of circles he is probably addressing—will give us a clue.

Arnold says that real men of genius are 'capable of emitting a life-giving stimulus'. In isolation 'life-giving stimulus' might mean almost anything; something that made one dance like a maenad, or stop telling lies, or practise self-control, or grow extra arms and legs like Shaw's 'ancients'. Knowing Arnold, we guess that the *life* which is stimulated will be urbanity or sweetness and light or something of that sort. As an anonymous quotation his dictum would convey very little.

Lawrence says that 'in life' we 'have got to live or we are nothing'.[2] Taken *au pied de la lettre*, this is, like Henley's, an identical proposition, but so to take it would

[1] *Ibid.* p. 246.
[2] *Selected Literary Criticism*, 'Why the novel matters', p. 107.

be silly and captious. 'To live' means 'to have or lead (or both) the sort of life that Lawrence values'. What that is we are to find out from our general knowledge of his books and behaviour.

So often in Dr Leavis, we read about the 'triumph over them (i.e. class-distinctions) of life',[1] or that 'the pride of class-superiority...appears as the enemy of life'.[2] A 'true moral sense' is 'one that shall minister to life'.[3] Or again: 'I have spent many years in a university English school, doing what I could to promote a study of literature that should be a discipline of intelligence, fostering life.'[4] And again: it is 'more important than ever that places of higher education should be fostering centres of responsibility, intelligence, and courage for life'.[5]

Perhaps my best way of diagnosing this semantic situation will be to say that I too could endorse all these utterances. I also could say that class-distinctions are the enemy of life (they are certainly a great bore). I also wish universities to encourage 'life'. But the trouble is that the context of the word *life*, the very pictures it arouses, might be quite different for Dr Leavis and for me. Each would be using the word to mean 'what I approve'. Until this blank cheque, this purely and therefore unspecifically evaluative term, had been placed on the index, nothing but cross-purposes could result from any discussion between us. And in the examples already quoted, is it not clear that the introduction of *life*, far from clarifying,

[1] *D. H. Lawrence*, p. 73.   [2] *Ibid.* p. 75.
[3] *Ibid.* p. 82.
[4] *Essays in Criticism* III, 2 (April 1953), p. 218.
[5] *Ibid.* p. 219.

inspissates? Do we not understand *intelligence* better than *intelligence fostering life*? Are not *responsibility and courage* clearer than *responsibility and courage for life*? For we may be sure that by adding 'for life' Dr Leavis does not mean to exclude courage for facing death. Where, if not in life, can death be faced?

Those who are in fact using *life* to mean 'what I approve'—which, by the way, is usually a very small part of *life* (*the Common Lot*)—do not always make quite clear to their readers what they are doing. They are perhaps not always clear themselves. Hence there can be confusion between *life* (= *what I approve*) and *life* (*Common Lot*), and the base word *life* can arouse favourable emotions even in those who have not asked themselves what, in the particular context, it means. The halo shines on them.

VII. 'REAL' LIFE

Life is sometimes an ellipsis for 'real life'. The distinction between 'real life' on the one hand and, on the other, day-dreams, expectations, theories, or ideals is very familiar, but very difficult to state in watertight form. Since we are not attempting philosophy, we must be content with a very rough and ready approximation.

In the previous section we noticed the use of the word *real* ('real poetry', 'real tennis') to mean 'good in its kind' or 'good enough to deserve the name'. But that is not what *real* usually means when we speak of 'real life'. The expression still implies disparagement of something else (named or implied) with which 'real life' is being contrasted, but it is a special sort of disparagement.

Except for certain metaphysical purposes the question 'Is this real?' had generally best be parried by the question 'Is it a real *what*?' This is not a real ghost, but it is a real dummy made out of a turnip and a dust sheet. That is not a real house, but it is a real bit of stage scenery. No real crocodile disturbed me in the night; a real nightmare did. Mr Chadband's piety was not real piety but real hypocrisy. Is this picture a real Rembrandt or a real forgery?

The statement that something is 'not real'—more strictly, that it is not a real *x* but is a real *y*—implies that it is either less important than we (or someone else) might suppose, or else is important in some quite different way. The turnip-ghost is not a proper object for awe and provides no evidence for the immortality of the soul. The canvas house on the stage is no protection against weather. We must not expect a high price for the forged Rembrandt. Mr Chadband's hypocrisy has importance, but not the same importance that genuine piety would have had; a different reaction on our part is appropriate.

In the vast majority of contexts, then, 'the unreal' is the discounted, what is set aside, what can and should be ignored. We have been deceived; we are now undeceived and can go ahead. If the deception was deliberately induced in us (say, by Mr Chadband or a forger) we feel some indignation: if it was self-induced, we may be angry with ourselves. Either way, these are pressures tending to make *unreal* a disparaging, and *real* a laudatory, term.

So, for the most part. But there can also be a recognition of (in some sense) unreality which involves no disparagement. This is in the realm of illusions that are not delusions; in art, or in play. The stage house which is not a real house may be praised as good scenery. Children who make believe they are drinking wine though it is really pepsicola do not scorn it. It must however be noticed that these exceptions have always weighed very little with the vast majority of the human race. And even the small minority who think art more important than play usually hold some theory of art which makes its importance depend on some, subtly defined, sort of 'reality'. For our present purpose it does not in the least matter whether they are right or not. The point is that the exceptional cases of play and art, thus handled, have hardly any effect on the laudatory quality of the word *real* or the disparaging quality of *unreal*.

Real life, then, no less than *life* in Henley or Lawrence, becomes a name for certain elements in our experience which the speakers value. But not necessarily the same elements nor the same valuation.

'Johnson', says Boswell, 'loved business, loved to have his wisdom actually operate on real life.'[1] Apparently any petty economic transaction is *Real Life*; the contrast is with the life of thought. A character in Rose Macaulay says 'These universities cram learning into our heads but teach us little enough of life'.[2] We read in Lawrence, 'to us who care more about life than scholarship'.[3] Arnold speaks of 'an Englishman who reads to live and does not live to read'.[4] Everyone remembers, though not all remember the context, Goethe's

[1] 20 March 1776.　　　[2] *They Were Defeated* (1960), p. 378.
[3] 'The Dragon of the Apocalypse.'
[4] *Marcus Aurelius.*

Grau, teurer Freund, ist alle Theorie,
Und grün des Lebens goldnes Baum.[1]

The *Leben* which Mephistopheles opposes to theory is the practical life of lucrative charlatanism.

The antithesis in all these between '(*real*) *life*' and thought or study is philosophically scandalous, for thought and study, no less than business or practice, are the activities of the living and therefore part of *life*. The popularity of the antithesis has, I believe, two sources. One of them is respectable. Those things which our thoughts are about are reasonably contrasted with our thoughts about them as 'real'—the reality the thoughts were trying or claiming to represent. Thus Wordsworth's Happy Warrior is the man who

> when brought
> Among the tasks of real life, has wrought
> Upon the plan that pleased his boyish thought.

Heroic action is real, in contrast to his boyish thought, because his boyish thought was about, was an anticipatory representation of, heroic action. But there is another and less respectable source. This is the deeply ingrained conviction of narrow minds that whatever things they themselves are chiefly exercised on are the only important things, the only things worth adult, informed, and thoroughgoing interest. This often means in practice that everything except acquisition and social success is excluded from the category of (*real*) *life* and relegated to the realm of play or day-dream.

[1] 'All theory, my friend, is grey, but green is the golden tree of life', *Faust. Studierzimmer* 2.

We noticed a moment ago that the admitted illusions of art had very little influence in moderating the strong approval conveyed by the word *real*. But we can now go further. Our usual language about one art, literature, actually helps to brighten the halo on *life* or *real life*. Literature is admired for representing 'life as it really is', and by an easy ellipsis the lifelikeness of persons and characters in fiction is often called simply *life*; just as in Neo-Classical criticism the likeness to 'Nature' was called simply 'nature'. Thus Raleigh credits Shakespeare with 'this amazing secret of life',[1] or Virginia Woolf complains that 'life escapes' Arnold Bennett, and adds that 'perhaps without life nothing else is worth while'.[2] No one, to be sure, misunderstands the expression in such contexts; but one more approving overtone is contributed to the word *life*.

VIII. 'LIFE' (BIOLOGICAL)

We now turn to that usage which, of all others, has contributed most to the rising temperature of the noun *Life*: the prime source of its magic.

'I shall assume', says Eddington (speculating about other planets) 'that the required conditions of habitability are not unlike those on the earth and that if such conditions obtain life will automatically make its appearance.'[3] *Life* in this sentence is, like *Life* (*Common Lot*), a high abstraction; but a very different one. *Life* (*Com-*

[1] *Shakespeare*, p. 143.
[2] *The Common Reader*, 'Modern Fiction'.
[3] *The Nature of the Physical World*, p. 170.

mon Lot) abstracts the common, characteristic features of terrestrial, human, and individual experiences, as we learn them directly or (much more) from biography, history, and some kinds of fiction. But *life* in Eddington's sense is 'what is common to all organisms': if you like, it is organisation, nutrition, growth, and reproduction—something we study in laboratories or learn of from text-books. I shall call it *Life* (*Biological*).

From the point of view of formal logic *Life* (*Biological*) is in the same position as any other universal: it is abstracted from particulars (from all particular organisms) just as *Blue* is abstracted from seas, skies, bluebells, kingfishers, and the rest, or *Shape* from all visible objects, or *Virtue* from all the actions we approve. On the prevalent modern view it would therefore be an *ens rationis* or 'creature of discourse'; that is to say, not a 'thing' as the particular organisms are things, but a linguistic gadget, a tool whereby we can conveniently manipulate the subject-matter of biology.

Such, I say, is the modern view of universals; but a very different view was once held. Plato, as everyone remembers, talked as if Justice or Goodness were entities not only as real as particular just acts or good men but incomparably more so. Most emphatically of all, he talked thus about Beauty. The place where he does so is hackneyed, but so germane that I must recall it. The pupil, we are told, should begin by loving beautiful bodies. He must then learn to love beautiful souls; then the beauty embodied in laws and manners; then, that in the sciences. He will then be ready to turn to 'the main sea of Beauty'.

After that comes the vision. He will 'see' a wonder; Beauty itself, which neither grows nor decays, which knows nothing of more and less, without body, without discourse of reason, 'itself in itself eternally existing in pure homogeneity'.[1]

To a transcendent entity of this character Plato gave the name *eidos* (plural *eidé*), and we may follow him.[2] An *eidos* is obviously very unlike the abstract universal of modern logic. Indeed the whole Platonic position has been judged so hopelessly alien to our mode of thought as to be dismissed with the amusing formula 'Plato thought abstract nouns were proper names'.

In reality, however, the modern usage of one privileged abstract noun often reveals a state of mind—not necessarily the best state of the best minds—which is startlingly close to the Platonic. If we want to know what it felt like to be Plato thinking about Beauty, we can get some inkling by noticing how people use *Life* (*Biological*).

C. E. B. Russell writes 'World-and-Life-Affirmation. This means that man has an inner conviction that life is a real thing'.[3] If life here were an abstract universal like *shape* or *equality*, a 'conviction that life is a real thing' would seem to mean merely a conviction that organisms exist, which is a conviction hardly worth mentioning. Clearly, the author is envisaging *Life* (*Biological*) as an *eidos*; not as an H.C.F. abstracted from organisms but as a transcendent force or entity which is immanent in them.

[1] *Symposium*, 210 b–211 b.
[2] The alternative names, 'Form' and 'Idea', have too many false associations.
[3] *The Path to Reconstruction* (1941), p. v.

This is confirmed a page or two later when she says that 'our guiding principle...should be reverence for that life which is the same divine, mysterious force in man or dog or flower or flea'.[1] But no one could reverence as 'divine' an abstract common quality.

Mr Speirs, writing of *Gawain*, says 'the ultimate source of the poem's actuality, strength, and coherence, is the knowledge...that there is life inexhaustible at the roots of the world even in the dead season, that there is perpetually to be expected the unexpected spring re-birth'.[2] It is beautifully said. But, after all, the poet didn't know, and Mr Speirs doesn't know, whether this planet or this universe will always contain organisms. The hyperbole, I suggest, comes naturally to Mr Speirs because he is really thinking of the *eidos*. The poet's vigorous delight in youth, feast, revelry, courage, and (above all) in the exuberant 'boisterousness' of the Green Knight himself, all become for the critic manifestations of *Life* (*Biological*). They arouse in him feelings which cry out for some such transcendent and ultimate object. And in that mood it is naturally—by an act rather of faith than of reason—saluted as 'inexhaustible'. It is, indeed, very unlikely that the poet even consciously thought about *life* (in this sense) at all; but Mr Speirs might reply 'thoughts beyond their thoughts to those high bards were given'.

We feel the presence of the *eidos* even more strongly when we read of 'the orgiastic, mystical sense of oneness,

[1] *The Path to Reconstruction* (1941), p. 3.
[2] *Medieval English Poetry: the Non-Chaucerian Tradition* (1957), p. 221.

of life as indestructibly powerful and pleasurable'.[1] If
Life here were an abstract universal, to call it *orgiastic* or
pleasurable would be nonsense. The existence of individual
organisms is sometimes orgiastic, sometimes pleasurable,
sometimes not, and many organisms (say, lichens)
probably know neither orgies nor pleasures. But you
must put into your concept of an abstract universal only
what is common to all the particulars. To make *Life*
(*Biological*) 'pleasurable' is like putting 'drawn in chalk'
or 'equilateral' into your idea of Triangle. And even if
one were determined to make this blunder, why 'pleasurable' rather than 'painful'? To be alive, so far as we know,
is the condition which alone makes pains and pleasures
possible; so that to call *life* 'pleasurable' is, to use our old
example, like calling a chessboard and a box of men a
good move. They make all good moves possible; and all
bad moves. But things are quite different if *Life* is an *eidos*;
for the true Platonic *eidos* is not only a 'thing' over and
above all the particulars but a better thing than they.
Beauty-in-itself is more beautiful than all beautiful
objects: they are indeed mere shadows of it. In order that
Life (*Biological*) can be called 'orgiastic' and 'pleasurable'
it must be given the same status as Plato's Beauty. It must
be the plenitude and perfection whereof only dim traces
are found in actual living things.

The 'mystical sense of oneness' also needs to be
pondered. No doubt all particulars which have been
classified together in virtue of a common quality have a

---

[1] Nietzsche, quoted by R. B. Sewall, 'The Tragic Form', *Essays in
Criticism* IV, 4 (1954), p. 350.

logical unity if the classification has been properly made. But this oneness hardly requires a 'mystical sense' to recognise it. Common sense tells me that if *ABC* is an isosceles triangle it will, in that respect, be one with all other isosceles triangles. Nietzsche's 'mystical sense of oneness' or Lawrence's 'intense apprehension of the unity of life'[1] must be something quite different. Two passages from Lawrence will help. He speaks of 'the gladness of a man in contact with the unknown in the female, which gives him a sense of richness and oneness with all life'.[2] And of the young couple copulating in the wood (*Sons and Lovers*, XIII) we read 'If so great a magnificent power could overwhelm them, identify them altogether with itself, so that they knew they were only grains in the tremendous heave that lifted every grass-blade its little height, and every tree and living thing, then why fret about themselves? They could let themselves be carried by life.'[3]

We all, I take it, recognise the feeling which Lawrence means to express, and neither moral nor literary criticism has any place in the present inquiry. Our sole concern is with the implied meaning of *life* which Lawrence uses to express the feeling. Neither passage will 'work' if *life* is an abstract universal. Our merely logical unity with all other living things, our membership of the class 'organisms', is nothing to the purpose; nor is it illustrated by

[1] *D. H. Lawrence: Novelist* (1957), p. 99. Dr Leavis, unlike many vitalists, wisely adds to 'the oneness of life' the 'separateness and irreducible otherness of lives' (p. 102).

[2] *Selected Literary Criticism*, ed. A. Beal (1955), 'Study of Thomas Hardy', p. 202.   [3] Penguin ed., pp. 430–1.

copulation any more (or less) than by nutrition, excretion, or death. As for a harmonious and co-operative unity with *life* in general, this is forever impossible. All organisms live in lethal competition with other organisms: man, with his pesticides and antiseptics and carnivorous diet, most of all. And with his contraceptives. Since the young people in *Sons and Lovers* never appear either to hope or fear fertility, we may assume that they have prudently taken measures to be 'carried by life' just so far as is convenient and no further. But all these cold and, as it were, profane cavils are silenced once you set up *Life* as the archetype, the *eidos*. In cold logic the fact that there was a great deal of organic life besides that of the two lovers in the wood is the most absurd argument for not 'fretting about themselves'; as they would have discovered if that other organic life had included a plentiful supply of adders, mosquitoes, or poison-ivy. But that is really beside the point. The lovers feel their own erotic appetites not as a mere *instance* of 'organic activity' but as something poured into them from a transcendent source. Many lovers in many ages have felt this. The Greeks would have said it was Aphrodite. A Renaissance poet might have said it was the far-travelled reminiscence of supra-mundane Beauty-itself. For Lawrence it is *Life* (*Biological*) conceived as a real supra-personal entity. All the other organic activity in the wood is mentioned to exalt that entity. It is as joint servants of *Life* that the grass-blades and the trees matter. Without that Queen these fellow-courtiers would be mere scenery.

In Lawrence this conception is merely implicit, but we

can find it explicit elsewhere. 'The individual drop of life', says Mr Findlay, 'returns after death to the reservoir from which it came.'[1] There is, then, a reservoir? The actual organisms do not contain all the life there is? 'A representation of the whole of life cannot consist in a combination of the simple ideas which life herself has deposited in us during the course of her evolution; how could the part be equivalent to the whole, the content to that which contains it, the residuum of the vital operation to the operation itself?'[2] This is very well if *Life* is a thing, a 'force', or a dæmon. But none of the metaphors will work if it is an abstract universal. Triangles are not related to Triangularity as parts to a whole, or content to container, or residuum to operation.

Though Plato did not personalise Beauty, the religious note in his language about it is unmistakable. That note becomes even louder in some modern utterances about *Life (Biological)*. It—or she—becomes a goddess. Evolutionary biology is 'the science of the everlasting transmutations of the Holy Ghost in the world'.[3] Creative Evolution is 'the religion of the Twentieth Century'.[4] This religion has its great commandment: 'Life must not cease. That comes before everything.'[5]

This commandment is very significant. An intense momentary conviction that one's own life must not cease and that its preservation 'comes before everything' is a familiar experience; the ordinary name for it is *terror*.

[1] S. Findlay, *Immortal Longings* (1961), p. 34.
[2] Bergson, *L'Évolution Créatrice* (1917), p. 53.
[3] Shaw (quoting Lorenz Oken), *Back to Methuselah*, p. xxix.
[4] *Ibid.* p. lxxviii.   [5] *Ibid.* p. 10.

The same conviction, steadily maintained and acted upon over a long period so that it becomes habitual, is also familiar. The ordinary name for it is *cowardice*. But I question whether we have by nature any similar feeling about *Life* (*Biological*) as such. Our spontaneous desire is that some lives should be preserved (which means, if we think it out, 'preserved at the expense of others'). But the proper name for this is *love* (of our friends, or class, or party, or nation, or species). We wish them to live because we love them: we do not love them because they are specimens of *life*. In other words, the Shavian religion must begin with a conversion, with new motives. We must turn away from all that instinct or experience has taught us to desire and learn to desire, to love 'before everything' an invisible, unimaginable object.

IX. THE 'TREE'

In the quotation from Eddington at the beginning of the previous section *Life* (*Biological*) was envisaged as something which will automatically turn up wherever suitable conditions arise. If life thus turned up on one of the planets of Sirius (supposing Sirius to have planets), that life and the life on Earth would be mutually independent. They would have like causes but no causal link with one another. They would simply be instances of the same thing, as the sphericity of Sirius and the sphericity of Sol are instances of the same shape.

If this had been for the last two centuries or so the way we usually thought about *Life* (*Biological*), the semantic situation which I have been trying to describe would probably never have arisen. But it was not. Naturally and inevitably biology has meant for us terrestrial biology. And it has long been held that terrestrial organisms are not merely independent instances of *Life* (*Biological*), but are factually, genetically, connected. 'All species of life upon Earth...are descended by slow continuous processes of change from some very simple, ancestral form of life.'[1] Or again, 'Life, from its beginnings, is the continuation of a single and identical drive (*élan*) which has divided itself among the divergent lines of evolution'.[2] This puts a very different complexion on the matter. In addition to the logical unity which organisms would in any case have had as members of a class, they now have unity of another sort.

It is in some degree like the unity of a family. We give the same name, say, to all the Postlethwaite-Joneses. This is not because we have, after inspection, discovered and abstracted a common quality of Postlethwaite-Jonesness (one could do that with some families, not with all), but because they are connected by an intricate web of causality. If they are an ancient and noble family they may speak of 'the blood of the Postlethwaite-Joneses'. They will set a high value on this 'blood'. They will indeed hypostatise it, treat it as though it were a thing over and above all the individual members of the family and valuable in itself. For while they may hope and believe that this 'blood' will by heredity produce heroic individuals, they will also work it the other way round

---

[1] H. G. Wells, *Short History* (1928), p. 15.
[2] Bergson, *L'Évolution Créatrice*, p. 57.

and say that all Postlethwaite-Joneses ought to be heroic in order to be worthy of their blood. In extreme cases every member of the family may be sacrificed to the Family. The 'blood' may become more important than the human beings who have it. Historically, we are rooted in centuries of such feeling. It is often extended to groups whose members are related far more loosely: to nationalities and to (largely imaginary) 'races'.

As soon as all terrestrial organisms are seen in their genetic unity, made into a kind of family tree, the same feeling which went out to the 'blood' of a family can apparently be transferred to *Life* (*Biological*). Two pressures, I suggest, encourage the transference.

(1) The popular picture of evolution—which differs in some respects from that of real biologists—is one that must deeply move any generous imagination. *Life* (*Biological*) begins as something very weak and humble with all the odds against it. Nevertheless it wins. It becomes Man. It conquers inanimate nature. It aspires to be the ancestor of super-Man. The story thus embodies one of the great archetypal patterns: the Ugly Duckling, the oppressed but finally triumphant Cinderella, the despised seventh son who outshines the six others, Jack the giant-killer. So moving a tale must not be that of a mere abstraction. It invites us first to reify, then to personify, finally to deify, *Life* (*Biological*).

(2) We all fear death for ourselves and for those we love, and to that extent (at least) we all value our lives and theirs. When we are thinking of individuals, *life* is therefore a rich, heart-warming word. It is the opposite

of death. By a firm association this rich quality, this halo, continues to cling to the word *life* even where it means *Life (Biological)*. It is not logically entitled to it. *Life (Biological)* is the opposite of the inanimate, not the opposite of death. On the contrary the reign of *Life (Biological)* coincides with the reign of death, for only what lives can die, and nothing lives that won't die. To say that 'there is life inexhaustible' in the universe is equally to say that there is death inexhaustible. The one will keep on occurring as long as the other, and no longer. But under the equivocal enchantment of the noun *Life* we ignore this. We talk, and therefore feel, as if *Life (Biological)*, the notional thread on which all living things are strung like beads, could itself be desired, enjoyed, or experienced.

And all the while Logic must ask 'Is *Life (Biological)* even alive?' After all, swiftness does not run about, and illness does not get ill, and death does not die.

X. APOLOGY

If anyone in Victoria's reign had tried to put himself outside the *mystique* of that society and, from outside, coldly to dissect the word *gentleman*, we can guess what would have happened to him. Wherever he had found confusion he would have been told 'But of course you can't understand. That is because you yourself are not a gentleman.' I am very well aware that in attempting to unravel the word *life* I risk a like fate. I have been handling a word which is still perhaps too hot to touch. I have had to put myself outside the *mystique* of our own age; and all that is said from outside will seem profane to those who are within. It will probably be useless to plead that I am not, in my private capacity, immune to all the appeals of this glowing word; that I am not more discontented than others with the Common Lot or that I feel no grandeur in popular conceptions of the Life Force. I shall probably be regarded as 'a doctor of death'. But I have thought the risk worth taking. It seems to me of practical importance that the analytical and critical bent of our age should not be expended entirely on our ancestors and that confusions should sometimes be exposed while they are still potent. It is more dangerous to tread on the corns of a live giant than to cut off the head of a dead one: but it is more useful and better fun.

11

I DARE SAY

In modern English this formula is never a strong affirmation. In that respect it is sharply distinguished from *I venture to say*, which, though modest in tone, ushers in a considered opinion that the speaker is prepared to defend. At its strongest, *I dare say* means something like 'Probably' or 'I shouldn't wonder if'; as when the doctor in *Bleak House*[1] looks at the dead opium-eater and says. 'He must have been a good figure when a youth, and, I dare say, good-looking', or when Mr Jarndyce says, 'Such wisdom will come soon enough, I dare say, if it is to come at all'.[2] When slightly weaker than this, it is roughly translatable by *perhaps*: 'I dare say you're right.'[3] It can be weakened still further to express, not an affirmation, but a mere refusal to deny, as in W. S. Gilbert's lines

> Yet *B* is worthy, I dare say,
> Of more prosperity than *A*—[4]

where *I dare say* is equivalent to 'for all I know to the contrary'. This usage often, perhaps usually, carries the implication that the proposition in question is not going to be denied nor indeed investigated chiefly because, even if true, it would be of no importance in the context.

[1] Ch. xi, Gadshill edn. vol. i, p. 169.
[2] *Ibid.* xiii, p. 217.
[3] E. Nesbit, *Five Children and It*, ch. ii.   [4] *Mikado* ii.

Thus in the story by Nesbit already quoted the children, who look as if they had no money, tell a shopkeeper that they would like to buy some of his stock, and he answers drily 'I daresay you would';[1] with the implication 'I couldn't care less'. Similarly in Dorothy Sayers's *The Man Born to be King*.[2] Philip who has allowed himself to be cheated by a tradesman to the detriment of the common purse says, 'I'm very sorry, everybody' and gets from Simon the retort 'I dare say you are, but—'. In other words, 'you may be sorry, but how does that mend matters?' In close argument *I dare say*, like the concessive *quidem* in Latin, grants for purposes of argument something which, if granted, leaves the speaker's case unimpaired: 'It is open to the noble lord to say that he would have decided differently. I dare say he would. But that doesn't mean to the rest of us that he would necessarily have decided more wisely.'[3] Finally *I dare say* can be ironical. In another of E. Nesbit's stories the children tell the cook 'We'll have a tinned tongue', and she replies 'I dare say';[4] that is, 'A likely story!' or 'Don't you wish you may get it?'

But if we extend our reading a few centuries backwards we shall discover that *I dare say* once bore a very different meaning. It was as strong as *I venture to say* and far less modest in tone, being in fact an assertion of the most uncompromising and resounding sort. Hence in some old contexts any intrusion of the weakened modern sense

---

[1] *Five Children and It*, ch. II.   [2] (1943), p. 117.
[3] *The Trial of Lady Chatterley* (1961), p. 281 (debate in the Lords).
[4] *The Phoenix and the Carpet*, ch. IX.

would produce absurdity. Sir Ector, 'when he beheld Sir Launcelot's visage, he fell down in a swoon. And when he waked it were hard any tongue to tell the doleful complaints that he made for his brother. Ah Launcelot, he said, thou were head of all Christian Knights, and now I dare say, said Sir Ector, thou Sir Launcelot, there thou liest, that thou were never matched of earthly Knight's hand.'[1] Sir Ector certainly does not mean that, for all he knows to the contrary, Launcelot may perhaps never have met his match. *I dare say* here means literally 'I dare to say. I take the full responsibility of saying', probably with the implication that he will prove his words 'in clean battle' on the body of anyone who offers to deny them.

Two centuries later Bunyan's Mrs Light-Mind speaks as follows: 'I was yesterday at Madam Wanton's...so there we had music and dancing and what else was meet to fill up the time with pleasure. And, I dare say, my lady herself is an admirably well-bred gentlewoman.'[2] The speaker is not putting forward what she regards as a merely probable opinion about Madam Wanton's good breeding. She is asserting it as strongly as she knows how. If we were doing a modernised version we should have to render her *I dare say* by something like 'Take it from me' or 'Upon my word'. Later in the same book, Christiana, as she pants up the Hill Difficulty, exclaims 'I dare say this is a breathing [i.e. a breath-taking] hill'. Something like 'I'll warrant you' is the nearest we can get to her sense.

[1] Malory, *Morte* XXI, xiii.　　　[2] *Pilgrim's Progress*, Pt II.

As usual in such developments, the two extremes—Malory and the modern usage—are easily distinguished; but during the long period between them almost every instance of *I dare say* requires careful scrutiny. Jane Austen uses the formula very often. I find in her works many places where, I think, it cannot bear the modern sense; some where it may; and none where it must.

I will take first those where I think it can't.

In *Northanger Abbey* the egregious Thorpe says of General Tilney, 'A very fine fellow; as rich as a Jew. I should like to dine with him. I dare say he gives famous dinners.'[1] Thorpe would not wish to dine with a man merely on the ground that, for all he knew to the contrary, the dinners might possibly be good. *I dare say* here means 'I bet' or 'I'll be bound'.

In *Emma*[2] old Woodhouse, speaking of his grandchildren to Harriet Smith, says 'They are very fond of being at Hartfield', and she replies, 'I dare say they are, Sir. I am sure I do not know who is not.' *I dare say* in any of the modern senses would be far too cold or too concessive for the gushing Harriet who herself finds Hartfield a social paradise. It would be almost pert. She means 'But *of course* they are!'

Later in the same book,[3] after Mrs Elton's visit. Mr Woodhouse says to Emma 'she seems a very pretty sort of young lady, and I dare say she was very much pleased with you'. Now Mr Woodhouse is the most doting and credulous of fathers, at once eager that Emma should be admired and very easily satisfied in the way of

[1] Ch. XII.   [2] Ch. IX.   [3] Ch. XXXII.

evidence for such admiration. That Mrs Elton should like Emma is not to him something merely possible, or even merely probable. His *I dare say* means something like 'Depend upon it' or 'You may be very sure'.

The following examples are debatable.

John Dashwood, who is hoping that Colonel Brandon may marry Elinor, shows him some of her pictures with the words 'These are done by my eldest sister and you, as a man of taste, will, I dare say, be pleased with them'.[1] He may be finessing, taking the view that advertisement is most effective when disguised in mock modesty. If so, the modern sense ('you may possibly care for them') will do. But John Dashwood is a coarse, insensitive creature. More probably he means 'I think I can predict', or even 'I don't mind betting'.

'I hope Mr Allen will put on his greatcoat when he goes,' says Mrs Allen, 'but I dare say he will not, for he had rather do anything in the world than walk out in a greatcoat.'[2] Here the modern sense will do very well. But so will the older and stronger. In view of her husband's normal practice, Mrs Allen may well mean it's a safe guess that he will go without his coat.

When Mrs John Dashwood is persuading Mr John Dashwood to disregard his father's dying words she says, 'He did not know what he was talking of, I dare say; ten to one, he was light-headed'.[3] Does *I dare say* mean 'for all we know', or is it nearly synonymous with 'ten to one'?

[1] *Sense and Sensibility* XXXIV.   [2] *Northanger Abbey* XI.
[3] *Sense and Sensibility* II.

Mrs Jennings in the same novel is also ambiguous. She is convinced that Colonel Brandon has an illegitimate daughter called Miss Williams. When he receives a letter and fails to tell the company anything about it, she says 'Perhaps it is about Miss Williams—and, by the by, I dare say it is because he looked so conscious when I mentioned her...I would lay any wager it is about Miss Williams'.[1] It will be noticed that *I dare say* is preceded by *perhaps* and followed by *I would lay any wager*. It could be synonymous with either. It could have a shade of meaning intermediate between the two, as if the speaker's conviction were increasing while she talked.

When Bingley urges Darcy to dance with Elizabeth[2] he points her out 'sitting down just behind you' and says she 'is very pretty and I dare say very agreeable'. Can this really have been the *I dare say* of modern conversation? It is just possible. But it is cold encouragement to say that a girl is 'perhaps' or 'possibly' or 'for all you know to the contrary' very agreeable, nor is it in keeping with the generous, sanguine, easily pleased Bingley. I think that if Bingley had been talking modern English he would have said, at the very least, 'no doubt', or (more probably) 'I don't mind betting'.

Perhaps hardly any of these passages would have struck us if we had not come to them with the examples from Malory and Bunyan in mind. Indeed I am ashamed to remember for how many years, as a boy and a young man, I read nineteenth-century fiction without noticing how often its language differed from ours. I believe it

[1] *Sense and Sensibility* xiv.   [2] *Pride and Prejudice* iii.

was work on far earlier English that first opened my eyes: for there a man is not so easily deceived into thinking he understands when he does not. In the same way some report that Latin or German first taught them that English also has grammar and syntax. There are some things about your own village that you never know until you have been away from it.

1 2

AT THE FRINGE
OF LANGUAGE

LANGUAGE exists to communicate whatever it can communicate. Some things it communicates so badly that we never attempt to communicate them by words if any other medium is available. Those who think they are testing a boy's 'elementary' command of English by asking him to describe in words how one ties one's tie or what a pair of scissors is like, are far astray. For precisely what language can hardly do at all, and never does well, is to inform us about complex physical shapes and movements. Hence descriptions of such things in the ancient writers are nearly always unintelligible. Hence we never in real life voluntarily use language for this purpose; we draw a diagram or go through pantomimic gestures. The exercises which such examiners set are no more a test of 'elementary' linguistic competence than the most difficult bit of trick-riding from the circus ring is a test of elementary horsemanship.

Another grave limitation of language is that it cannot, like music or gesture, do more than one thing at once. However the words in a great poet's phrase interinanimate one another and strike the mind as a quasi-instantaneous chord, yet, strictly speaking, each word must be read or heard before the next. That way, language is as unilinear as time. Hence, in narrative, the great difficulty of presenting a very complicated change which happens suddenly. If we do justice to the complexity, the time the reader must take over the passage will destroy the feeling of suddenness. If we get in the suddenness we shall not be able to get in the complexity. I am not saying that genius will not find its own ways of palliating this defect in the instrument; only that the instrument is in this way defective.

One of the most important and effective uses of language is the emotional. It is also, of course, wholly legitimate. We do not talk only in order to reason or to inform. We have to make love and quarrel, to propitiate and pardon, to rebuke, console, intercede, and arouse. 'He that complains', said Johnson, 'acts like a man, like a social being.' The real objection lies not against the language of emotion as such, but against language which, being in reality emotional, masquerades—whether by plain hypocrisy or subtler self-deceit—as being something else.

All my generation are much indebted to Dr I. A. Richards for having fully called our attention to the emotional functions of language. But I am hardly less indebted to Professor Empson for having pointed out that the conception of emotional language can be very easily extended too far.[1] It was time to call a halt.

We must obviously not call any utterance 'emotional' language because it in fact arouses, even because it must arouse, emotion. 'It is not cancer after all', 'The Germans have surrendered', 'I love you'—may all be true state-

[1] *Op. cit.* ch. i.

ments about matter of fact. And of course it is the facts, not the language, that arouse the emotion. In the last the fact communicated is itself the existence of an emotion but that makes no difference. Statements about crime are not criminal language; nor are statements about emotions necessarily emotional language. Nor, in my opinion, are value-judgements ('this is good', 'this is bad') emotional language. Approval and disapproval do not seem to me to be emotions. If we felt at all times about the things we judge good the emotion which is appropriate, our lives would be easier. It would also be an error to treat 'I am washed in the blood of the Lamb' as emotional language. It is of course metaphorical language. But by his metaphor the speaker is trying to communicate what he believes to be a fact. You may of course think the belief false in his particular case. You may think the real universe is such that no fact which corresponded to such a statement could possibly occur. You may say that the real cause which prompts a man to say things like that is a state of emotion. But if so, an emotion has produced erroneous belief about an impossible fact, and it is the fact erroneously believed in which the man is stating. A man's hasty belief that the Germans had surrendered (before they did) might well be caused by his emotions. That would not make 'The Germans have surrendered' a specimen of emotional language. If you could find a man nowadays capable of believing, and saying, 'The Russians have all been annihilated by magic', even this would not be emotional language, though his belief in magic might be a belief engendered by emotion.

All this is fairly plain sailing. We reach something harder in the things said by poets. For there the purpose of the utterance would be frustrated if no emotion were aroused. They do not merely, like the sentences cited above, arouse emotion in fact; it is their purpose—at any rate, part of their purpose—to do so. But we must be very careful here. Having observed that a poetical utterance in fact arouses emotion, and is intended to arouse emotion, and that if taken as a statement about reality—or even about the make-believe 'realities' of a fictitious narrative —it would be nonsensical or at least false, can we conclude that it communicates nothing but emotion? I think not.

Nothing will convince me that 'My soul is an enchanted boat'[1] is simply a better way—however much better—of doing what might be done by some exclamation like 'Gee!' Asia has risen from the dark cave of Demogorgon. She is floating upwards. She is saluted as 'Life of Life!' The reversed temporal process in ll. 97–103 ('We have passed Age's icy caves' etc.), borrowed from Plato's *Politicus* (269^c *sq.*), marks the fact that at this moment the whole cycle is reversed and cosmos begins anew. She is undergoing apotheosis. What did it feel like? The poet says to us in effect 'Think of going in a boat. But quite effortless' ('Like a sleeping swan' gliding with the current, he adds in the next line), 'Like a boat without sail or oar; the motive power undiscoverable. Like a magic boat— you must have read or dreamed of such things—a boat drawn on, drawn swiftly on, irresistibly, smoothly, by enchantment.' Exactly. I know now how it felt for Asia.

[1] *Prometheus Unbound* II, v, 72.

The phrase has communicated emotion. But notice how. By addressing in the first instance my imagination. He makes me imagine a boat rushing over waves, which are also identified with sounds. After that he need do no more; my emotion will follow of itself. Poetry most often communicates emotions, not directly, but by creating imaginatively the grounds for those emotions. It therefore communicates something more than emotion; only by means of that something more does it communicate the emotion at all.

Burns compares his mistress to 'a red, red rose'; Wordsworth his to 'a violet by a mossy stone Half hidden from the eye'. These expressions do communicate to me the emotion each poet felt. But it seems to me that they do so solely by forcing me to imagine two (very different) women. I see the rose-like, overpowering, midsummer sweetness of the one; the reticent, elusive freshness, the beauty easily overlooked in the other. After that my emotions may be left to themselves. The poets have done their part.

This, which is eminently true of poetry, is true of all imaginative writing. One of the first things we have to say to a beginner who has brought us his MS. is, 'Avoid all epithets which are merely emotional. It is no use *telling* us that something was "mysterious" or "loathsome" or "awe-inspiring" or "voluptuous". Do you think your readers will believe you just because you say so? You must go quite a different way to work. By direct description, by metaphor and simile, by secretly evoking powerful associations, by offering the right stimuli to our nerves (in the right degree and the right order), and by the very beat and vowel-melody and length and brevity of your sentences, you must bring it about that we, we readers, not you, exclaim "how mysterious!" or "loathsome" or whatever it is. Let me taste for myself, and you'll have no need to *tell* me how I should react to the flavour.'

In Donne's couplet

> Your gown going off, such beautious state reveals
> As when from flowry meads th'hills shadow steales[1]

beautious is the only word of the whole seventeen which is doing no work.

There are exceptions to this principle. By very successful placing, a great author may sometimes raise such words to poetic life. Wordsworth's lines are a specimen:

> Which, to the boundaries of space and time,
> Of melancholy space and doleful time,
> Superior—[2]

Here we have almost the reverse of the process I have been describing. The object (space and time) is in one way so familiar to our imaginations and in another so unimaginable—we have read so many tedious attempts to exalt or over-awe us with mere superlatives or even with simple arithmetic—that nothing can be made of it. This time, therefore, the poet withdraws the object (the ground for emotion) altogether and appeals directly to our emotions; and not to the quite obvious ones. Another exception is naturally to be found in drama or very dramatic lyric,

Elegy XIX, 13.   [2] *Prelude* VI, 134.

where the poet—with discretion and a proper use of illusion—imitates the speech of people in some highly emotional situation—even, at need, their inarticulate cries. This in its purity, which purity a good poet never sustains for long, belongs to poetry not in so far as poetry is a special use of language but in so far as poetry is *mimesis*. In themselves the 'Ah! Ah!' or 'Otototoi' or 'Iou! Iou!' of characters in a Greek tragedy are not specimens of poetry any more than the 'Bé, bé' of the lamb or the 'Au! Au!' of the dog in Aristophanes.

In general, however, the poet's route to our emotions lies through our imaginations.

We must also exclude from the category 'emotional language' words such as I have taken *supernatural* to be. The class of things which they refer to may be bound together chiefly by a common emotion; but the purpose of using the words is to assign something to that class, not merely to communicate the emotion which led to the classification.

Having thus narrowed the field, we can now make a new start. It will be noticed that I have throughout used the word *emotional* rather than *emotive*. This is because I think the latter word applicable to only one aspect of emotional language. For an 'emotive word' ought to mean one whose function is to arouse emotion. But surely we ought to distinguish utterances which arouse, from those which express, emotion? The first is directed towards producing some effect on a (real or imagined) hearer; the second discharges our own emotion, cleanses our stuffed bosom of some perilous stuff.

The distinction will seem straw-splitting if we have in mind the language of love. For, as Samson says, 'love seeks to have love', and it would be hard to say whether endearments serve more as expressions of love in the speaker or incitements to it in the beloved. But that tells us more about the nature of love than about the nature of language. One of my old headmasters once wisely said it was a pity that *amare* was the first Latin verb we all learn. He thought this led to an imperfect grasp of the difference between the active and the passive voice. It might be better to begin with *flagellare*. The difference between flogging and being flogged would come home to the business and bosoms of schoolboys far more effectively than that of loving and being loved. On the same principle, we can best see the distinction between the stimulant and the expressive functions of emotional language in a quarrel; and best of all where the same word performs both. The man who calls me a low hound both expresses and (actually or intentionally) stimulates emotion. But not the same emotion. He expresses contempt; he stimulates, or hopes to stimulate, the almost opposite emotion of humiliation.

Again, in the language of complaint we often find the expressive without the stimulant. When two people who have missed the last train stand on the silent platform saying 'Damn' or 'Bloody' or 'Sickening', they neither intend nor need to stimulate each other's disappointment. They are just 'getting it off their chests'.

The vocabulary of endearment, complaint, and abuse, provides, I think, almost the only specimens of words that are purely emotional, words from which all imaginative or conceptual content has vanished, so that they have no function at all but to express or stimulate emotion, or both. And an examination of them soon convinces us that in them we see language at its least linguistic. We have come to the frontier between language and inarticulate vocal sounds. And at that frontier we find a two-way traffic going on.

On the one hand we find inarticulate sounds becoming words with a fixed spelling and a niche in the dictionary. Thus English *heigh-ho* and Latin *eheu* are clearly formalised imitations of the sigh; *ah*, of the gasp; *tut-tut*, of the tongue clicked against the hard palate. These are general. In particular situations the 'verbification' of the inarticulate may occur *ad hoc*. A voluntary scream may become a cry for mercy. A voluntary groan, from a wounded man, uttered to attract the attention of the stretcher-bearers, may be the equivalent of a sentence ('There is a wounded man in this ditch').

But we also see the frontier being crossed in the opposite direction. In the vocabulary of abuse and complaint we see things that once were words passing out of the realm of language (properly so called) and becoming the equivalents of inarticulate sounds or even of actions; of sighs, moans, whimperings, growls, or blows.

The 'swear-words'—*damn* for complaint and *damn you* for abuse—are a good example. Historically the whole Christian eschatology lies behind them. If no one had ever consigned his enemy to the eternal fires and believed that there were eternal fires to receive him, these ejaculations would never have existed. But inflation, the spontaneous hyperboles of ill temper, and the decay of religion, have long since emptied them of that lurid content. Those who have no belief in damnation—and some who have—now damn inanimate objects which would on any view be ineligible for it. The word is no longer an imprecation. It is hardly, in the full sense, a word at all when so used. Its popularity probably owes as much to its resounding phonetic virtues as to any, even fanciful, association with hell. It has ceased to be profane. It has also become very much less forceful. You may say the same of *sickening* in its popular, ejaculatory, use. There are alarms and disappointments which can actually produce nausea, or, at least, emotions which we feel to be somehow similar to it. But the man who says *sickening!* when he has missed the train is not thinking about that. The word is simply an alternative to *damn* or *bloody*. And of course far weaker than it would be if it still carried any suggestion of vomiting.

So with abusive terms. No one would now call his schoolfellow or next door neighbour a *swine* unless someone had once used this word to make a real comparison between his enemy and a pig. It is now a mere alternative to *beast* or *brute* or various popular unprintable words. They are all interchangeable. *Villain*, as we know, once really compared your enemy to a *villein*. Once, to call a man *cad* or *knave* assigned to him the status of a servant. And it did so because, earlier still, these words meant 'boy' or 'junior' (you address a slave as 'boy' in Greek and a waiter as *garçon* in French).

Thus all these words have come down in the world.

None of them started by being *merely* abusive, few of them by being abusive at all. They once stimulated emotion by suggesting an image. They made the enemy odious or contemptible by asserting he was like somebody or something we already disliked or looked down on. Their use was a sort of passionate parody of the syllogism: pigs (or servants or my juniors) are contemptible—John is like a pig (or servant or adolescent)—therefore John is contemptible. That was why they really hurt; because hurting was not the whole of what they did. They stimulated emotion because they also stimulated something else; imagination. They stimulated emotion in the particular case because they exploited emotions which already existed towards whole classes of things or persons. Now that they are nothing whatever but emotional stimulants, they are weak emotional stimulants. They make no particular accusation. They tell us nothing except that the speaker has lost his temper.

And even this they do not tell us linguistically, but symptomatically; as a red face, a loud voice, or a clenched fist, might do equally well. The fact of the other person's anger may hurt or frighten us; hurt us if we love him, or frighten us if he is larger and younger than ourselves and threatens violence. But his language as such has very little power to do the only thing it is intended to do. It would have been far more wounding to be called *swine* when the word still carried some whiff of the sty and some echo of a grunt; far more wounding to be called a *villain* when this still conjured up an image of the unwashed, malodorous, ineducable, gross, belching, close-

323

fisted, and surly boor. Now, who cares? Language meant solely to hurt hurts strangely little.

This can be seen clearly when we catch a word 'just on the turn'. *Bitch* is one. Till recently—and still in the proper contexts—this accused a woman of one particular fault and appealed, with some success, to our contempt by calling up an image of the she-dog's comical and indecorous behaviour when she is on heat. But it is now increasingly used of any woman whom the speaker, for whatever reason, is annoyed with—the female driver who is in front of him, or a female magistrate whom he thinks unjust. Clearly, the word is far more wounding in its narrower usage. If that usage is ever totally lost— as I think it will be—the word will sink to the level of *damn her*. Notice, too, how *cat* (of a woman) is still strong and useful because the image is still alive in it.

An important principle thus emerges. In general, emotional words, to be effective, must not be solely emotional. What expresses or stimulates emotion directly, without the intervention of an image or concept, expresses or stimulates it feebly. And in particular, when words of abuse have hurting the enemy as their direct and only object, they do not hurt him much. In the field of language, however it may be in that of action, hatred cuts its own throat, and those who are too 'willing to wound' become thereby impotent to strike. And all this is only another way of saying that as words become exclusively emotional they cease to be words and therefore of course cease to perform any strictly linguistic function. They operate as growls or barks or tears.

'Exclusively' is an important adverb here. They die as words not because there is too much emotion in them but because there is too little—and finally nothing at all—of anything else.

In this there is not much to be lamented. If a mother with a baby, or lovers in each other's arms, use language so emotional that it is really not language at all, I see no ground for shame or offence; and if men in an orgy of resentment, though (in the physical sense) they articulate, are really no more speaking—are saying no more—than a snarling animal, this is perhaps all for the best. The real corruption comes when men whose purpose in speaking is in fact purely emotional conceal this from others, and perhaps from themselves, by words that seem to be, but are not, charged with a conceptual content.

We have all heard *bolshevist*, *fascist*, *Jew*, and *capitalist*, used not to describe but merely to insult. Rose Macaulay noticed a tendency to prefix 'so called' to almost any adjective when it was used of those the speaker hated; the final absurdity being reached when people referred to the Germans as 'these so-called Germans'. *Bourgeois* and *middle class* often suffer the same fate.

A literary man of my acquaintance, on reading an unfavourable reference to his own works, called it *vulgar*. The charge brought against him was one that only highly educated people ever bring; the tone of the passage not otherwise offensive than by being unfavourable; the phrasing perfectly good English. If he had called it false, unintelligent, or malicious, I could have understood, though I might have disagreed. But why *vulgar*? Clearly, this word was selected solely because the speaker thought it was the one that the enemy, if he could hear it, would most dislike. It was the equivalent of an oath or a growl. But that was concealed from the speaker because 'This is vulgar' sounds like a judgement.

When we write criticism we have to be continually on our guard against this sort of thing. If we honestly believe a work to be very bad we cannot help hating it. The function of criticism, however, is 'to get ourselves out of the way and let humanity decide'; not to discharge our hatred but to expose the grounds for it; not to vilify faults but to diagnose and exhibit them. Unfortunately to express our hatred and to revenge ourselves is easier and more agreeable. Hence there is a tendency to select our pejorative epithets with a view not to their accuracy but to their power of hurting. If writing which was intended to be comic has set our teeth on edge, how easily the adjectives *arch* or *facetious* trickle out of the pen! But if we do not know exactly what we mean by them, if we are not prepared to say how comic work which errs by *archness* and *facetiousness* differs from comic work which errs in any other way, it is to be feared that we are really using them not to inform the reader but to annoy the author—*arch* or *facetious* being among the most effective 'smear-words' of our period. In the same way work which obviously aspires and claims to be mature, if the critic dislikes it, will be called *adolescent*; not because the critic has really seen that its faults are those of adolescence but because he has seen that adolescence is the last thing the author wishes or expects to be accused of.

The best protection against this is to remind ourselves again and again what the proper function of pejorative words is. The ultimate, simplest and most abstract, is *bad* itself. The only good purpose for ever departing from that monosyllable when we condemn anything is to be more specific, to answer the question 'Bad in what way?' Pejorative words are rightly used only when they do this. *Swine*, as a term of abuse is now a bad pejorative word, because it brings no one accusation rather than another against the person it vilifies; *coward* and *liar* are good ones because they charge a man with a particular fault—of which he might be proved guilty or innocent. As applied to literature, *dull, hackneyed, incoherent, monotonous, pornographic, cacophonous*, are good pejoratives; they tell people in what particular way we think a book faulty. *Adolescent* or *provincial* are not so good. For even when they are honestly used, to define, not merely to hurt, they really suggest a cause for the book's badness instead of describing the badness itself. We are saying in effect 'He was led into his faults by being immature' or 'by living in Lancashire'. But would it not be more interesting to indicate the faults themselves and leave out our historical theory about their causes? If we find words like these— and *vulgar*, and others—indispensable to our criticism, if we find ourselves applying them to more and more different kinds of things, there is grave reason to suspect that—whether we know it or not—we are really using them not to diagnose but to hurt. If so, we are assisting in verbicide. For this is the downward path which leads to the graveyard of murdered words. First they are purely descriptive; *adolescent* tells us a man's age, *villain*, his status. Then they are specifically pejorative; *adolescent* tells us that a man's work displays 'mawkishness and all the thousand bitters' confessed by Keats, and *villain* tells that a man has a churl's mind and manners. Then they become *mere* pejoratives, useless synonyms for *bad*, as *villain* did and as *adolescent* may do if we aren't careful. Finally they become terms of abuse and cease to be language in the full sense at all.

As this book is now almost done, what would otherwise be a digression—for it carries us beyond the subject of vocabulary—may perhaps be excused as a sort of *coda*. In the last few paragraphs we have had to touch on criticism. I would be very glad if I could transfer to even one reader my conviction that *adverse* criticism, far from being the easiest, is one of the hardest things in the world to do well. And that for two reasons.

Dr I. A. Richards first seriously raised the problem of badness in literature. And his singularly honest wrestling with it shows how dark a problem it is. For when we try to define the badness of a work, we usually end by calling it bad on the strength of characteristics which we can find also in good work. Dr Richards began by hoping he had found the secret of badness in an appeal to stock responses. But Gray's *Elegy* beat him. Here was a good poem which made that appeal throughout. Worse still, its particular goodness depended on doing so. This happens again and again. The novel before you is bad—a transparent compensatory fantasy projected by a poor, plain woman, erotically starving. Yes, but so is *Jane Eyre*. Another bad book is amorphous; but so is *Tristram Shandy*. An author betrays shocking indifference to all the great political, social, and intellectual upheavals of his age; like Jane Austen. The solution of the problem is, I suspect, still far away.

The other difficulty lies within. As I said before, what we think thoroughly bad, we hate. If, besides being bad, it enjoys great popularity and thereby helps to exclude works that we approve from their 'place in the sun', hatred of a somewhat less disinterested sort will creep in. Lower and still lower levels of hatred may open; we may dislike the author personally, he and we may belong to opposed literary 'parties' or factions. The book before us becomes a symbol of *l'infâme*. Hence a perpetual danger of what is called criticism (judgement) becoming mere action—a blow delivered in a battle. But if it does, we are lost as critics.

Everyone who remembers Arnold's 'Literary Influence of Academies' will see why we are lost. But its lesson has been forgotten. There has been in our time a determined, and successful, attempt to revive the *brutalité des journaux anglais*. Reviews so filled with venom have often been condemned socially for their bad manners, or ethically for their spite. I am not prepared to defend them from either charge; but I prefer to stress their inutility.

They can, no doubt, be enjoyed if we already agree with the critic. But then, you know, we are not reading them to inform our judgement. What we enjoy is a resounding blow by our own 'side'. How useless they are for any strictly critical function becomes apparent if

we approach them with an open mind. I had this forced
upon me when I read some unusually violent reviews
lately which were all by the same man. My mind could
not but be open. The books he reviewed were not by me
nor by any close friend of mine. I had never heard of the
critic. I read (at first—one soon learned to skip his pro-
ductions) to find out what the books were like and
whether I should consider buying them. But I found
I could learn nothing about the books. In the first
hundred words the critic had revealed his passions. What
happened to me after that is, I think, what must happen
to anyone in such circumstances. Automatically, without
thinking about it, willy-nilly, one's mind discounts everything he says; as it does when we are listening to a drunk
or delirious man. Indeed we cannot even think about the
book under discussion. The critic rivets our attention on
himself. The spectacle of a man thus writhing in the
mixed smart and titillation of a fully indulged resentment
is, in its way, too big a thing to leave us free for any
literary considerations. We are in the presence of tragi-
comedy from real life. When we get to the end we find
that the critic has told us everything about himself and
nothing about the book.

Thus in criticism, as in vocabulary, hatred over-reaches
itself. Willingness to wound, too intense and naked,
becomes impotent to do the desired mischief.

Of course, if we are to be critics, we must condemn as
well as praise; we must sometimes condemn totally and
severely. But we must obviously be very careful; in their
condemnations great critics long before our time have

exposed themselves. Is there any way in which we—lesser men than they—can avoid doing the same? I think perhaps there is. I think we must get it firmly fixed in our minds that the very occasions on which we should most like to write a slashing review are precisely those on which we had much better hold our tongues. The very desire is a danger signal. When an author whom we admire in general, writing in a *genre* we thoroughly enjoy, produces a disappointing work, we may proceed with tolerable safety. We know what we had hoped for. We see, and would have relished, what he was trying to do. By that light we may possibly diagnose where the book has gone wrong. But when an author we never could stand is attempting (unsuccessfully—or, worse still, successfully) 'exactly the sort of thing we always loathe', then, if we are wise, we shall be silent. The strength of our dislike is itself a probable symptom that all is not well within; that some raw place in our psychology has been touched, or else that some personal or partisan motive is secretly at work. If we were simply exercising judgement we should be calmer; less anxious to speak. And if we do speak, we shall almost certainly make fools of ourselves.

Continence in this matter is no doubt painful. But, after all, you can always write your slashing review now and drop it into the wastepaper basket a day or so later. A few re-readings in cold blood will often make this quite easy.

INDEX

ADDISON, *wit*, 105; *sense*, 154; *sensibility*, 159; *simple*, 174; *world*, 265

ÆLFRED, *gecynde* (adj.), 27; *gecynd* (sbst.), 48; *freora*, 114; *woruld*, 214, 218, 221–2

ÆLFRIC, *gecynde* (sbst.), 26; *cynd* (gender), 26; *worulda*, 214, 244–5, 247

AESCHYLUS, *aion* (world), 226; *aion* (life), 270

AGLIONBY, on conscience, 197–8

ALANUS AB INSULIS, 41 n., 44

ANDREWES, LAUNCELOT, *villains*, 118

APULEIUS, *simplex*, 171–7

AQUINAS, THOMAS, 61; *simpliciter*, 168; *synteresis* and *conscientia*, 194

ARISTOPHANES, *xunoida*, 187; *bé* and *au*, 319

ARISTOTLE, *phusis*, 34, 39, 56; history—tragedy, 57; *phusis*, 65; classification of his works, 68; *phusike*, 70; quoted, 110; *eleutheria*, 126; *eleuthera* by analogy, 127; *koine aisthesis*, 147; on sense and motion, 151; *haplôs*, 167–8; *aion*, 226; *kosmos*, 252; *bios*, 275, 276, 277

ARNOLD, 18, 229; *world*, 241–2, 243, 248, 260, 265; *life*, 278, 286–7, 291

ASCHAM, *wits*, 88

'ASSEMBLY OF GODS, THE', *synderesis*, 196

'ASSEMBLY OF LADIES', *world*, 255

AUDEN, W. H., 94

AUGUSTINE, ST, 112; *communis sensus*, 150

AULUS GELLIUS, *senserint*, 137

AUSTEN, JANE, *sad*, 83, 84; *sense—sensibility*, 164; *conscious*, 186; *I dare say*, 307–11

AUTHORISED VERSION, THE, *freedom*, 125; *single*, 171; *harmless*, 172; *lowly*, 176; *thought*, 182; *know by myself*, 187; *world*, 218, 224–5, 233

AXIOCHUS, *eleutheriotaten*, 126

BACON, *sense*, 142; *conscious*, 139; *world*, 259

BAXTER, *physically*, 70–1; *world*, 240–1

333

INDEX

INDEX

INDEX

INDEX

INDEX

INDEX

341

INDEX